D0221874

Strategy: A View from the Top

Strategy:

A View from the Top
(An Executive Perspective)
THIRD EDITION

Cornelis A. de Kluyver

Masatoshi Ito Professor of Management
Peter F. Drucker and Masatoshi Ito Graduate School of Management
Claremont Graduate University

John A. Pearce II

VSB Endowed Chair in Strategic Management and Entrepreneurship, and
Professor of Management
Villanova School of Business
Villanova University

Upper Saddle River, New Jersey 07458

Library of Congress Cataloging-in-Publication Data

de Kluyver, Cornelis A.

   Strategy : a view from the top (an executive perspective)/
Cornelis A. de Kluyver, John A. Pearce II.–3rd ed.

      p. cm.

   Includes bibliographical references and index.

   ISBN 978-0-13-604140-5 (pbk. : alk. paper)

1. Executives. 2. Leadership. 3. Management. I. Pearce, John A. II. Title.

  HD38.2.D425 2008

  658.4′012–dc22

                               2007051165

Associate Vice President/Editor in Chief: David Parker
Editorial Assistant: Elizabeth Davis
Marketing Manager: Nikki Jones
Marketing Assistant: Ian Gold
Senior Managing Editor: Judy Leale
Assistant Editor: Kristen Varina
Production Project Manager: Ruth Ferrera-Kargov
Permissions Supervisor: Charles Morris
Senior Operations Supervisor: Arnold Vila
Cover Design Manager: Jayne Conte
Cover Illustration/Photo: Getty Images, Inc.
Full-Service Project Management: BookMasters, Inc.
Composition: Integra Software Services
Printer/Binder: RR Donnelley–Harrisonburg

Credits and acknowledgments borrowed from other sources and reproduced, with permission, in this textbook appear on appropriate page within text.

Copyright © 2009, 2006 by Pearson Education, Inc., Upper Saddle River, New Jersey, 07458. All rights reserved. Printed in the United States of America. This publication is protected by Copyright and permission should be obtained from the publisher prior to any prohibited reproduction, storage in a retrieval system, or transmission in any form or by any means, electronic, mechanical, photocopying, recording, or likewise. For information regarding permission(s), write to: Rights and Permissions Department.

Pearson Prentice Hall™ is a trademark of Pearson Education, Inc.
Pearson® is a registered trademark of Pearson plc
Prentice Hall® is a registered trademark of Pearson Education, Inc.

Pearson Education Australia PTY, Limited
Pearson Education North Asia Ltd
Pearson Educación de Mexico, S.A. de C.V.
Pearson Education Malaysia, Pte. Ltd.

Pearson Education LTD.
Pearson Education Singapore, Pte. Ltd
Pearson Education, Canada, Ltd
Pearson Education–Japan

10 9 8 7 6 5 4 3 2 1
ISBN-13: 978-0-13-604140-5
ISBN-10:   0-13-604140-X

BRIEF CONTENTS

CONTENTS

PREFACE

Strategy: A View from the Top, **Third Edition, is written for practicing executives getting ready to assume executive responsibilities and for MBA and EMBA students who aspire to top management responsibilities.**

Corporate success depends to a considerable degree on the ability to craft and implement effective strategies. Companies that enjoy a competitive advantage over their rivals typically have a better grasp of what their customers prefer, how they can create value, and who their competitors are and how they behave.

Formulating a sound strategy requires both analysis and synthesis; therefore, it is as much a rational as it is a creative act. Successful strategies reflect a solid grasp of relevant forces in the external and competitive environment, a clear strategic intent, and a deep understanding of an organization's core competencies and assets. Generic strategies rarely propel a company to a leadership position. Knowing where you want to go and finding carefully considered, creative ways of getting there are the hallmarks of successful strategy.

NEW TO THE THIRD EDITION

The organization of the third edition reflects the many constructive suggestions we received from readers all over the world. We have reordered some topics to accommodate new material and improve the flow of the subject matter for teaching purposes and have updated the numerous examples and vignettes used throughout the book. At the same time, we have taken care to retain the differentiating characteristics of the first edition—its brevity, conversational style, and executive orientation.

Chapter 1, "What Is Strategy?" defines strategy as the act of positioning a company for competitive advantage by focusing on unique ways to create value for customers. It differentiates between crafting a strategy and enhancing an organization's operational effectiveness, introduces the concept of a competitive advantage cycle, and defines such commonly used terms as *mission, vision, strategic intent,* and *stretch.* We then discuss the process by which strategies are formulated and the importance of organizational learning as part of this process. **The third edition includes a new section on strategic "ecosystems" and an enhanced discussion of the importance of embedding corporate values in strategy formulation.**

Chapter 2, "Strategy and Performance," has been expanded. **We have added a discussion of two widely cited studies on the subject of how companies achieve greatness as measured by superior, sustained performance.** The first, by Jim Collins, entitled *Good to Great: Why Some Companies Make the Leap . . . and Others Don't*, originally published in 2001, focused on what good companies can do to become truly great. Its findings have inspired many CEOs to change their views about what drives success. The second, *What Really Works: The 4+2 Formula for Sustained Business Success*, by Joyce, Nohria, and Roberson, in association with McKinsey & Company, is a groundbreaking, 5-year study aimed at identifying the must-have management practices that truly produce superior results. The third edition also includes an expanded section on the board's role in strategy formulation.

Chapter 3, "Analyzing the External Strategic Environment," has several new features. First, we include a section on **global tectonics**—the process by which developing trends in technology, nature, and society slowly revolutionize the business environment, much like Earth's tectonic plates shift the ground beneath our feet. We have also revised our discussion of **scenario analysis**, a technique for defining and analyzing alternative futures, and end the chapter with a **new section on the oft-asked question whether the compact between business and society** is changing and what impact this is likely to have on strategy formulation and corporate behavior.

Chapters 4, 5, and 6—"Analyzing an Industry,""Analyzing an Organization's Strategic Resource Base," and "Formulating Business Unit Strategy"—have been edited for readability, but their content is essentially unchanged.

Chapter 7, "Business Unit Strategy: Contexts and Special Dimensions," has been expanded to include a **deeper discussion of strategic issues peculiar to a deregulating environment**, such as pricing dilemmas and patterns of competitive reaction, and a **broader discussion of the challenges associated with strategies based on innovation** and their impact on profitability.

Chapter 8, "Global Strategy Formulation," has been enhanced to include a more thorough discussion of **country/region analysis**. The section on how **Wal-Mart goes global** has been updated to chronicle the company's recent challenges and disappointments in Germany, the U.K., and elsewhere. The revised chapter concludes with a discussion of **how a focus on similarities between countries and markets can obscure opportunities rooted in advantage based on differences**.

Chapter 9, "Corporate Strategy: Shaping the Portfolio," has undergone several revisions. The third edition includes a revised and expanded discussion of the strategic logic behind vertical integration, additional material on alliances, and discusses **DaimlerChrysler's decision to spin off its U.S. auto operations to a private equity firm**.

Chapter 10, "Corporate Strategy: Managing the Portfolio," has undergone three major changes. First, the discussion of portfolio models was **expanded to include McKinsey's MACS model**. Like McKinsey's old nine-box matrix, MACS includes a measure of each business unit's stand-alone value within the corporation, but it adds a measure of a business unit's fitness for sale to other companies. This new measure is what makes MACS especially useful. The key contribution of the MACS framework is that it recognizes that a corporation's ability to extract value from a business unit should be benchmarked externally relative to that of other potential owners and should be a key determinant in deciding whether to sell or hold onto the unit in question. It holds that such a decision should not be made on the basis of a valuation of the business unit in isolation. Thus, under the MACS point of view, decisions about whether to sell off a business unit might have less to do with how unattractive it really is (the main concern of the nine-box matrix) and more with whether a company is, for whatever reason, well suited to run it. Second, the concept of **portfolio management of alliances** is introduced. Finally, we updated the discussion on **corporate strategic planning** to reflect the new competitive dynamics faced by multinationals in the twenty-first century.

INSTRUCTOR'S SUPPLEMENTS

The third edition text includes a case map on the inside front and back covers that identifies specific cases for the different topics and chapters in the book.

Additionally, a complete set of **PowerPoint** presentations accompanies the third edition to assist adopters in preparing for classroom and executive presentations. These PowerPoint presentations can be found at www.prenhall.com/irc. Registration is simple and gives you immediate access to new titles and new editions. As a registered faculty member, you can download resource files and receive immediate access and instructions for installing course management content on your campus server. If you never need assistance, our dedicated technical support team is ready to help with the medial supplements that accompany this text. Visit www.247.prenhall.com. for answers to frequently asked questions and toll-free user support phone numbers.

COURSESMART eTEXTBOOKS ONLINE

CourseSmart Textbooks Online is an exciting new choice for students looking to save money. As an alternative to purchasing the printed textbook, students can subscribe to the same content online and save up to 50 percent off the suggested list price of the print text. With a CourseSmart eTextbook, students can search the text, make notes online, print out reading assignments that incorporate lecture notes, and bookmark important passages for later review. For more information or to subscribe to the CourseSmart eTextbook, visit www.coursesmart.com.

ACKNOWLEDGMENTS

Writing a book is a mammoth undertaking. Fortunately, we had a lot of encouragement along the way from current users of the book, our publisher, family members, colleagues, and friends. We take this opportunity to thank them all for their constructive criticisms, their time, and words of encouragement. We are grateful to all of them and hope the result meets their high expectations.

We are particularly indebted to our families: Louise de Kluyver and sons Peter and Jonathan, and Susie Pearce and sons David and Mark. We thank them for their unwavering support.

We especially thank the following individuals who provided valuable comments and suggestions to improve this edition:

Sheldon Weinig	Columbia University
Yusaf Akbar	Southern New Hampshire University
Michael K. Mulford	Buena Vista University
Phaedon Papadopoulos	Houston Baptist University
Michel Mestre	Biola University
Bruce Kusch	Brigham Young University, Idaho

Cornelis A. "Kees" de Kluyver
John A. "Jack" Pearce II
January 2008

About the Authors

Cornelis A. "Kees" de Kluyver is the Masatoshi Ito Professor of Management and former dean at the Peter F. Drucker and Masatoshi Ito Graduate School of Management at Claremont Graduate University. He also served as Executive Director of the Peter F. Drucker Research Library and Archives and as Governor of the Peter F. Drucker Foundation for Non-Profit Management.

He has held prior academic appointments at George Mason University, at the University of Virginia, and at Purdue University, and for several years was a principal with Cresap Management Consultants, a Towers Perrin Company, in the firm's strategy and organizational effectiveness practice. In this position, he served a wide range of clients in the high technology and service industries on various international strategy issues including the impact of European unification on North American business and the globalization of multinational operations.

Dr. de Kluyver's areas of research include global strategy and corporate governance. He has published extensively in the areas of Operations Research, Marketing, and Strategic Management and his writings can be found in such journals as *Management Science*, the *Journal of Marketing Research*, the *European Journal of Operational Research*, the *Sloan Management Review*, and *Long Range Planning*. He serves on a number of corporate, foundation, and advisory boards; is a frequent speaker to professional audiences; and holds a Ph.D. in Operations Research from Case Western Reserve, an MBA for the University of Oregon, and undergraduate degrees from the University of Oregon and the Netherlands School of Business.

John A. "Jack" Pearce II is the VSB Endowed Chair in Strategic Management and Entrepreneurship at Villanova University. A two-time recipient of the Fulbright International Professional Award, Jack has taught at Pennsylvania State University, West Virginia University, the University of South Carolina, and George Mason University. He received a Ph.D. in Strategic Management from Penn State. Jack is coauthor of 36 additional books including *Strategic Management: Formulation, Implementation, and Control*, 11th edition (with Richard B. Robinson, Jr.), Irwin, 2009. He has authored or coauthored 100 articles and 126 refereed professional papers.

The first Chairman of the Academy of Management's Entrepreneurship Division, Jack is the recipient of several awards in recognition of his accomplishments in teaching, research, scholarship, and professional service, including the Richard Beckhard Prize in 2006, awarded for research on corporate social responsibility by the *MIT Sloan Management Review*. Sponsors of other awards include the National Association of Small Business Investment Companies, the Association of Management Consulting Firms, and a record four Outstanding Research awards by Divisions of the Academy of Management. A frequent leader of executive development programs, an active consultant to businesses, and an experienced expert witness, Jack is frequently interviewed by the print media for his views on contemporary business issues.

Strategy: A View from the Top

Chapter

1

What Is Strategy?

INTRODUCTION

How did Google become the world's number one search engine? What is the secret to Toyota's success? Can Wal-Mart continue its relentless growth? Why does Southwest Airlines consistently out-perform its many rivals? What makes the Starbucks brand so powerful? How important is it for a company to be first in developing a new product or entering a new market? Which elements of a company's strategy can be globalized? These kinds of questions go to the heart of strategy formulation.

Understanding how a strategy is crafted is important, because there is a proven link between a company's strategic choices and its long-term performance. Successful companies typically have a better grasp of customers' wants and needs, their competitors' strengths and weaknesses, and how they can create value. Successful strategies reflect a company's clear strategic intent and a deep understanding of its core competencies and assets—generic strategies rarely propel a company to a leadership position. Therefore, formulating a sound strategy requires both analysis and synthesis and is as much a rational act as it is a creative one. Knowing where to go and finding carefully considered, creative ways of getting there are the hallmarks of successful strategy development.

STRATEGY DEFINED

It is hard to imagine a business conversation that does not include the word *strategy*. We talk about Wal-Mart's distribution strategy, Coca-Cola's strategy in China, Amazon's e-business strategy, McDonald's human resource strategy, IBM's marketing strategy, Intel's technology strategy, and so on. Its frequent use would suggest that the term *strategy* is unambiguous and its meaning well understood. Unfortunately, it is not; much of what is labeled strategy in fact has little to do with it. Although numerous attempts have been made at providing a simple, descriptive definition of *strategy*, its inherent complexity and subtlety preclude a one-sentence description. There is substantial agreement about its principal dimensions, however. Strategy is about *positioning* an organization for *competitive advantage*. It involves making *choices* about *which industries to participate in, what products and services to offer,* and *how to allocate corporate resources*. Its primary goal is to *create value for shareholders and other stakeholders* by providing *customer value*.

Strategic Thinking Continues to Evolve

Defining strategy in terms of positioning an organization for competitive advantage with the goal of creating value is useful in framing a number of key questions. What do we mean by positioning an organization for competitive advantage? How should value be defined? The answers to these questions are complex. What is more, they change as the context in which strategy is developed continues to change. Today's competitive environment is very different from the one executives faced 25 years ago. A few decades from now, the strategic environment will once again have changed considerably.

The evolution of strategic thinking over the last 50 years reflects these changes and is characterized by a gradual shift in focus from an *industrial economics* to a *resource-based* perspective to a *human and intellectual* capital perspective (Figure 1-1). It is important to understand the reasons underlying this evolution, because they reflect a changing view of what strategy is and how it is crafted.

The early *industrial economics* perspective held that environmental influences—particularly those that shape industry structure—were the primary determinants of a company's success. The competitive environment was thought to impose pressures and constraints, which made certain strategies more attractive than others. Carefully choosing where to compete—selecting the most attractive industries or industry segments—and controlling strategically important resources, such as financial capital, became the dominant themes of strategy development at both the business unit and corporate levels. The focus, therefore, was on *capturing economic value* through adept positioning. Thus, industry analysis, competitor analysis, segmentation, positioning, and strategic

Figure 1-1 The Evolving Focus of Strategy

Competitive Focus	Products and Markets	Resources and Competencies	Talents and Dreams
Strategic objective	Defensible product-market positions	Sustainable advantage	Continuous self-renewal
Tools/perspectives	• Industry analysis; competitor analysis	• Core competencies	• Vision/values
	• Segmentation and positioning	• Resource-based strategy	• Flexibility and innovation
	• Strategic planning	• Networks	• Entrepreneurship
Key strategic resource	Financial capital	Organizational capability	Human and intellectual capital

Source: Reprinted from "Building Competitive Advantage Through People," by Christopher A. Bartlett and Sumantra Ghoshal, *MIT Sloan Management Review,* Winter 2002, pp. 34–41, by permission of publisher. Copyright © 2002 by Massachusetts Institute of Technology. All rights reserved.

planning became the most important tools for analyzing strategic opportunity.[1]

As globalization, the technology revolution, and other major environmental forces picked up speed and began to radically change the competitive landscape, key assumptions underlying the industrial economics model came under scrutiny. Should the competitive environment be treated as a constraint on strategy formulation, or was strategy really about shaping competitive conditions? Was the assumption that businesses should control most of the relevant strategic resources needed to compete still applicable? Were strategic resources really as mobile as the traditional model assumed, and was the advantage associated with owning particular resources and competencies therefore necessarily short-lived?

In response to these questions, a *resource-based* perspective of strategy development emerged. Rather than focusing on positioning a company within environment-dictated constraints, this new school of thought defined strategic thinking in terms of building core capabilities that transcend the boundaries of traditional business units. It focused on creating corporate portfolios around *core businesses* and on adopting goals and processes aimed at enhancing *core competencies*.[2] This new paradigm reflected a shift in emphasis from capturing economic value to creating value through the development and nurturing of key resources and capabilities.

The current focus on *human and intellectual capital* as a company's key strategic resource is a natural extension of the resource-based view of strategy and fits with the transition of global commerce to a knowledge-based economy. For a majority of companies, access to physical or financial resources no longer is an impediment to growth or opportunity; not having the right people or knowledge has become the limiting factor. Microsoft scans the entire pool of U.S. computer science graduates every year to identify and attract the few it accepts. It recognizes that competency-based strategies are dependent on people, that scarce knowledge and expertise drive product development, and that personal relationships with clients are critical to market responsiveness.[3]

It is interesting to note that researchers are reintroducing the idea of a company's environment as a determinant of performance, albeit in a different way. A study into how Wal-Mart and Microsoft have achieved dominance in their respective industries revealed that a substantial portion of their success is attributable to the success of their *ecosystems*, the loose networks of suppliers, distributors, contract manufacturers, makers of related products and services, technology providers, and others that play an important role in the creation and the delivery of their products and services. Thoughtful strategy formulation, therefore, should look beyond a company's immediate opportunities and capabilities and also promote its ecosystem's overall health.[4] Wal-Mart's procurement system, for example, also offers suppliers valuable real-time information on customer preferences and demand that they could not gather for themselves at the same level of cost.

Strategy Versus Tactics

New business concepts, technologies, and ideas are born every day. The Internet, innovation, total quality, flexibility, and speed, for example, all have come to be recognized as essential to a company's competitive strength and agility. As a result, corporations continue to embrace initiatives such as six-sigma, quality management, time-based competition, benchmarking, outsourcing, partnering, reengineering, and a host of other concepts in an all-out effort to enhance competitiveness.

Some of these initiatives have produced dramatic results. Automobile manufacturers have spent billions of dollars reengineering their design and production processes. As a result, unit costs have fallen dramatically, quality has gone up, relationships with component manufacturers and other suppliers are stronger, and the time needed to take a new car from concept to production has been cut in half. Though such results are gratifying, it is important to put them in their proper context. Enhancing operational effectiveness is crucial in today's cutthroat competitive environment, but it is no substitute for sound strategic thinking.

There is a difference between *strategy* and the application of operational tools and managerial philosophies focused on *operational effectiveness.* Both are essential to competitiveness. But whereas the application of managerial tools is aimed at doing things *better* than competitors and therefore *tactical* in nature, *strategy* focuses on doing things *differently.* Understanding this distinction is critical, as recent history has shown. Companies that embraced the Internet as "the strategic answer" to their business rather than just another, if important, new tool were in for a rude awakening. By focusing too much on e-business options at the expense of broader strategic concerns, many found themselves chasing customers indiscriminately, trading quality and service for price, and, with it, losing their competitive advantage and profitability.[5]

Long-term, sustainable superior performance—the ultimate goal of strategy—can only occur if a company can *preserve* meaningful differences between itself and its rivals. E-business initiatives, total quality management, time-based competition, benchmarking, and other tactics aimed at improved operational performance, however desirable and necessary, are generally fairly easily imitated. Enhanced performance attributable to such actions is at best temporary.

Strategy Forces Trade-offs

Strategic thinking, instead, focuses on taking *different* approaches to delivering customer value; on choosing *different* sets of activities that cannot easily be imitated, thereby providing a basis for an enduring competitive advantage. When Dell pioneered its highly successful direct sales, made-to-order business model, it carefully designed every aspect of its manufacturing, sourcing, and inventory system to support its low-cost, direct-sales strategy. In the process, it redefined value for many customers in terms of speed and cost and created major barriers to imitation. Its competitors, stuck with traditional distribution networks and manufacturing models, faced a difficult choice: abandon their traditional business model or focus on alternative ways of delivering customer value.

Thus, whereas operational effectiveness tools can improve competitiveness, they do not by themselves force companies to choose between entirely different, internally consistent *sets* of activities. IBM and other competitors could have responded to Dell's innovative strategy by also selling directly to end users, but they would have had to dismantle their traditional distribution structures to reap the benefits Dell realizes from its strategy. Thus, choosing a *unique competitive positioning*—the essence of strategy—forces trade-offs in terms of what to do and, equally important, of what *not* to do, and creates *barriers to imitation.*

Positioning choices should not only dictate what activities a company chooses to perform and how it will perform them; they also should specify how they interrelate to form a coherent set that differentiates the chosen activity set from competitive bundles of activities. Figure 1-2 shows how Southwest Airlines' strategy is based on a carefully integrated set of activities that is more than just a collection of parts. The different activities *fit* together and *reinforce* each other to create real economic value. Collectively, they deter imitators, who are forced to duplicate the entire chain of value-creating activities rather than individual components if they wish to achieve similar results.

Strategy Should Focus on Value Creation

A good strategy focuses on creating *value*—for shareholders, partners, suppliers, employees, and the community—by satisfying the needs and wants of customers better than anyone else. If a company can deliver value to its customers better than its rivals can over a sustained period of time, that company likely has a superior strategy. This is not a simple task. Customers' wants, needs, and preferences change, often rapidly, as they become more knowledgeable about a product or service, as new competitors enter the market, and as new entrants redefine what value means. As a result, what is valuable today might not be valuable tomorrow. The moral of this story is simple but powerful: *The value of a particular product or service offering, unless constantly maintained, nourished, and improved, erodes with time.*

The PC market provides a good example. The business model developed some years ago by Dell to eliminate intermediaries and sell direct provided a significant competitive advantage to

Figure 1-2 Southwest Airlines' Activity System

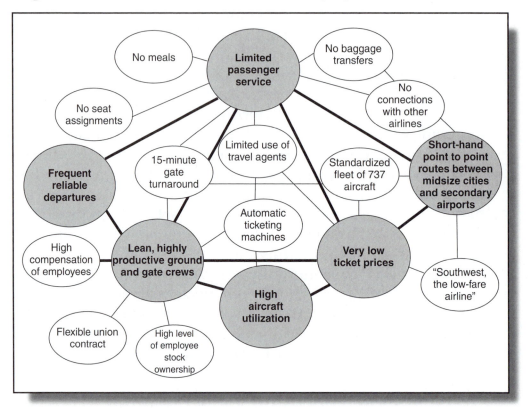

Source: Reprinted by Permission of *Harvard Business Review.* From "What Is Strategy" by Michael Porter, Nov/Dec. 1996. Copyright © 1996 by the Harvard Business School Publishing Corporation; all rights reserved.

the company. Competitors such as IBM and HP had a hard time responding, because their business models depended on extensive distribution systems. Customers valued the direct approach. Personalizing your own machine was appealing when the typical PC cost between $2,000 and $3,000. Customers could focus their purchasing dollars on the features that mattered most to them. If you were a gamer, you bought a powerful video card.

As the market evolved, so did the definition of value. Today, digital photographers demand an oversized hard drive to store their images. Users of big mathematical models or elaborate spreadsheets want rapid computing power, multiple processors, and lots of memory. An office worker who only needs email and

Word is satisfied with a stripped-down machine or gets by with a PDA. Prices of processors, memory, graphics, hard drives, keyboards, wireless modems, and so on have all collapsed over the last decade. As the markets for computers, cell phones, PDAs, and other communication devices converge, customers face an increasing array of choices. Today, the most expensive part of a computer may well be the software. Although IBM has abandoned the PC market, HP has reinvented itself and now produces high-performance, homogenized machines, built with just about everything anyone would want, and makes them easily available in local stores.

This has created a major dilemma for Dell. Margins have fallen, the market has fragmented, and the definition of value has changed. How should Dell respond? Should it offer a reliable, full-featured machine aimed at a global market? Should it sell in its own stores, through resellers, as well as direct? Should it design its machines to compete with Apple? Should it enter the mobile device market?

As it creates a new value proposition, Dell knows that reliability, dependability, and accessible service have become increasingly important to customers. Battery recalls, hours in a service queue to get help, high prices, and confusing catalogs all serve to drive customers away. A decade ago, offering promotional machines was an effective strategy for building market share. Today's customer values a more personalized approach as well as immediate , knowledgeable, local customer service.

Figure 1-3 depicts this competitive advantage cycle. It shows that at any given point in time companies compete with a particular mix of resources. Some of a company's assets and capabilities are better than those of its rivals; others are inferior. The superior assets and capabilities are the source of positional advantages.[6] Whatever competitive advantage a firm possesses, it must expect that ongoing change in the strategic environment and competitive moves by rival firms continuously work to erode it. Competitive strategy thus has a dual purpose: (1) slowing down the erosion process by protecting current sources of advantage against the actions of competitors and (2) investing in new capabilities that form the basis for the next position of

Figure 1-3 The Competitive Advantage Cycle

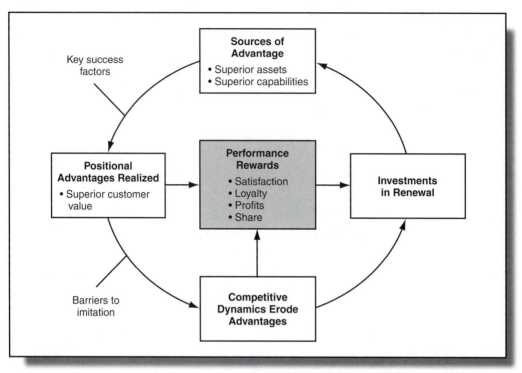

Source: WHARTON on Dynamic Competitive Strategy by George S. Day and David J. Reibstein. Copyright © 1997 by John Wiley & Sons, Inc. This material is used by permission of John Wiley & Sons, Inc.

competitive advantage. The creation and maintenance of advantage is therefore a continuous process.

Strategy Is About Creating Options

When we characterize strategy formulation as positioning an organization for competitive advantage, we do not mean deciding on a detailed long-term plan and following it to the letter. Rapid change in the competitive environment makes such a view of strategy untenable. At the time a strategy is crafted some outcomes are more predictable than others. When Motorola invests in a new technology, for example, it might know that this technology holds promise in several markets. Its precise returns in different applications, however, might not be known with any degree of certainty until much later.[7] Therefore, strategy formulation is about crafting a long-term *vision* for an organization while maintaining a degree of flexibility about how to get there and creating a portfolio of options for adapting to change. *Learning* is an essential component of this process. As soon as a company begins to implement a chosen direction, it starts to learn—about how well attuned the chosen direction is to the competitive environment, about how rivals are likely to respond, and about how well prepared the organization is to carry out its competitive intentions.

Strategy: An Ecosystem Perspective[8]

In our increasingly interconnected world, a single company focus often is not strategically viable. Most companies rely heavily on networks of partners, suppliers, and customers to achieve market success and sustain performance. These networks function like a biological ecosystem, in which companies succeed and fail as a collective whole.

Business ecosystems have become a widespread phenomenon within industries such as banking, biotechnology, insurance, and software. As with biological systems, the boundaries of a business ecosystem are fluid and sometimes difficult to define. Business ecosystems cross entire industries and can encompass the full range of organizations that influence the value of a product or service.

To achieve a sustainable competitive advantage, companies need to leverage the competencies of their entire network and use highly sophisticated technology to connect the various components. A good strategy improves the overall health of the business ecosystem and sustains the performance of the individual company. Companies such as Charles Schwab, eBay, and Wal-Mart effectively use ecosystem strategies to coordinate behavior and influence outcomes within their own networks.

Technology increasingly is the connective tissue that lets the ecosystem function, grow, and develop in widely diverse ways. Corporations planning to craft an effective ecosystem strategy must have a technical infrastructure in place that allows them to share information and encourage collaboration, as well as integrate systems within the ecosystem. Wal-Mart's success as the world's largest retailer, for example, is based, in part, on information technology decisions that are closely tied to its understanding of the ecosystem on which it depends. Wal-Mart maintains a vast supply-chain ecosystem that stretches from manufacturer to consumer. This centralized supply chain brings efficiencies to Wal-Mart and also creates value for its suppliers, both large and small, by providing a massive new channel for them to reach consumers worldwide.

An ecosystem-based strategy perspective makes clear the importance of interdependency in today's business environment. Stand-alone strategies often no longer suffice, because a company's performance is increasingly dependent on its ability to influence assets outside its direct control.

Strategy as Alignment

Strategies call for implementing numerous activities ranging from acquiring and allocating resources to building capabilities to shaping corporate culture to installing appropriate support systems. These activities are aimed at *aligning* an organization's resources and capabilities with the goals of a chosen strategic direction. Strategic alignment can be directed at *closing strategic capability gaps* or at *maintaining strategic focus.*

Strategic capability gaps are substantive disparities in competences, skills, and resources between what customers demand or are likely to demand in the future and what the organization currently can deliver. This strategic alignment dimension, therefore, focuses on closing the gap between *what it takes* to succeed in the marketplace and *what the company currently can do.* Examples of activities in this category are developing better technologies, creating faster delivery mechanisms, adopting a stronger branding, and building a stronger distribution network.

A second dimension of alignment is concerned with *maintaining strategic focus.* Strategy formulation and implementation are human activities and thus are subject to error, obstruction, or even abuse. Therefore, to successfully execute a chosen strategy an organization must find ways to ensure that *what is said*—by groups and individuals at all levels of the organization—*is in fact done*. Making sure strategic objectives are effectively communicated, allocating the necessary resources, and creating proper incentives for effective alignment are examples of activities in this category.

Is All Strategy Planned?

Even the best-laid plans do not always result in the intended outcomes. Between the time a strategy is crafted—that is, when *intended* outcomes are specified—and the time that strategy is implemented, a host of things can change. For example, a competitor might introduce a new product or new regulations might have been passed. Thus, the *realized* strategy can be somewhat different from the *intended* strategy.[9]

Multiple Levels of Strategy

Strategy formulation occurs at the *corporate, business unit,* and *functional* levels. In a multibusiness, diversified corporation, *corporate* strategy is concerned with what kinds of businesses a firm should compete in and how the overall portfolio of businesses should be managed. In a single-product or single-service business or in a division of a multibusiness corporation, *business unit* strategy is concerned with deciding what product or service to offer, how to manufacture or create it, and how to take it to the market place. *Functional* strategies typically involve a more limited domain, such as marketing, human resources, or technology. All three are part of strategic management—the totality of managerial processes used to guide the long-term future of an organization.

The Role of Stakeholders

Most companies rely, to a great extent, on a network of external *stakeholders*—suppliers, partners, and even competitors—in creating value for customers. The motivation of internal stakeholders—directors, top executives, middle managers, and employees—also is critical to success. A misstep in managing suppliers, a major error in employee relations, or a lack of communication with principal shareholders can set back a company's progress for years. The importance of different stakeholders to a company's competitive position depends on the *stake* they have in the organization and the kind of *influence* they can exert. Stakeholders can have an *ownership stake* (shareholders, directors, among others), an *economic stake* (creditors, employees, customers, suppliers), or a *social stake* (regulatory agencies, charities, the local community, activist groups).[10] Some have *formal power,* others *economic* or *political power.* Formal power is usually associated with legal obligations or rights; economic power is derived from an ability to withhold products, services, or capital; and political power is rooted in an ability to persuade other stakeholders to influence the behavior of an organization.

Vision and Mission

A *vision* statement represents senior management's long-range goals for the organization—a description of what competitive position it wants to attain over a given period of time and what core competencies it must acquire to get there. As such, it summarizes a company's broad strategic focus for the future. A *mission* statement documents the purpose for an organization's existence. Mission statements often contain a code of corporate conduct to guide management in implementing the mission.

In crafting a *vision* statement, two important lessons are worth heeding. First, most successful companies focus on relatively few activities and do them extremely well. McDonald's is successful precisely because it sticks to hamburgers, H&R Block because it concentrates on tax preparation, and Microsoft because it focuses on software. This suggests that effective strategy development is as much about deciding *what not to do as it is about choosing what activities to focus on.* The second lesson is that most successful companies achieved their leadership position by adopting a vision far greater than their resource base and competencies would allow. To become the market leader, a focus on the drivers of competition is not enough; a vision that paints "a new future" is required.

With such a mind-set, gaps between capabilities and goals become challenges rather than constraints, and the goal of winning can sustain a sense of urgency over a long period of time.[11]

A vision statement should provide both strategic guidance and motivational focus. A good vision has the following characteristics:

- It is clear, but not so constraining that it inhibits initiative.
- It meets the legitimate interests and values of all stakeholders.
- It is feasible; that is, it can be implemented.[12]

Vision statements help frame strategic action. When Jack Welch became CEO of General Electric in 1981, the U.S. economy was in recession. High interest rates and a strong dollar exacerbated the problem. To get the company moving and to leverage performance in GE's diverse portfolio of businesses, the new CEO challenged each business to be "better than the best." This challenge led to the adoption of the vision statement that each business become. . . "the number one or number two competitor in its industry—or to disengage."[13]

Increasingly, companies around the world are adopting formal statements of corporate *values*, the core of a *mission* statement, and senior executives now routinely identify ethical behavior, honesty, integrity, and social concerns as top issues on their companies' agendas. A recent survey by consultants Booz Allen Hamilton, Inc. showed that of the 89 percent of companies surveyed that had a written corporate values statement, 90 percent specified ethical conduct as a key guiding principle. Further, 81 percent believed their management practices encouraged ethical behavior among staff. Ethics-related language in formal statements not only sets corporate expectations for employee behavior; it also serves as a shield companies are using in an increasingly complex and global legal and regulatory environment. The survey also showed that the importance of particular values and how companies align those values with their strategies vary significantly by region. Asian and European companies are more likely than North American firms to emphasize values related to the corporation's broader role in society, such as social and environmental responsibility. Finally, in implementing a values-based strategy, the CEO's tone matters. Eighty-five percent of the respondents say their companies rely on explicit CEO support to reinforce values, and 77 percent say such support is one of the "most effective" practices for reinforcing the company's ability to act on its values. It is considered the most effective practice among respondents in all regions, industries, and company sizes.[14]

The usefulness of a carefully crafted *mission* statement is illustrated by the history of Johnson & Johnson. For more than 50 years, its Credo—a statement of fundamental beliefs about how the company defines its corporate responsibilities—has guided Johnson & Johnson in all its actions. It begins "We believe our first responsibility is to the doctors, nurses, and patients, to mothers and fathers and all others who use our products and services . . . ." and continues to explicitly define the company's responsibilities to employees, the community and shareholders. Its value was reaffirmed during the Tylenol crises of 1982 and 1986 when the company's product was adulterated with cyanide. With Johnson & Johnson's name and reputation at stake, executives made important decisions that were inspired by the company's Credo. It helped the company preserve its reputation and regain its Tylenol acetaminophen business.

Strategic Intent and Stretch

A related concept is a company's *strategic intent*. A statement of strategic intent is at once an executive summary of the strategic goals a company has adopted and a motivational message. Properly articulated, a statement of strategic intent does more than paint a vision for the future; it signals the desire to win and recognizes that successful strategies are built as much around what can be as around what is. It focuses the organization on key competitive targets and provides goals about which competencies to develop, what kinds of resources to harness, and what segments to concentrate on. Instead of worrying about the degree of fit between current resources and opportunities, it shifts the focus to how to close the capability gap. Current resources and capabilities become starting points for strategy development, not constraints on strategy formulation or its implementation.[15]

A related idea is the concept of *stretch*. Stretch reflects the recognition that successful strategies are built as much around *what can be* as around *what is*. Ultimately, every company must create a fit between its resources and its opportunities. The question is over what time frame? Too short a time frame encourages a focus on *fit* rather than *stretch*, on resource *allocation* rather than on getting more value from existing resources. The use of too long a time horizon, however, creates an unacceptable degree of uncertainty and threatens to turn stretch objectives into unrealistic goals.

Strategy and the Nonprofit Sector

The nonprofit sector has grown and now includes over 1 million organizations. Collectively, nonprofit organizations contribute significantly to the national economy. Like their for-profit counterparts, they also are experiencing fundamental shifts in their environmental conditions—shifts that could threaten their future well-being. This explains the growing interest on the part of nonprofit organizations in becoming more strategic in how they operate.

Like for-profit corporations, every nonprofit organization, no matter what its mission or scope, needs three kinds of performance metrics: (1) a measure of its success in mobilizing the necessary resources, (2) an evaluation of the effectiveness of its people in doing their assigned jobs, and (3) an assessment of its progress toward fulfilling its chosen mission. For example, an environmental organization might evaluate the performance of its staff by whether a specific piece of clean-air or clean-water legislation was adopted, whereas a charity might choose to measure how many people attended its fundraisers.

The first two of these metrics are relatively easy to create and implement. Metrics for the mobilization of a nonprofit organization's resources include such measures as fund-raising performance, membership growth, and market share. The number of people served by a particular program and the number of projects that an organization completes are examples of simple staff-related performance measures.

Defining and implementing the third kind of metric—measuring the success of the organization in achieving its mission—is a major challenge for nonprofit organizations. In the for-profit sector, value creation is relatively easy to measure. Companies can focus on measures such as shareholder value, profitability, and return on investment. In contrast, nonprofit organizations usually have broad, qualitative missions that are much more difficult to measure. How, for example, can we determine whether the Girl Scouts of the USA make progress toward its mission—to help young girls reach their full potential as citizens?

Research conducted at McKinsey & Co. has shown that nonprofit organizations, despite these difficulties, can measure their success in achieving their mission.[16] Three different approaches have been identified. The first option is to define a mission sufficiently narrow so that progress can be measured directly. The mission of Goodwill Industries, for example, is to raise people out of poverty through work. Goodwill can therefore measure its success simply by counting the number of people who participate in its training programs and find jobs.

A second approach is to invest in research to determine whether the organization's activities actually do help in achieving its stated mission. The Jump$tart Coalition, which is dedicated to improving the educational outcomes of poor children, follows this approach. It periodically commissions independent statistical studies to show that Jump$tart graduates enter kindergarten better prepared than children who do not participate in the program.[17]

For many nonprofit organizations, however, narrowing the scope of the mission is not a viable option and commissioning research into outcomes is prohibitive or infeasible. How, for example, can the Nature Conservancy measure the impact of its efforts on the Earth's total biodiversity? In such cases, a third option for measuring success should be considered: the development of a comprehensive set of "micro-level" goals that, if achieved, imply success on a broader scale. Consider what the Chesapeake Bay Foundation has done. Its mission is to preserve the health of the Chesapeake estuary. To make this goal more concrete, it created nine indicators of the bay's health, such as water clarity, levels of dissolved oxygen, migratory fish populations, and the size of the surrounding wetlands. To measure progress, it collected baseline data for each indicator and then set specific 10-year targets representing significant progress for the bay.[18] A major advantage of this approach is that it is easily understood by the general public and potential donors, and it thereby benefits fund-raising and attracting other forms of support.

THE STRATEGY FORMULATION PROCESS

Steps

The process of crafting a strategy can be organized around three key questions: *Where are we now? Where do we go?* and *How do we get there?* (Figure 1-4). Each question defines a part of the process and suggests different types of analyses and evaluations. It also shows that the components of a strategic analysis overlap, and that feedback loops are an integral part of the process.

1. The *Where are we now?* part of the process is concerned with assessing the current state of the business or the company as a whole. It begins with revisiting such fundamental issues as what the organization's mission is, what management's long-term vision for the company is, and who its principal stakeholders are. Other key components include a detailed evaluation of the company's current performance; of pertinent trends in the broader sociopolitical, economic, legal, and technological environment in which the company operates; of opportunities and threats in the industry environment; and of internal strengths and weaknesses.

2. *Where do we go?* questions are designed to generate and explore strategic alternatives based on the answers obtained to the first question. At the business unit level, for example, options such as concentrating on growth in a few market segments or adopting a wider market focus, whether to go-it-alone or partner with another company, or whether to focus on value-added or

Figure 1-4 The Strategy Formulation Process

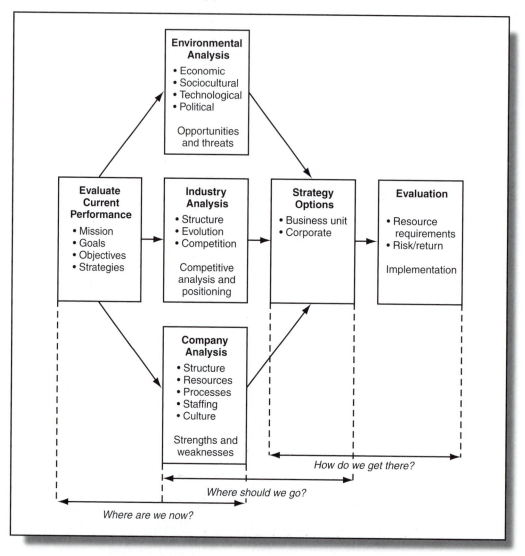

low-cost solutions for customers might be considered. At the corporate level, this part of the process is focused on shaping the portfolio of businesses the company participates in and on making adjustments in parenting philosophies and processes. At both levels, the output is a statement of *strategic intent,* which identifies the guiding business concept or driving force that will propel the company forward.

3. The *How do we get there?* component of the process is focused on how to achieve the desired objectives. One of the most important issues addressed at this stage is how to bridge the *capability gap* that separates current organizational skills and capabilities from those that are needed to achieve the stated strategic intent. It deals with the "strategic alignment" of *core competences* with *emerging market needs* and with identifying *key success factors* associated with successfully implementing the chosen strategy. The end product is a detailed set of initiatives for implementing the chosen strategy and exercising strategic discipline and control.

Strategy and Planning

A strategy review can be triggered by a host of factors—new leadership, disappointing performance, changes in ownership, the emergence of new competitors or technologies—or be part of a scheduled, typically annual, review process.

Most companies employ some form of strategic planning. The impetus for imposing structure to the process comes from two main pressures: (1) the need to cope with an increasingly complex range of issues—economic, political, social, and legal on a global scale—and (2) the increasing speed with which the competitive environment is changing. A formal system ensures that the required amount of time and resources are allocated to the process, that priorities are set, that activities are integrated and coordinated, and that the right feedback is obtained.

This planning process is usually organized in terms of a *planning cycle*. This cycle often begins with a review at the corporate level of the overall competitive environment and of the corporate guidelines to the various divisions and businesses. Next, divisions and business units are asked to update their long-term strategies and to indicate how these strategies fit with the company's major priorities and goals. Third, divisional and business unit plans are reviewed, evaluated, adjusted, coordinated, and integrated in meetings between corporate and divisional/business unit managers. Finally, detailed operating plans are developed at the divisional/business unit level, and final approvals are obtained from corporate headquarters.

A formal strategic planning system or planning cycle, by definition, attempts to structure strategy development and implementation as a primarily linear, sequential process. Environmental and competitive changes do not respect a calendar-driven process, however. When a significant new competitive opportunity or challenge emerges, a company cannot afford to wait to respond. This does not mean that formal processes should be abandoned altogether. Rather, it underscores that even though strategy is about crafting a long-term *vision* for an organization, it should maintain a degree of flexibility about how to get there and preserve options for adapting to change.

EVALUATING STRATEGIC OPTIONS

Criteria

The ultimate test of any strategy is whether it produces a competitive advantage with above-average returns. Thus, it is not surprising that, to many executives, strategy evaluation is principally a matter of how well a business or company performs. Although intuitive, this perspective is not satisfactory because measures of current performance are not necessarily indicative of future performance. Strategy evaluation should focus on a firm's future competitiveness and ask whether long-term objectives are appropriate; whether strategies chosen to attain such objectives are consistent, bold enough, and achievable; and whether these strategies are likely to produce a sustainable competitive advantage with above-average returns.

Quantifying such judgments is difficult. Though financial returns are important, the key issue is whether strategic intent and specific proposals aimed at realizing intent always can be reduced to a cash-flow forecast. Clearly, the financial effect on the corporation of specific strategy options, such as acquisitions at the corporate level or specific new product or market entries at the business unit level, can and should be quantified. A good argument can be made, however, that strategic thinking does not lend itself to purely quantitative assessments. Historically, corporate and business unit strategies were limited to market-based, competitive initiatives. Today, analysis of political and other nonmarket forces is becoming a more important component of strategic thinking.

Executives face enormous pressure from within the organization and from external sources such as the financial community to forecast business unit and corporate performance and, implicitly, to quantify anticipated strategic outcomes. Traditionally, *return on investment* (ROI) was the most common measure for evaluating a strategy's efficacy. Today, *shareholder value* is one of the most widely accepted yardsticks.

Shareholder Value

The *shareholder value approach* (SVA) to strategy evaluation holds that the value of the corporation is determined by the discounted future cash flows it is likely to generate. In economic terms, value is created when companies invest capital at returns that exceed the cost of that capital. Under this model, new strategic initiatives are treated as any other investment the company makes, and evaluated on the basis of shareholder value. A whole new managerial framework—*value-based management* (VBM)—has been created around it.[19]

The use of shareholder value or related measures, such as *economic value added* (EVA), defined as after-tax operating profit minus the cost of capital, as the principal yardstick for evaluating alternative strategy proposals is somewhat contentious. Besides implementation problems, there are issues of transparency in the relationship between shareholder value on the one hand and positioning for sustained competitive advantage on the other. Even though shareholder value and strategy formulation are ultimately about the same thing—generating long-term sustained value—they use different conceptions of value and view the purpose of strategy from a fundamentally different point of view.

Strategists focus on creating a sustainable competitive advantage through *value delivered to customers*. But SVA measures *value to shareholders.* Though in the long run the two should be highly correlated, individual strategy proposals can force short-term trade-offs between the two. It is not surprising, therefore, that shareholder value has not been universally embraced as the preferred method for measuring a strategy's potential. It also explains why less restrictive, but possibly less rigorous evaluation schemes, such as the Balanced Scorecard, discussed later in this book, have gained in acceptance in the last few years.[20]

NOTES

1. Christopher A. Bartlett and Sumantra Ghoshal, 2002, "Building Competitive Advantage Through People," *Sloan Management Review,* 43(2), 34–41.
2. C. K. Prahalad and G. Hamel, 1990, "The Core Competence of the Corporation," *Harvard Business Review,* May–June, 79–91.
3. Christopher A. Bartlett and Sumantra Ghoshal, 2002, op. cit., 35.
4. Marco Iansiti and Roy Levien, 2004, "Strategy as Ecology," *Harvard Business Review,* March, pp. 68–78.
5. Michael E. Porter, 1996, "What Is Strategy?" *Harvard Business Review,* November–December, pp. 61–78.
6. George S. Day, 1997, "Maintaining the Competitive Edge: Creating and Sustaining Advantages in Dynamic Competitive Environments," Chapter 2, p. 52, in George S. Day and David J. Reibstein (Eds.), *Wharton on Dynamic Competitive Advantage* (New York: John Wiley & Sons).
7. These ideas are based on Timothy A. Luehrman, 1998, "Strategy as a Portfolio of Real Options," *Harvard Business Review,* September–October, 89–99.
8. This section is based on Marco Iansiti, 2004, *The Keystone Advantage: What the New Dynamics of Business Ecosystems Mean for Strategy, Innovation, and Sustainability* (Boston: Harvard Business School Press).
9. Henry Mintzberg, 1985, "Of Strategies, Deliberate and Emergent," *Strategic Management Journal,* 6(3), 257–272.
10. R. E. Freeman, 1984, *Strategic Management: A Stakeholder Approach* (Boston: Pittman).
11. Gary Hamel and C. K. Prahalad, 1989, "Strategic

Intent," *Harvard Business Review,* May– June, 63–76.

12. John Kotter, 1990, *A Force for Change* (New York: Free Press).

13. "GE's Two-Decade Transformation: Jack Welch's Leadership," Harvard Business School Case Study 9–399–150, Harvard Business School, 2005.

14. Reggie Van Lee, Lisa Fabish, and Nancy McGaw, 2005, "The Value of Corporate Values," *Strategy and Business,* Summer, Booz Allen Hamilton, Inc.

15. Gary Hamel and C. K. Prahalad, 1989, op. cit.

16. John Sawhill and David Williamson, 2001, "Measuring What Matters in Nonprofits," *The McKinsey Quarterly,* 2.

17. Ibid.

18. Ibid.

19. See, e.g., Tom Copeland, Tim Koller, and Jack Murrin, 1995, *Valuation: Measuring and Managing the Value of Companies* (New York: John Wiley & Sons).

20. R. S. Kaplan and D. P. Norton, 1996, "Using the Balanced Scorecard as a Strategic Management System," *Harvard Business Review,* January–February, 75–85; and R. S. Kaplan and D. P. Norton, 1992, "The Balanced Scorecard—Measures That Drive Performance," *Harvard Business Review,* January–February, 71–79.

Strategy and Performance

INTRODUCTION

Carefully crafted strategies often only deliver a fraction of their promised financial value. Why should this be so? Is it because CEOs press for better execution when they really need a sounder strategy? Or is it because they focus on crafting a new strategy when execution is the organization's true weakness? Are there other reasons? And how can such errors be avoided? A good starting point is a better understanding of how strategy and performance are linked.

We begin this chapter with a discussion of two widely cited studies on the subject of how companies achieve greatness as measured by superior, sustained performance. The first, by Jim Collins, entitled *Good to Great: Why Some Companies Make the Leap. . . and Others Don't*, originally published in 2001, focused on what good companies can do to become truly great. Its findings have inspired many CEOs to change their views about what drives success. It showed that factors such as CEO compensation, technology, mergers and acquisitions, and change management initiatives played relatively minor roles in fostering the *Good to Great* process. Instead, successes in three main areas—*disciplined people, disciplined thought, and disciplined action*—were likely the most significant factors in determining a company's ability to achieve greatness.

The second, *What Really Works: The 4+2 Formula for Sustained Business Success*, by Joyce, Nohria, and Roberson, in association with McKinsey & Co., is a groundbreaking study aimed at identifying the must-have management practices that truly produce superior results. As part of this so-called Evergreen Project, more than 200 well-established management practices were evaluated as they were employed over a 10-year period by 160 companies. It concluded that eight management practices—four primary and four secondary—are directly correlated with superior corporate performance as measured by total return to shareholders. Winning companies achieved excellence in all four of the primary practices, plus any two of the secondary practices, suggesting the *4+2 Formula* title. Losing companies failed to do so.

Although the two studies differ substantially in terms of their methodology, there is substantial agreement in the findings. As it turns out, a company's strategy, execution, leadership and talent pool, organization, process, and corporate culture *all* are critical to sustained success. What is more, they *all* are inextricably linked and *together* determine performance. To understand how these variables interact with each other, the third section of this chapter presents a conceptual framework that links strategy to performance.

Next, we introduce the concept of a "Balanced Scorecard" as a way of creating focus in a company's efforts to implement a chosen strategy. The Balanced Scorecard framework forces executives to address four key issues on an ongoing basis: (1) How do customers see us? (2) At what must we excel? (3) Can we continue to improve and create value? (4) How do we look to our company's shareholders? and highlights any gaps in employee skill sets, information technology, and processes that can hamper an organization's ability to execute a given strategy.

The chapter concludes with a look at the role of an organization's board of directors in creating a high-performance environment, monitoring corporate progress, and ensuring compliance.

FROM GOOD TO GREAT—
ABOUT HEDGEHOGS AND
FLYWHEELS[1]

Jim Collins conducted two widely cited, detailed studies of companies' sustainable, superior performance. The first, published as *Built to Last* and co-authored with Jerry Porras, explored what makes great companies great and how they sustain that greatness over time. The second, the aforementioned *Good to Great: Why Some Companies Make the Leap. . . and Others Don't*, originally published in 2001, addressed a more vexing question: What can merely good companies do to become truly great? In this context, Collins defined "great" in terms of a number of metrics, including financial performance that exceeded the market average by several orders of magnitude over a sustained period of time. Using these criteria, a handful of companies—Abbott, Fannie Mae, Circuit City, Gillette, Kimberly-Clark, Kroger, Nucor, Philip Morris, Pitney Bowes, Walgreens, and Wells Fargo—were selected and analyzed in detail.

The quality and nature of the *top leadership* defined a significant difference between good and great companies. Collins identifies what he calls "Level 5 leadership" as a common characteristic of the great companies assessed in the study. This type of leadership forms the top level of a five-level hierarchy that ranges from merely competent supervision to strategic executive decision making. Level 5 leaders displayed an unusual mix of intense determination and profound humility. These leaders often have a long-term personal sense of investment in the company and its success, often cultivated through a career-spanning climb up the company's ranks. Personal ego and individual financial gain are not as important as the long-term benefit of the team and the company to true Level 5 leaders.

The next important factor is the *nature of the leadership team*. Specifically, Collins advances the idea that the process of securing high-quality, high-talent individuals with Level 5 leadership abilities must be undertaken *before* an overarching strategy can (and should) be developed. With the right people in the right positions, many of the management problems that plague companies and sap valuable resources will automatically dissipate. Thus, firms seeking to make the *Good to Great* transition might find it worthwhile to expend extra energy and time on personnel searches and decision making.

A third element of some companies' unique ability to make the transition from *Good to Great* is the *willingness to identify and assess defining facts in the company and in the larger business environment*. In today's market, trends in consumer preferences are constantly changing, and the inability to keep apace with these changes often results in company failure.

In considering the importance of strategy, Collins uses the metaphor of the hedgehog to illustrate the seemingly contradictory principle that simplicity can sometimes lead to greatness. When confronted by predators, the hedgehog's simple, but surprisingly effective, response is to roll up into a ball. Whereas other predators, such as the fox, might be more clever, few can devise a strategy that is effective enough to overcome the hedgehog's simple, repetitive response. Similarly, Collins asserts that the way to make the transformation from *Good to Great* often is *not doing many things well, but instead, doing one thing better than anyone else in the world*. It might take time to identify the single function that will be a particular firm's "hedgehog concept," but those who do successfully identify it often are rewarded with singular success. To expedite this process, Collins suggests using three criteria: (1) Determine what the company can and cannot be best at in the world; (2) determine what drives the company's economic engine; and (3) determine what the company's people are deeply passionate about.

Collins also notes the importance of an *overarching organizational culture of discipline*. This means creating an organization in which each manager and staff member is driven by an unrelenting inner sense of determination. In this type of organization, each individual functions as an entrepreneur, with a deeply rooted personal investment in both their own work and the company's success. Discipline manifests itself in an almost fanatical devotion to objectives, to sticking to the script outlined by the company's "hedgehog concept" that will foster the transformation from merely *Good to Great*.

Businesses should not depend on *technology* alone to increase efficiency, reduce overhead, and maximize competitive advantage. Good-to-great companies approach the prospect of new and emerging technologies with the same prudence and careful deliberation that characterizes all of their other business decisions. Further, these companies tend to apply technology in a manner that is reflective of their "hedgehog concepts"—typically by selecting and focusing solely on the development of a few technologies that are fundamentally compatible with their established strengths and objectives. Collins characterizes the ideal approach to technology with the following cycle: "Pause—Think—Crawl—Walk—Run."

A significant part of the value in the *Good to Great* study is in its orientation toward *process*. Collins describes two cycles that demonstrate the way that business decisions tend to accumulate incrementally in either an advantageous or a disadvantageous manner. Both accrue—more slowly that most people think—over time. The first is the *advantageous business cycle* that, in some cases, can foster the transition from *Good to Great*; Collins calls this the "the flywheel effect." By making decisions and taking actions that reinforce and affirm the company's "hedgehog" competencies, executives initiate positive momentum. This, in turn, results in the accumulation of tangible positive outcomes, which serve to energize and earn the investment and loyalty of the staff. This revitalization of the team serves to further build momentum. If the cycle continues to repeat in this manner, the transition from *Good to Great* is likely to transpire. In contrast, the *doom loop* is characterized by reactive decision making, an overextension into too many diverse areas of concentration, following short-lived trends, frequent changes in leadership and personnel, loss of morale, and disappointing results.

Linking these results to his previous work, *Built to Last*, Collins concludes that companies need a set of *core values* in order to achieve long-term, sustainable success; a quest for profits is not enough. This purpose does not have to be specific; even if the shared values that compel the company toward success are as open-ended as being the best at what they do and achieving excellence consistently, that may be sufficient as long as the team members are equally dedicated to the same set of values.

THE 4+2 FORMULA FOR SUSTAINED BUSINESS SUCCESS[2]

In association with McKinsey & Co., Joyce, Nohria, and Roberson also conducted a groundbreaking study aimed at identifying the must-have management practices that truly produce superior results. They examined more than 200 well-established management practices as they were employed over a 10-year period by 160 companies.

The study shows that—without exception—companies that outperformed their industry peers excelled at four primary management practices—strategy, execution, culture, and structure—and augmented their strengths in those areas with a mastery of (any) two of four secondary management practices—talent, innovation, leadership, and mergers and partnerships (hence the 4+2 designation). The results clearly show that it does not matter whether a company implements a particular software system or whether it chooses to centralize or decentralize its business processes. What matters is how it implements such decisions; that whatever technology it selects, it implements it flawlessly; that whatever form of organization it chooses, it pays attention to the impact of that decision on its ability to execute. This requires strength in *all* four primary and *two or more* secondary practices. A winning performance, therefore, depends on much more than having the right strategy; it calls for achieving excellence on six or more dimensions of success at once. What is more, a single misstep on any of the six can severely depress a company's performance, or worse, be fatal.

Excelling at Four Primary Practices

What does it mean to excel in setting strategy, execution, shaping culture, and forging structure? Numerous tools, techniques, and frameworks—some of which are described in this book—have been developed to help executives master these practices. To improve execution, for example, executives have used Total Quality Management (TQM), Kaizen, and Six Sigma, among other techniques. The study by Nohria et al. shows that although such tools and techniques are helpful, and even necessary, in say, streamlining execution or developing strategy, no single, obvious choice will bring a company success. There are, however, "hallmarks" of effective strategy—execution, culture, and structure—which virtually all of the most consistently successful companies demonstrated for more than 10 years.

Strategy: Devise and Maintain a Clearly Stated, Focused Strategy

Whether a company chooses to compete on low prices, top quality, or great service, it must be clear what the chosen strategy is and it should be consistently communicated to customers, employees, shareholders, and other stakeholders. Successful strategies also tend to focus on growth; doubling the size of the core business and building a new business about half the size of the core business every 7 years appeared to be the norm for high-performance companies. Finally, a clear hallmark of success was that effective strategies begin with a simple, focused value proposition that is rooted in deep, certain knowledge about a company's target customers and a realistic appraisal of the firm's capabilities.

Execution: Develop and Maintain Flawless Operational Execution

Flawless execution, the study found, is as important as having a sound strategy. Winning companies consistently exceeded customer expectations. They also increased productivity by about twice the industry's average and were realistic about what could be achieved. No company can outperform its competitors in every facet of its operations. Identifying which processes are most important to meeting customer needs and focusing the company's energies and resources on making those processes as efficient as possible therefore becomes paramount.

Culture: Develop and Maintain a Performance-Oriented Culture

Culture plays a significant role in corporate success. Building the right culture—one that champions high-level performance and ethical behavior rather than merely promoting a fun environment—is key. In winning companies, the study found, everyone works at the highest level. They function with a culture that encourages outstanding individual and team contributions, one that holds employees—not just managers—responsible for success. Also important, winners do not just compare themselves to their immediate competitors; they look outside the industry for a suitable benchmark. For example, once a winning company has overmatched its rivals in, say, the effectiveness of its logistics, it may ask "Why can't we do it better than FedEx?" Even if the goal is unreachable, it still may represent a significant opportunity for high-performing employees and managers by asking: "If we can't be the best at logistics, why not outsource it to a partner that can?"

Structure: Build and Maintain a Fast, Flexible, Flat Organization

Too great a focus on protocols and procedures and too much red tape can impede progress, dampen employees' enthusiasm, and sap energy. High-performance companies try to eliminate unnecessary bureaucracy—extra layers of management, an abundance of rules and regulations, outdated formalities. They strive to make their structures and processes as simple as possible, not only for their employees, but also for their vendors and customers. Again, these findings confirm that the "how" is often more important than the "what" of organizational structure. No particular organizational structure differentiated winning companies from the others. It made little difference whether they were organized by function, geography, or product, or whether they gave their business units P&L responsibility. What did matter was whether the organizational structure simplified the work.

Embracing Two of Four Secondary Practices

In many ways, the study's findings about the four primary business practices are both unsurprising and intuitive. In contrast, the conclusions about the secondary practices of business success—talent, innovation, leadership, and mergers and partnerships—are more surprising. In particular, many executives tend to believe that excellence in two of the factors—talent and leadership—is at least as important to sustained success as excellence in each of the four primary practices. The study draws different conclusions. Winning companies complemented their strengths in the four primary practices with superior performance in *any two* of the secondary practices. It did not matter which two; no dominant patterns in the combinations were found. What is more, it made no difference if a company excelled in all four secondary practices rather than just two; going beyond "4+2" was not rewarded.

Talent: Hold on to Talented Employees and Find More
The best test of the quality of a company's talent base is the ease with which any executive who leaves to join a competitor can be replaced from within. Winning companies hired chief executives from the outside half as often as underperforming firms. Growing talent in-house often is cheaper, more reliable, and promotes continuity and loyalty. Companies that focus on talent building dedicate major resources—including personal attention from top executives—to building and retaining an effective workforce and management team.

Innovation: Make Industry-transforming Innovations
Companies that excel at innovation are focused on finding new product ideas or technological breakthroughs that have the potential to transform their industries, not just marginal improvements.

At these companies, innovation encompasses more than developing new products and services; they also apply new technologies to their business processes, which can yield huge savings and sometimes have the power to transform an industry.

Leadership: Find Leaders Who Are Committed to the Business and Its People

Choosing the right CEO can raise performance significantly. Among a CEO's most important qualities are the ability to build relationships with people at all levels of the organization and to inspire the rest of the management team to do the same Another is a leader's ability to spot opportunities and problems early. Some rely on intuition; others create special groups within the organization that are assigned to stay abreast of changes in everything from politics to demographics. Still others engage outside consultants or academics to watch for changes in the marketplace. Though their methods vary, effective leaders help their companies remain winners by seizing opportunities before their competitors do and tackling problems before they impair ongoing performance.

Mergers and Partnerships: Seek Growth Through Mergers and Partnerships

After innovation, pursuit of mergers and partnerships is the second most popular avenue of growth. Although many of the companies studied engaged in some merger activity, only a small number—less than a quarter—were able to make this a winning practice. Companies that do relatively small deals on a consistent basis are likely to be more successful than those that do large, occasional deals. Winners made better choices: They created value in most of the deals they struck, generating returns in 3 years that exceeded the premium paid. By contrast, underperformers destroyed shareholder value in most of the deals they did. Winning companies did not treat acquisitions and partnerships casually or as one-off deals. They invested substantial financial and human resources in developing an efficient, ongoing process for deal making; for example, establishing dedicated teams composed of individuals with the requisite investigative, financial, business, and negotiation skills. Winning companies often have codified principles—lessons drawn from experience—that enable them to more consistently choose the right partners and integrate them quickly.

STRATEGY AND PERFORMANCE: A CONCEPTUAL FRAMEWORK

Although some of the conclusions of the studies cited differ in emphasis or detail, there is a remarkable consistency to these findings. They clearly show that in today's complex business environment, no single individual—or even the top two or three people—can do all that is required to make a company successful. Corporate success increasingly depends on the willingness and ability of every manager to not just meet their own functional or divisional responsibilities, but to think about how their actions influence the performance of the company as a whole. Viewed this way, organizational performance is ultimately the result of thousands of decisions and trade-offs made every day by individuals at all levels of an organization. The choices that these individuals make reflect their aspirations, knowledge, and incentives, and usually are sensible in the context of what each knows, sees, and understands.[3]

When strategies are not effective, it is therefore not very useful to question peoples' rationality. Merely restating the organization's aspirations or exhorting employees to do better is equally unproductive. Instead, the focus should be on changing the organizational environment to encourage decision making that is aligned with the overall objectives of the company. This means reexamining who makes what decisions and what information, constraints, tools, and incentives affect the way they evaluate those decisions. Understanding why and where suboptimal decisions are made is the first step to realigning the organizational environment with the chosen strategy.

Success requires that the right people—armed with the right information and motivated by the right incentives—have clear authority to make critical decisions. Developing the right organizational model thus requires identifying which activities are critical to achieving a chosen strategy, and then defining the organizational attributes that must be present to encourage the right behaviors. Therefore, companies must focus on three critical dimensions: people, knowledge, and incentives.

Figure 2-1 shows a conceptual framework for understanding the complex links between strategy and a company's performance. It has three interrelated components. The first links corporate purpose to strategy and leadership. The second describes the organizational environment in terms of five interacting components: structure, systems, processes, people, and culture. The third links a company's definition of performance with two distinct philosophies of exercising control. This framework is helpful in identifying actual or potential challenges and

Figure 2-1   Strategy and Performance: A Conceptual Framework

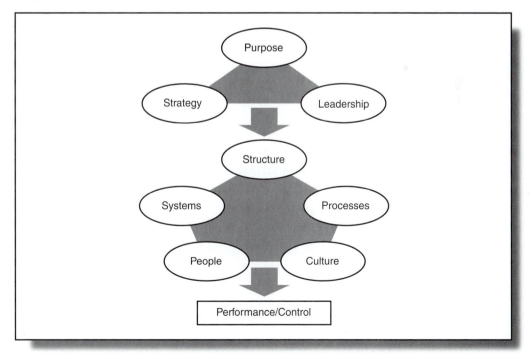

obstacles to successfully implementing a chosen strategic direction. It can also be used to analyze the process of strategic change.

Strategy, Purpose, and Leadership

The so-called *strategy–structure–systems* paradigm dominated thinking about the role of corporate leaders for many years. Developed in the 1920s, when companies such as General Motors began to experiment with diversification strategies, it held that the key to successfully executing a complex strategy was to create the right organizational structure and disciplined planning and control support systems. Doing so, it was thought, would systematize behavior and minimize ineffective and countereffective actions, thereby helping managers cope with the increased complexity associated with a multibusiness enterprise.

This doctrine remained dominant for most of the twentieth century. It helped companies cope with high growth, integrate their operations horizontally, manage their diversified business portfolios, and expand internationally. The advent of global competition and the technology revolution greatly reduced its effectiveness, however. What had been its principal strength—minimizing human initiative—became its major weakness; the new competitive realities called for a different managerial thrust that was focused on developing corporate competencies such as innovation, entrepreneurship, horizontal coordination, and decentralized decision making.[4]

To deal with more-intense global competition, corporate leaders began to articulate a broader, long-term strategic intent rooted in a clear sense of corporate purpose. In effect, they redefined their task from being the "chief strategist" to being the "chief facilitator" and sought ways to involve employees at all levels in the strategic management process. Top executive agendas started to include such items as creating organizational momentum, instilling core values, developing human capital, and recognizing individual accomplishment. In the process, the preoccupation with structural solutions was replaced by a focus on process, and the rationale behind systems was redirected toward supporting the development of capabilities and unleashing human potential rather than guiding employee behavior.[5] This broader, more humanistic view of strategic leadership recognizes that strategic discipline and control are secured through commitment, not compliance.

The top portion in Figure 2-1 summarizes these important relationships among a company's *strategy, leadership, and sense of purpose*. Successful strategy development and implementation require that these elements mutually reinforce each other as a basis for obtaining commitment, focus, and control at all levels of the organization.

Strategy and Organizational Change

A host of factors—from structural and cultural rigidities to a lack of adequate resources to an adherence to dysfunctional processes—can reduce a company's capacity for absorbing change. It is important, therefore, for executives charged with developing and implementing new strategic directions to understand the dynamics of the various organizational forces at work.

The middle portion of Figure 2-1 shows five organizational variables—*structure, systems, processes, people*, and *culture*—that are key to creating effective organizational change. As shown, they are interrelated, which explains why the successful implementation of a new strategy often requires change in all variables. In other words, an implementation effort or corporate reorganization that is focused on just one of these variables is doomed to fail. Style, skills, and superordinate goals—values around which a business is built—are as important as strategy or structure in bringing about fundamental change in an organization.

Structure

To become more competitive, many companies have shed layers of management and adopted flatter organizational structures. As organizations became leaner, the problem of "how to organize" changed from one of dividing up tasks to one focused on issues of coordination. The issue of *structure*, therefore, is not just one of deciding whether to centralize or decentralize decision making. Rather, it involves identifying dimensions that are crucial to an organization's ability to adapt and evolve strategically and then adopting a structure that allows it to refocus as and when necessary.

Choosing the right organizational model is difficult. Most organizations were not created to support a specific strategy, but evolved over time in response to a host of known, as well as unknown, market forces. Finding the right model becomes more difficult as companies become larger, because growth increases complexity. As complexity increases, aligning the interests of an individual with the interests of the company becomes much more difficult. Nevertheless, the goal should be to create an organizational environment that allocates resources effectively and is naturally self-correcting as strategic changes need to be made.[6]

In considering structural options, it is important to realize that there is no "one right form of organization"; each structural solution has specific advantages and drawbacks. What is more, organizations are not homogeneous entities; what is right for one part of an organization or set of tasks might not be the preferred solution for another. No matter what form of organization is used, however, *transparency* is critical; effective strategy implementation cannot occur if lines of authority are blurred or responsibility is ill defined.

Corporate structures typically reflect one of five dominant approaches to organization: (1) *Functional* organizational structures make sense when a particular task requires the efforts of a substantial number of specialists. (2) *Geographically* based structures are useful when a company operates in a diverse set of geographical regions. (3) *Decentralized* (divisional) structures have been found to reduce complexity in a multibusiness environment. (4) *Strategic business units* help define groupings of businesses that share key strategic elements. (5) *Matrix structures* allow multiple channels of authority and are favored when coordination among different interests is key.

The growing importance of human and intellectual capital as a source of competitive advantage has encouraged companies to experiment with new organizational forms. Some companies are creating organizational structures centered on knowledge creation and dissemination. Others, in a drive to become leaner and more agile, are restricting ownership or control to only those intellectual and physical assets that are critical to their value-creation process. In doing so, they are becoming increasingly virtual and more dependent on an external network of suppliers, manufacturers, and distributors.

Systems and Processes

Having the right *systems* and *processes* enhances organizational effectiveness and facilitates coping with change. Misaligned systems and processes can be a powerful drag on an organization's ability to adapt. Checking what effect, if any, current systems and processes are likely to have on a company's ability to implement a particular strategy is therefore well advised.

Support *systems,* such as a company's planning, budgeting, accounting, information, and reward and incentive systems, can be critical to successful strategy implementation. Although they do not by themselves define a sustainable competitive advantage, superior support systems help a company adapt more quickly and effectively to changing requirements. A well-designed *planning* system ensures that planning is an orderly process, gets the right amount of attention by the right executives, and has a balanced external and internal focus. *Budgeting and accounting* systems are valuable in providing accurate historical data, setting benchmarks and targets, and defining measures of performance. A state-of-the-art *information* system supports all other corporate systems, and it facilitates analysis as well as internal and external communication. Finally, a properly designed *reward and incentive* system is key to creating energy through motivation and commitment.

A *process* is a systematic way of doing things. Processes can be formal or informal; they define organizational roles and relationships, and they can facilitate or obstruct change. Some processes look beyond immediate issues of implementation to an explicit focus on developing a stronger capacity for adapting to change. Processes aimed at creating a learning organization and at fostering continuous improvement are good examples.

People

Attracting, motivating, and retaining the right *people* have become important strategic objectives. After several episodes of mindless downsizing and rightsizing, many companies have recognized how expensive it is to replace knowledge and talent. As a result, much greater emphasis is being placed on attracting, rewarding, and retaining talent at all levels of the organization. A focus on continuous improvement through skill development is an important element of this strategy. Many companies have come to realize that developing tomorrow's skills—individually and collectively—is key to strategic flexibility. Leadership skills, in particular, are in increasing demand. Increased competitive intensity has created a greater need for leadership at all levels of the organization. The rapid pace of change and greater uncertainty in the strategic environment also have increased the difficulty of providing effective leadership.[7]

Culture

Performance is linked to the strength of a company's corporate culture. Common elements of strong culture include leaders who demonstrate strong values that align with the competitive conditions; a company commitment to operating under pervasive principles that are not easily abandoned; and a concern for employees, customers, and shareholders. Conversely, below-average profit performance is associated with weak corporate cultures. Employees in these cultures report experiencing separateness from the organization, the development of fiefdoms, the prevalence of political maneuvering, and hostility toward change.

A company's corporate culture is a shared system of values, assumptions, and beliefs among a firm's employees that provides guidance on how to think, perceive, and act. It is manifested through artifacts, shared values, and basic assumptions. *Artifacts* are visible or audible processes, policies, and procedures that support an important cultural belief. *Shared values* explain why things should be as they are. Shared values often reinforce areas of competitive advantage and can be found in internal corporate language. The words can be well defined within mission statements and codes of ethics or ambiguously embedded within company lingo. Either way, these words and phrases are used to define the image a firm wants to portray. Microsoft, for example, supports a culture of high energy, drive, intellect, and entrepreneurship. The day-to-day company language is filled with "nerdisms" such as "supercool" and "totally random." Employees touted as having "high bandwidth" (energetic and creative thinkers) are the most respected.[8] Finally, *basic assumptions* are invisible reasons why group members perceive, think, and feel the way they do about operational issues. They are sometimes demonstrated in corporate myths and stories that highlight corporate values. These legends are of considerable value because employees can identify with them and easily share them with others.

Because of its pronounced effect on employee behavior and effectiveness, companies increasingly recognize that corporate culture can set them apart from competitors. At UPS, for instance, culture is considered a strategic asset, ever growing in importance: "Managing that culture to competitive advantage involves three key priorities: recruiting and retaining the right people, nurturing innovation, and building a customer mindset."[9] UPS executives believe that the firm's culture is so important that the company spends millions of dollars annually on employee training and education programs, with a great deal of the expenditures involving the introduction of the company's culture to new employees.

A pronounced corporate culture can be an advantage or an impediment in times of rapid change. On the one hand, the continuance of core values can help employees become comfortable with or adjust to new challenges or practices. On the other hand, a company's prevailing organizational culture can inhibit or defeat a change effort when the consequences of the change are feared. For example, in a company in which consensus decision making is the norm, a change to more top-down decision making is likely to be resisted. Similarly, an organization focused on quarterly results will culturally resist a shift to a longer-term time horizon. These reactions do not constitute overt resistance to change. Rather, they represent expected responses fostered by the cultural elements ingrained over a long period of time in the organization. The failure to recognize and work within the prevailing cultural elements can doom a change agenda. For example, a large global pharmaceutical company discovered that R&D professionals resisted their promotions to management. An examination revealed that the resistance stemmed from an organizational culture bias that prevented them from competing with their peers for career rewards.[10]

The Balanced Scorecard

Traditional performance management systems often are designed around the annual budget and operating plan and tend to promote short-term, tactical behavior. To create effective strategic change, such traditional systems might have to be replaced by a carefully selected set of measurements that promote performance- and strategy-focused behavior.

The Balanced Scorecard is a set of measures designed to provide strategists with a quick, yet comprehensive, view of the business (Figure 2-2).[11] Developed by Robert Kaplan and David Norton, the Scorecard asks managers to look at their business from customer, company capability, innovation and learning, and financial perspectives. It provides answers to four basic questions:

1. How do customers see us?
2. At what must we excel?
3. Can we continue to improve and create value?
4. How do we look to our company's shareholders?

The Balanced Scorecard requires managers to translate a broad *customer-driven* mission statement into factors that directly relate to customer concerns such as product quality, on-time delivery, product performance, service, and cost. Measures are defined for each factor based on customers' perspectives and expectations, and objectives for each measure are articulated and translated into specific performance metrics. Apple Computer Corporation uses the Balanced Scorecard to introduce customer satisfaction metrics. Historically, Apple was a

Figure 2-2 The Balanced Scorecard

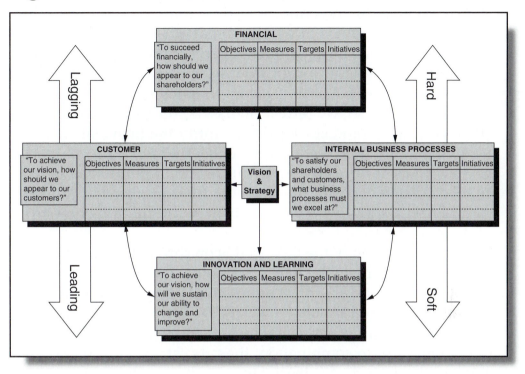

Source: Reprinted by Permission of *Harvard Business Review.* From "Using the Balanced Scorecard as a Strategic Management System," Jan/Feb 1996. Copyright © 1996 by the Harvard Business School Publishing Corporation; all rights reserved.

technology and product-focused company that competed by designing better computers. Getting employees to focus on customer satisfaction metrics enabled Apple to function as a customer-driven company.

Customer-based measures are important, but they must be translated into measures of what the company must do *internally* to meet its customers' expectations. Once these measures are translated into operational objectives such as cycle time, product quality, productivity, and cost, managers must focus on the internal business processes that enable the organization to meet the customers' needs.

Customer-based and internal business process measures directly relate to competitive success. The ability to create new products, provide value to customers, and improve operating efficiencies provides the basis for entering new markets that drive incremental revenue, margins, and shareholder value. Financial performance measures signal whether the company's strategy and its implementation are achieving the company objectives that relate to profitability, growth, and shareholder value. Measures such as cash flow, sales growth, operating income, market share, return on assets, return on investment, return on equity, and stock price quantify the financial effects of strategies and link them to other elements of the Balanced Scorecard. A failure to convert improved operational performance, as measured in the Scorecard, into improved financial performance should spur executives to rethink the company's strategy.

The application of the Balanced Scorecard has evolved into an overall management system. In essence, the Scorecard encompasses four management processes: translating a vision, communicating goals and linking rewards to performance, improving business planning, and gathering feedback and learning. Separately, and in combination, the processes contribute to linking long-term strategic objectives with short-term actions.[12]

The objective of *translating a vision* is to clarify and gain employee support for that vision. For people to be able to act effectively on a vision statement, that statement must be expressed in terms of an integrated set of objectives and measures that are based on recognized long-term drivers of success. The application of the Scorecard also is useful in highlighting gaps in employee skill sets, information technology, and processes that can hamper an organization's ability to execute a given strategy.

Thorough and broad-based *communication* is essential to ensure that employees understand the firm's objectives and the strategies that are designed to achieve them. Business unit and individual goals must then be aligned with those of the company to create ownership and accountability. *Linking rewards* to the Balanced Scorecard is a direct means of measuring and rewarding contributions to strategic performance. Clearly defined, objective performance measures and incentives are key to creating the right motivational environment.

Creating a Balanced Scorecard forces companies to *integrate* their strategic planning and budgeting processes. The output of the business-planning process consists of a set of long-term targets in all four areas of the Scorecard (customer, internal, innovation/learning, and financial), a set of clearly defined initiatives to meet the targets, an agreed-upon allocation of resources to support these initiatives, and a set of appropriate measures to monitor progress. In this process, financial budgeting remains important but does not drive or overshadow the other elements. Finally, managers must constantly gather *feedback* on the Balanced Scorecard's short-term measurements to monitor progress in achieving the long-term strategy and to *learn* how performance can be improved. Deviations from expected outcomes indicate that assumptions regarding market conditions, competitive pressures, and internal capabilities need to be revisited. As such, this feedback assists in assessing whether a chosen strategy needs to be revised in light of updated information about competitive conditions.

Performance and Control

Most methods for measuring and evaluating performance at different levels in the organization—from economic value added to gap analysis to the Balanced Scorecard—are focused on *outcome control,* the attainment of specific targets in pursuit of specific goals. Outcome control is principally achieved by altering the incentive structure for business units, executive teams, and individual managers. However, when changing an existing corporate culture is key to enhancing performance or implementing a new strategic direction, for example, in the case of a merger or acquisition, outcome management might not be enough. Rather, a *behavior control* style of management might be called for. Under behavior control, the company directly monitors the behavior of specific business units, executive teams, or individual managers, for example, through the approval of capital expenditure requests or specific hiring or promotion decisions.

THE ROLE OF THE BOARD

Creating a culture of high performance is central to a board of directors' fundamental mandate, which is to "direct the affairs of the company." The first and fundamental responsibility for a board in "directing" is to determine and prioritize just what it is the board should focus its attention and efforts on, given the unique circumstances of the particular company.[13] Specifically, to create a high performance culture, a board should:

1. *Define its role, agenda, and information needs.* Boards must define their priorities and a view of what matters most to the success of the enterprise. Doing so enables a board to provide management with meaningful guidance and support. The board needs to get to know the business of the company and the competitive environment in which it operates, in collaboration with—but not unduly dependent on—management. This task is important, because even the best managers will have potential conflicts or blind spots about performance, strategy, and/or risks.

2. *Ensure that management not only performs, but performs with integrity.* Selecting, monitoring, and compensating management and, when necessary, replacing management continue to lie at the heart of board activity. Directors should assess management's integrity not only at the outset in their hiring decisions, but also continuously when considering matters proposed and presented by management, assessing management performance, determining management compensation, and planning for succession and management development.

3. *Set expectations about the tone and culture of the company.* Related to its ongoing assessment of management integrity, the board has an important role to play in assuring that management is promoting an appropriate ethical culture within the company. Only the board is positioned to assess whether senior management is setting the appropriate tone and culture, both in the messages management sends throughout the company and as exhibited in management behavior.

The standards of ethics and business conduct that are followed—or not followed—throughout a company impact the bottom line in many ways. "Tone at the top" should be a priority throughout the company and not viewed simply as a compliance matter.

4. *Formulate corporate strategy with management.* Once the board has hired the best and most trustworthy management team available, it should challenge the team to propose and continually fine-tune the corporate strategy. After agreeing to a strategic course with management through an iterative process, the board should determine the benchmarks that will evidence success or failure in achieving strategic objectives and then regularly monitor performance against those objectives. This all requires significant understanding and information about the company, its industry and competitive conditions, and it requires active control by the board of the board's agenda and the information available to it. It also requires the development of a clear understanding between the board and the senior management team of just what issues come to the board and in what time frame and under what circumstances the board expects to be informed of a critical emerging issue.

5. *Ensure that the corporate culture, the agreed strategy, management incentive compensation, and the company's approach to audit and accounting, internal controls, and disclosure are consistent and aligned.* A board that is actively engaged in strategic oversight, that has a deep understanding of the key drivers of corporate performance and the corporate culture, is in a good position to ensure that the company's approach to compensation, financial disclosure, internal controls, risk, and compliance all complement one another.

6. *Help management understand the expectations of shareholders and regulators.* Boards add significant value when they help management cope with the complex context in which the company operates and when they support management in focusing on the long-term interests of the company and its shareholders.

Kocourek et al. suggest 12 questions boards should ask in the course of discharging their oversight responsibilities:

1. Does management have a comprehensive strategy and operating plan for the company to realize its performance potential? (Strategic Direction)
2. Are the necessary human, financial, physical, and other supporting resources provided and properly allocated to achieve success? (Resource Allocation)
3. Does the CEO provide the leadership required by the company, and does the organization have a succession plan for this position? (Management)
4. Are financial information systems, control processes, decision delegations, and reporting responsibilities established and audited? (Financial Accountability)
5. Does management utilize an effective system of key performance indicators to monitor and control operating performance? (Operating Controls)
6. Are mechanisms in place to ensure conformance with legislations and regulations protecting customers, employees, and the community? (Constituency Protection)
7. Does management adequately report, control, and provide for all material disputes of a legal, financial, or regulatory nature? (Litigation and Disputation)
8. Are effective risk management processes in place to prevent or correct physical or financial crises? (Crises and Contingencies)
9. Does the board adequately understand and support the resolution of near-term, intermediate, and long-term priorities of management? (Management Priorities)
10. How does the company's financial and market performance compare with its historical performance, projected performance, and competitors' performance? (Past and Present Performance)
11. What specific competitive strengths and weaknesses, market forces, or drivers of profit dynamics determined performance results? (Underlying Causes)
12. What are the reasonable objectives for, and limits to, the company's growth, profitability, and appreciation of shareholder's value? (Performance Potential)[14]

As these questions suggest, a narrow focus on accounting data is inadequate; directors must have access to a broad mix of indicators to be able to judge how a corporation is performing. This requires a "push and pull" approach to information sharing in which companies provide directors with regular, standardized briefing books of summarized information that is timely, comprehensive, and presented in order of importance, and in which directors can request—and expect to receive with reasonable speed—any other information they want.

NOTES

1. Jim Collins, *Good to Great: Why Some Companies Make the Leap. . . and Others Don't*, New York, Harper Collins, 2001; and Jim Collins and Jerry I. Porras, *Built to Last: Successful Habits of Visionary Companies*, New York, Harper Collins, 1994.
2. William Joyce, Nitin Nohria, and Bruce Roberson, *What Really Works: The 4+2 Formula for Sustained Business Success*, New York, Harper Collins, 2003.
3. Jeffrey W. Bennett, Thomas E. Pernsteiner, Paul F. Kocourek, and Steven B. Hedlund, "The Organization vs. The Strategy: Solving the Alignment Paradox," *Strategy + Business*, 2000, Fourth Quarter.
4. Christopher Bartlett and Sumantra Goshal, "Changing the Role of Top Management: From Strategy to Purpose," *Harvard Business Review*, November 1994, p. 79.
5. It is, of course, no coincidence that during this same period the resource-based view of strategic thinking overtook the industrial economics perspective. See Chapter 1.
6. Gary Neilson, David Kletter, and John Jones, "Treating the Troubled Corporation," *Strategy + Business*, 2003, First Quarter.
7. John P. Kotter, *The Leadership Factor*, New York, The Free Press, 1988, p. 12.
8. K. Rebello and E. I. Schwartz, "Microsoft: Bill Gates's Baby Is on Top of the World. Can It Stay There?" *BusinessWeek*, April 19, 1999.
9. L. Soupata, "Managing Culture for Competitive Advantage at United Parcel Service," *Journal of Organizational Excellence*, 20(3) (2001): pp. 19–26.
10. J. R. Ross, 2000, "Does Corporate Culture Contribute to Performance?" *American*

International College Journal of Business, Spring 2000, pp. 4–9.

11. R. Kaplan and D. P. Norton, 2001, "Building a Strategy Focused Organization," *Ivey Business Journal,* May–June 2001, pp. 12–17.

12. R. Kaplan and D. P. Norton, 2001, "Leading Change with the Balanced Scorecard," *Financial Executive,* September 2001, pp. 64–66.

13. Ira M. Millstein, Holly J. Gregory, and Rebecca C. Grapsas, "Six Priorities for Boards in 2006," Weil Briefing: Corporate Governance, January 2006.

14. P. F. Kocourek, C. Burger, and B. Birchard, 2003, "Corporate Governance: Hard Facts about Soft Behaviors," *Strategy + Business,* 2003, First Quarter.

Chapter 3

Analyzing the External Strategic Environment

INTRODUCTION

Changes in the broader *economic, technological, political, and sociocultural environment*, which often are beyond the control of any single company, can have a profound effect on a company's success. Globalization has increased the interdependence between the world's major economies and intensified competition in many industries. In the process, entire industries have been restructured based on deconstructed value chains, new forms of competition have emerged, and "virtual corporations" have become a reality. Demographic and social changes such as the aging of the population, the entry of large numbers of women into the labor force, and renewed interest in quality-of-life issues have created new opportunities and threaten a number of existing businesses. The technology revolution has changed the way we live, work, and unwind, spawning entirely new industries.

As global competition becomes even more intense, the winners will not be those who control natural resources and physical capital, but rather those who master ideas and technology—resources that are not bound by ownership or geography or governed by traditional rules of scarcity and scale economics. At the same time, the center of gravity of economic activity will continue to shift. In years to come, global business growth is less likely to originate in the United States, Western Europe, or Japan and more likely to come from the China, India, and developing countries.

In this chapter, we analyze how the process of globalization in general and specific global trends such as an aging world population, urbanization, and the use of information technology are reshaping the strategic business environment and introduce a framework for analyzing uncertainty, which is key to effective strategy development in a context of change. We also introduce scenario analysis, a technique for defining and analyzing alternative futures. We conclude by considering the oft-asked question whether the compact between business and society is changing and what impact this is likely to have on strategy formulation and corporate behavior.

GLOBALIZATION

Globalization, as a political, economic, social, and technological force, seems unstoppable. Whereas boundaries between countries and regions might be meaningful in political terms, they have all but disappeared on the global competitive map. The ever-faster flow of information across the world has made people aware of the tastes, preferences, and lifestyles of citizens in other countries. Through this information flow we are all becoming—at varying speeds and at least in economic terms—global citizens. This "Californiazation of need" is controversial, even offensive, to some who consider globalization a threat to their identity and way of life. It is not surprising, therefore, that globalization has evoked counter forces aimed at preserving, if not deepening, a sense of local identity. Yet, at the same time, we increasingly take advantage of what a global economy has to offer—we use Nokia cell phones, drive BMW cars, wear Nike sneakers, drink Starbucks coffee and Coca-Cola, eat McDonald's hamburgers, and buy on eBay. This is equally true for the buying habits of businesses. The market boundaries for

IBM services or GE aircraft engines are no longer defined in political or geographic terms. Rather, it is their intrinsic value that defines their appeal. Like it or not, we are living in a global economy.

Understanding Globalization

When we speak of "globalization," it is important to define terms. Economists focus on trade and regard the free flow of capital as the defining issue. A different characterization of globalization centers on the flow of high technology and real-time information as defining traits of the modern world economy. Still others point to nonstate actors' growing influence relative to that of nation states, whether nongovernmental organizations (NGOs), multinational corporations, or supranational organizations. There also are numerous religious and cultural characterizations.[1]

Underlying these sentiments is a differentiation between political, economic, technological, and now psychological aspects of globalization. Although it been with us for more than a hundred years, the idea of globalization as a primary process reshaping the world approximately coincides with the collapse of communism in 1989, because it marked the beginning of *political globalization*.[2] In its aftermath, many countries opted for democracy and market-driven economies; they deregulated industries, privatized formerly state-run enterprises, and liberated capital flows. Trade and cross-country investment increased, and free enterprise began to flourish on a worldwide scale, thereby setting in motion *economic globalization*. The rapid pace of economic globalization that ensued could not have occurred without a third potent force: *technological globalization*. Over the past 20 years, these three components of the globalization process have become mutually reinforcing, and together they have created a new force that shapes many of today's global strategic challenges: *psychological globalization*, defined as the *gradual convergence of human expectations on a global scale*.

Regionalism: A Stepping Stone on the Path Toward a Global Economy?

Globalization is still very much a work in progress. Trade and foreign investment among and within the so-called Triad countries—the United States, the European Union, and Japan—still account for the bulk of global economic activity, and more than four-fifths of the world's 500 largest publicly traded companies are headquartered in the Triad.[3]

World bank data show that *regional trading blocks* account for almost 60 percent of world trade. The recently enlarged European Union (EU) has grown to account for almost a quarter of the world's trade. NAFTA currently only has three members—Canada, the United States, and Mexico—but accounts for nearly 8 percent of world trade. ASEAN coordinates trade policies and promotes economic cooperation in Southeast Asia. EUROMED is a group of 12 Mediterranean countries that have agreed to establish a free-trade zone by 2010. APEC consists of 18 countries around the Pacific Rim that hope to create "free trade and investment in the region" by 2010 for its higher income members, and by 2020 for the rest. Finally, Mercosur, a small trading club founded by Argentina, Brazil, Paraguay, and Uruguay, represents 0.3 percent of world trade.

Some analysts view regionalism as a stepping stone toward a truly global economy; others argue regionalism is simply a proxy for "real solutions" to the problems and pressures created by the globalization process. If the latter is true, regionalism may actually increase tensions as "like" countries and societies forge economic and political structures that will be hard to change later. It would also signal that free trade on a global scale is not likely to become a reality any time soon.

New Powerhouses: India and China

In the second half of the twentieth century, Japan rose to economic prominence. Today, India and China stand at the threshold of a similar breakthrough. India's GDP has grown more than 5 percent annually in the last 5 years, and, by some measures, China's economy is already larger than Germany's.

In India, investment is growing, foreign capital and technology are coming in, Western-style competition is taking hold, and state intervention is diminishing. India has become the location of choice for software development and many other services for Western and Asian companies alike.

China has become a preferred location for manufacturing. Its huge population provides a continuing supply of low-cost labor. With the conclusion of the Uruguay Round of trade talks, along with China's inclusion in the World Trade Organization, most of the classic barriers to the global flow of goods and capital were removed. By widely opening the doors to foreign investment, emphasizing the education of technologists, and providing major incentives for technology transfer, China has combined inexpensive labor with technology to create a major, global competitive advantage. China is already the biggest trading partner for Japan, Korea, and many other key Asian economies.

China's economic progress is still uneven, however. In some areas, Coca-Cola is available—but is delivered by mule; a majority of deliveries are still made by bicycle or motor scooter. Nevertheless, recognizing its vast potential, a substantial number of U.S. companies, including Wal-Mart, KFC, Motorola, Elizabeth Arden, and Nike, have begun doing business in China. Guangdong is Procter & Gamble's largest overseas market for shampoo. Coca-Cola dominates the soft drink market, with bottlers at two dozen locations, and more planned. Other U.S. firms that have made major investments in China are ARCO, Amoco, United Technologies, Pepsico, Lucent Technologies, General Electric, General Motors, HP, and IBM.

A key challenge for Western companies doing business in China is that the government still controls many aspects of the business environment. Companies that try to compete against domestic firms for the Chinese market might not find the path as easy as those that generate the high-tech products and exports Chinese leaders are so eager to see expand. Motorola is encouraged to sell cellular telephones as long as it produces them in China. Boeing sells jet airplanes in China, but must involve local subcontractors and train local maintenance people. The challenge of developing a presence in China is therefore very different from that at home or in Western Europe. In China, there are few wholly American-owned companies. Most are joint ventures, often with Chinese middlemen either from the mainland or elsewhere in Southeast Asia.

China also does not yet have a consistent, easily understood, universally enforced judicial system. There are only rudimentary and limited legal protections that foreign ventures can draw on. This makes large investments in what is fundamentally a very attractive market extremely risky.

As the Asian economies take off, traditional Western multinationals increasingly will face strong competition from newly emerging Asian rivals intent on making major inroads in Western as well as Asian markets. Ranbaxy Laboratories, for example, India's leading pharmaceutical company, already has become a leading generics producer in Europe and the United States. Samsung Electronics and HSBC followed a similar path to global success; each developed unique competencies in their home markets and then successfully transferred these skills to Europe and the United States.

GLOBAL TECTONICS AND THEIR STRATEGIC IMPLICATIONS[4]

Whereas 20 years ago only a few businesses could be called global, today almost all businesses are affected by globalization. The maturity of many Western markets has forced firms to expand beyond the confines of the developed world into areas with greater potential that carry a level of risk far greater than that to which they are accustomed. Greater participation in international markets means venturing into other, often unfamiliar, cultures, dealing with different regulatory agencies and structures, and accepting a higher level of exposure to political and currency risk. Geopolitical uncertainty has become an increasingly important factor in corporate strategy formulation. Multinational corporations are now active in at least 70 countries rated at "medium" to "extreme" risk, and more than $150 billion is invested in 50 countries rated "fairly" to "very" corrupt in the *Transparency International Corruption Perceptions Index*, according to *Control Risks Group*, a London-based international consulting firm.[5]

Global Tectonics

The Penn State Center for Global Business Studies recently completed a comprehensive study of the global trends that are likely to present the most significant challenges to business leaders in the years to come. The authors use the term "global tectonics" to describe the process by which developing trends in technology, nature, and society slowly revolutionize the business environment, much like Earth's tectonic plates shift the ground beneath our feet.

The project categorizes tectonic shifts as societal, technological, or environmental. *Environmental tectonics* arise from the interactions between people and their environment, such as the growth in the world's population or the phenomenon of urbanization. They impact resource management, health, and the quality of life for people around the world. *Technological tectonics*—advances in biotechnology, nanotechnology, information systems—power economic growth and development, global integration, and the speed by which the global economy is becoming a "knowledge" economy. *Societal tectonics* represent shifts in international governance and political and cultural values, such as the current wave of democratization, deregulation, and governance reform.

12 Global Trends

The project identified 12 global trends that are likely to present the most significant challenges for companies in the next 30 years. Developments in areas such as demography, infectious diseases, resource degradation, economic integration, nanotechnology, international conflict, and governance all will have major consequences for corporate strategy. They might shake up individual companies or entire industries. Companies that are attuned to these challenges, prepare for them, and respond appropriately will likely thrive; those that ignore them do so at their peril.

1. *Population trends.* Across the planet, demographic trends are transforming societies, changing patterns of economic activity, creating new economic and social dependencies, and altering the geopolitical landscape:

- The world population is rising—fast—from 6.4 billion today to an expected 7.8 billion by 2025 and 9 billion by 2050.
- At the same time, the rate of global population growth is decreasing, especially in developed countries, making a "global population explosion" unlikely.
- Growth is highest in those areas of the world least capable of supporting such growth.
- Asymmetric global growth will change the global political equation and could create frictions.
- New migration and immigration patterns will emerge.
- Aging populations in Europe, the United States, and Japan will present key challenges for the public as well as the private sector.

The strategic implications of these shifts are far reaching. As markets in developed nations mature, the economies of developing nations will take off, thereby shifting economic growth, the flow of capital, the tastes and preferences of consumers, as well as the use of the world's natural and "strategic" resources, including food, water, and energy.

In the developed nations, where markets were largely shaped by the values, habits, and preferences of the younger population, a new, potentially highly lucrative over-50 market is emerging for a growing number of products and services. In financial services, this split has already occurred. The under-45s—with a long-term outlook and a different risk profile from that of pensioners—have very different investment objectives from those over 50, who are mainly interested in mutual funds or deferred annuities. Similarly, older people spend a higher proportion of their consumption in services and other intangibles, whereas their younger counterparts prefer to buy more tangible products.

The gradual aging of the population in developed countries also is creating a split in the labor market into two distinct workforces, broadly made up of the under-50s and the over-50s, respectively. These two workforces are likely to differ markedly in their needs and behavior and in the jobs they occupy. The younger group will seek a steady income from a permanent job, or at least a succession of full-time jobs. The rapidly growing older group will have more choices and will be able to combine traditional jobs, unconventional jobs, and leisure in whatever proportion suits them best. Women, who now outnumber men in American higher education, increasingly look for flexible work opportunities in the new knowledge technologies. A nurse, a computer technologist, or a paralegal now can take a few years off to rear children and then return to full-time work. Such jobs are the first in human history to be well adapted to the special needs of women and to their increasing longevity.

2. *Urbanization.* Migration from rural to urban areas is rapidly becoming a major challenge. Whereas today less than half of the world's population lives in cities, by 2030 this number is expected to increase to nearly 60 percent. What are some of the implications?

- Local and federal governments will be hard pressed to provide the necessary infrastructure and social services.
- Rising potential for social, health-related, economic, and security volatility.
- Mega cities—with 10 million or more inhabitants—will become commonplace; rural development might languish.

These trends offer large opportunities for business. To make mega cities livable requires innovation, investment, and economic growth. Sectors such as transportation, housing, waste management, and recycling will have to respond. There will also be opportunities in rural areas to bridge the widening gap between the urban and rural economies.

3. *The spread of infectious disease.* As levels of migration and cross-border flow of labor and goods increase, the likelihood of epidemics and the spread of infectious disease becomes greater. Its impact on economic growth and development can be enormous; in many developing countries, HIV/AIDS has impaired the labor force and all but overwhelmed social systems such as education and health care. The threat of biological terrorism is also becoming more real with every passing day.

Many of the solutions to these problems will have to be provided by the private sector—from providing a health care infrastructure to developing new generations of drugs to developing disaster response systems.

4. *Resource management.* The strategies of many companies around the world depend on the availability of such critical resources as water, food, and energy. Access to plentiful fresh water is a key concern in many areas and is a major determinant of local growth and investment. Prudent forecasts suggest that future conflict over water resources is increasingly likely. The availability of food is impacted by and affects population growth, technology, and governance. Increasing crop yields, enhancing foods with vitamins, and improving distribution systems will be critical. Energy availability is an ongoing concern in many industries and has spawned innovation and investment in a whole new range of renewable sources of energy.

5. *Environmental degradation.* "Global warming" once was an uncommon term used by a few scientists who were growing concerned over the effects of decades of pollution on long-term weather patterns. Today, the idea of global warming is well known, if not always well understood. Possible effects of global warming include the inundation of low-lying countries due to rising sea levels, increased frequency of severe storms, and the retreat of glaciers and icecaps. Less abrupt changes could also occur as average temperatures increase. In temperate areas with four seasons, the growing season might become longer and include more precipitation. Less temperate parts of the world will likely see increasing temperatures and a sharp decrease in precipitation, causing long droughts and potentially creating deserts.

The most devastating effects, and also the hardest to predict, will be the effects on the world's living ecosystems. Many species of plants and animals will adapt or move to deal with the shift in climate, but many might become extinct. The human cost of global warming is hard to quantify. Thousands of lives per year could be lost as the elderly or ill suffer from heat stroke and other heat-related trauma. Poor people and underdeveloped nations would suffer the worst effects, because they would not have the financial resources to deal with the problems that come with an increase in temperature. Huge numbers of people could die from starvation if a decrease in precipitation limits crop growth and from disease if coastal flooding leads to widespread water-borne illness.

Global warming is not the only environmental concern. Water pollution, deforestation, desertification, and erosion also pose significant threats to the environment. Solutions to these problems will require a partnership between the private sector and regulatory authorities on a global scale. A small beginning has been made. Smaller, more fuel-efficient cars and non-fossil-fuel energy sources, such as hydroelectric power, solar power, hydrogen engines, and fuel cells, all promise big cuts in greenhouse gases if they become more common. At the international level, the Kyoto Treaty was written to reduce carbon dioxide and other greenhouse gas emissions worldwide. Thirty-five industrialized nations have committed to reducing their output of these gases to varying degrees.

6. *Economic integration.* Higher levels of cross-border economic activity have increased interdependence among the world's economies and created a fully integrated economic system on a global scale. The Airbus Consortium provides a good example. The aircraft's wings are manufactured in Britain, its fuselage and tail in Germany. A Spanish company produces the doors, and cockpit construction and final assembly take place in France. In all, more than 2,000 companies, located in more than 30 different countries, supply components, spare parts, or provide services. This picture increasingly is repeated in industry after industry and illustrates the powerful role multinational corporations (MNCs) play today in the global economy.

Some industries are more regulated than others. In the steel industry, for example, the presence or absence of favorable trade policies, technical standards, policies and regulations, and government-operated or subsidized competitors or customers have a direct influence on a company's global strategic options. In the past, multinationals almost exclusively relied on governments to negotiate the rules of global competition. However, as the politics and economics of global competition have become more closely intertwined, companies are paying greater attention to the nonmarket dimensions of their global strategies aimed at shaping the global competitive environment to their advantage. In the telecommunications industry, falling trade barriers and other deregulatory moves have encouraged companies to pursue more global approaches to their business. The threat of protectionism or re-regulation in the steel industry, however, inhibits industry globalization and causes companies to take a less-global approach.

7. Knowledge dissemination. The emergence of a global economy based on knowledge and ideas has changed the very *nature* of strategic opportunity and risk. Knowledge is changing the *nature* of the products and services companies bring to market and the *business models* they use to develop and manage such offerings. In a knowledge-based Internet economy, ideas spread all across the world almost overnight at an extremely low cost, making it easier for small companies, new ones, and those from developing countries to compete with established firms from industrially advanced countries. So-called *smart* products—interactive products that become smarter the more they are used and that can be customized—are a primary focus of modern product development.[6] A tire that notifies the driver of its air pressure and a garment that heats or cools in response to temperature changes are early versions of knowledge-based, or *smart*, products already on the market. Knowledge also is changing *how* companies do business. Farmers use Massey Ferguson's yield-mapping system to maximize the yield of each square yard in every field. The system links the farmer's tractor to a satellite-based Global Positioning System, which records the latitude, longitude, and yield of every square yard. The data are automatically sent to the farmer's desktop computer, allowing the farmer to investigate selected areas and analyze variations in productivity. Over time, this knowledge-based system has become more valuable than Massey Ferguson's primary business.

8. *Information technology.* Three decades ago, the Internet was still a dream. Today, customers routinely tap into FedEx's package-tracking database to check the status of their shipment, "googling" has become an accepted verb in the English language, and remote monitoring is becoming a reality in health care delivery. Meanwhile, many companies have created intranets for their information bases so that employees can reallocate investments in their 401(K) plans, work together with corporate offices around the globe, and connect to their homes.

Information technology also is changing the quality of peoples' lives. For many, the days of the maddening commute through endless streams of traffic and congestion are already over. Flexible work hours, the emergence of the fully equipped home office, and new forms of communication are making new lifestyles possible, allowing for a blend of work with family life.

9. *Biotechnology.* Rapid advances in humankind's ability to understand and manipulate the basic elements of life are likely to fundamentally alter scientific inquiry and offer solutions to problems that could not be solved before. The biotechnology revolution is likely to have the greatest potential in three areas: medicine, agriculture, and the environment. One day, farmers will be able to grow plants that make plastic—enough to lessen our dependence on oil; whole families of new drugs will eradicate many types of disease, and major advancements in pollution cleanup will become possible. In the long run, advances in the biosciences will also likely shake up the world of electronics and make silicon obsolete. Companies such as Motorola have already begun to investigate the potential of genetic engineering in computing—the first step toward a DNA-based computer.

10. *Nanotechnology.* The ability to create new materials one atom at a time is fundamentally reshaping our vision of the future, with stronger and lighter materials that will reduce the cost of transportation and reduce pollution; the advent of molecular manufacturing that reduces waste; and "nanomedicines" that will be able to monitor, repair, and control human biological systems.

11. *Conflict.* The fall of the Berlin Wall in 1989 changed the nature of international conflict from being primarily a bilateral clash between superpowers to multiple civil and intracountry conflicts, most of them clustered in the developing world. Terrorism has become a major threat—for business as well as civil society—and continues to threaten the stability of the international political and economic order.

The business implications of these sources of uncertainty are far reaching—companies must develop security standards and policies around the world, protect their information systems and computer networks against cyber attacks, and create redundancies in their supply chains, all at significant cost.

12. *Governance.* Societies and corporations are connected by two interrelated sets of laws. The first is the rule of law as defined by local and national legislatures, multilateral agreements, and an emerging body of international law. These legal structures vary greatly from one part of the world to another. Most have deep and ancient societal roots; were shaped through centuries of cultural, political, and economic change; and exhibit a high degree of inertia. Proactive convergence of these structures therefore is unlikely, but a new global regulatory framework may well be needed.

The market defines the second set of laws. Here we see a very different picture. No matter where a company operates or what it produces, these laws affect, or even determine, its fate. It should not come as a surprise, therefore, that this second set of laws is becoming—within the boundaries of applicable legal structures—the dominant force in the evolution of corporate governance practices around the world.

The market-led movement toward at least a partial convergence of corporate governance practices has several dimensions. First, corporations have adapted their *management* structures and practices to compete in increasingly global product and capital markets and to deal with emerging global regulatory frameworks. Related to this development is a second, subtler trend. As the pace of globalization increases, *business culture* is starting to change. In a growing part of the world, government interference in day-to-day business affairs is waning; "product market" realities increasingly define the rules of competitive engagement. At the same time, executives must explicitly deal with the potential consequences of higher levels of global economic volatility and carefully balance global and local identities, allegiances, and conflicts. A third market-based force putting pressure on governance is the recent, substantial increase in cross-border investment. Worldwide cross-border merger and acquisition transactions now top $500 billion, somewhere between 1 and 2 percent of world Gross Domestic Product, and are widely expected to rise further. Many such transactions involve companies, facilities, and infrastructure investments in developing countries, which carry substantial risks. Such investment patterns are the natural outgrowth of the fourth force—the need to seek revenues abroad. For most global companies today, a substantial and rising portion of their revenues and profits come from outside their "home" country. To accommodate an increasingly global presence, they also need to tap more and more into international debt and equity markets. Such global expansion gave rise to a fifth source of pressure on corporate governance. Marketing to new cultures, global risk management, and gaining credibility in new political and regulatory environments requires a global savvy few boards possess. Finally, the sometimes-unrealistic demands of global investors for meaningful involvement in the governance process *and* instant liquidity, for consistent short-term *and* long-term results and for entrepreneurial behavior, and for risk-taking *and* predictable performance illustrate the enormity of the global governance dilemma.

A GLOBAL KNOWLEDGE ECONOMY—STRATEGIC IMPLICATIONS

The emerging global knowledge economy has a number of characteristics that have profound strategic implications:

1. The new economy is not governed by the laws of economics of scarcity, but by the laws of abundance. Unlike most resources that deplete when used, information and knowledge can be shared, and actually grow through application.

2. The effect of location is diminished. Using appropriate technology and methods, virtual marketplaces and virtual organizations can be created that offer benefits of speed and agility, of round-the-clock operation, and of global reach.

3. National laws, barriers, and taxes are difficult to apply. Knowledge and information "leak" to where demand is highest and the barriers are lowest.

4. Knowledge-enhanced products or services can command price premiums over comparable products with low embedded knowledge or knowledge intensity, but pricing and value depend heavily on context. Thus, the same information or knowledge can have different value to different people at different times.

5. Knowledge, when locked into systems or processes, has higher inherent value than when it can "walk out of the door" in people's heads.

6. Human capital—in the form of acquired skills and competencies—is the key component of value in a knowledge-based company.[7]

Faster technology transfer on a global scale also implies shorter product life cycles and smaller windows of opportunity to bring products to market. As supply chains have become multinational, firms can focus on specific parts of the value chain or play expanded roles as strategic partners, providing not just manufacturing services but also sharing in the design and development of products. Virtual corporations, based only on a sophisticated knowledge of customer wants and how best to deliver that value without manufacturing or other in-house facilities, are likely to become more viable, common, and multinational as the use of networked technology expands.

Fragmentation of markets and the reduced appeal of mass-marketing approaches also are a hallmark of the new global economy. Procter & Gamble, a pioneer in mass marketing, is shifting its focus from selling to a vast, anonymous crowd to selling to millions of particular consumers. And so are Coca-Cola, McDonald's, General Motors, Unilever Group, American Express, and many other consumer-products giants. McDonald's now devotes less than a third of its U.S. marketing budget to network television, compared with two-thirds 5 years ago, with the remainder being spent on media such as closed-circuit sports programming, custom-published magazines, and in-store video.[8]

RISK AND UNCERTAINTY

Many strategic choices involve future events that are difficult to predict. The success of a new product introduction, for example, can depend on such factors as how current and potential competitors will react, the quality of components procured from outside suppliers, and the state of the economy. To capture the lack of predictability, decision-making situations often are described along a continuum of states ranging from *certainty* to *risk* to *uncertainty*. Under conditions of certainty, accurate, measurable information is available about the outcome of each alternative considered. When an event is risky, we cannot predict its outcome with certainty but have enough information to assess its probability. Under conditions of uncertainty, little is known about the alternatives or their outcomes.

To make analysis of the strategic environment actionable, we must be able to assess the degree of *uncertainty* associated with relevant events, the *speed* with which changes are likely to occur, and the possible *outcomes* they foreshadow. Conditions of certainty and risk lend themselves to formal analysis; uncertainty presents unique problems. Some changes take place gradually, and are knowable, if not predictable. We might not be able to determine exactly when and how they affect a specific industry or issue, but their broad effect is relatively well understood. The globalization of the competitive climate and most demographic and social trends fall into this category. The prospect of new industry regulations creates a more immediate kind of uncertainty—the new regulatory structure will either be adopted or it will not. The collapse of boundaries between industries constitutes yet another scenario: the change forces themselves may be identifiable, but their outcomes might not be totally predictable. Finally, there are change forces such as the sudden collapse of foreign governments, outbreaks of war, or major technological discoveries that are inherently random in nature and cannot easily be foreseen.

Scenario Analysis

Originally developed at Royal Dutch/Shell in London, *scenario analysis* is one of the most widely used techniques for constructing alternative plausible futures of a business' external environment. Its purpose is to analyze the effects of various uncontrollable change forces on the strategic playing field and to test the resiliency of specific strategy alternatives. It is most heavily used by businesses, such as energy companies, that are highly sensitive to external forces.

Scenario analysis is a disciplined method for imagining and examining possible futures.[9] It divides knowledge into two categories: (1) things we believe we know something about and (2) elements we consider uncertain or unknowable. The first category mainly focuses on the forward projection of knowable change forces. For example, we can safely make assumptions about demographic shifts or the substitution effects of new technologies. Obvious examples of uncertain aspects—the second category—are future interest rates, oil prices, results of political elections, and rates of innovation. Because scenarios depict possible futures but not specific strategies to deal with them, it makes sense to invite into the process outsiders, such as major customers, key suppliers, regulators, consultants, and academics. The objective is to see the future broadly in terms of fundamental trends and uncertainties and to build a shared framework for strategic thinking that encourages diversity and sharper perceptions about external changes and opportunities.

The scenario-building process involves four steps:

1. Deciding what possible future developments to probe, which trends—technological change, demographic change, or resource issues—to include, and what time horizon to consider.
2. Identifying what forces or developments are likely to have the greatest ability to shape the future.
3. Constructing a comprehensive set of future scenarios based on different combinations of possible outcomes. Some combinations will be of greater interest than will others, either because they have a greater effect on the strategic issue at hand, or because they are more or less likely to occur. As a result, a few scenarios usually emerge that become the focus of a more-detailed analysis.
4. Generating scenario-specific forecasts that allow an assessment of the implications of the alternative futures for strategic postures and choices.

Global Futures: The Global Scenario Group[10]

A good example of the power of scenario analysis is provided by the work of the Global Scenario Group, convened by the Stockholm Environment Institute in 1995. To examine the prospects for world development in the twenty-first century, it created a number of scenarios based on three fundamentally different social visions of the future: *Conventional Worlds*, *Barbarization*, and *Great Transitions*.

Conventional Worlds envision the global system of the twenty-first century evolving without major surprises, sharp discontinuities, or fundamental transformations in the basis for human civilization. Dominant values and institutions shape the future, the world economy grows rapidly, and developing countries gradually converge toward the norms set by highly industrial countries. Scenarios include:

- *Scenario 1: Market Forces.*   This scenario incorporates mid-range population and development projections and typical technological change assumptions. The problem of resolving the social and environmental stress arising from global population and economic growth is left to the self-correcting logic of competitive markets.
- *Scenario 2: Policy Reform.*   This variant adds strong, comprehensive, and coordinated government action, as called for in many policy-oriented discussions of sustainability, to achieve greater social equity and environmental protection. The political will evolves for strengthening management systems and rapidly diffusing environmentally friendly technology, in the context of proactive pursuit of sustainability as a strategic priority.

Scenarios under the second social vision—*Barbarization*—envision the grim possibility that the social, economic, and moral underpinnings of civilization deteriorate, as emerging problems overwhelm the coping capacity of both markets and policy reforms.

- *Scenario 3: Breakdown*.   In this scenario, crises combine and spin out of control, leading to unbridled conflict, institutional disintegration, and economic collapse.
- *Scenario 4: Fortress World.*   This variant features an authoritarian response to the threat of breakdown. Ensconced in protected enclaves, elites safeguard their privilege by controlling an impoverished majority and managing critical natural resources, while outside the fortress there is repression, environmental destruction, and misery.

Great Transitions explore visionary solutions to the sustainability challenge, including new socioeconomic arrangements and fundamental changes in values. They depict a transition to a society that preserves natural systems, provides high levels of welfare through material sufficiency and equitable distribution, and enjoys a strong sense of social solidarity. Population levels are stabilized at moderate levels and material flows through the economy are radically reduced through lower consumerism and massive use of green technologies.

- *Scenario 5: Eco-Communalism.* This scenario incorporates the green vision of bioregionalism, localism, face-to-face democracy, small technology, and economic autarky.
- *Scenario 6: New Sustainability Paradigm.* This variant shares some of the goals of the *Eco-Communalism* scenarios, but would seek to change the character of the urban, industrial situation, rather than to replace it, to build a more humane and equitable global civilization rather than retreat into localism.

A NEW COMPACT BETWEEN BUSINESS AND SOCIETY?

As will be evident from the foregoing discussion, societal considerations increasingly force companies to rethink their approach to core strategy and business model design. Dealing more effectively with a company's full range of stakeholders is another emerging strategic imperative. Historically, the amount of attention paid to stakeholders, other than directly affected parties, such as employees or major investors, in crafting strategy has been limited. Issues pertaining to communities, the environment, the health and happiness of employees, human rights violations of global supply chains, and activist nongovernmental organizations (NGOs), among numerous other issues, were dealt with by the company's public relations department or its lawyers.

In this emerging environment, companies will find that "business as usual" might no longer be an option and that traditional strategies for companies to grow, cut costs, innovate, differentiate, and globalize are now subject to a set of new laws of doing business in relationship to society:[11]

1. *Size means scrutiny.* The bigger a company is, and the more market dominance it achieves, the more attention and demand

it faces for exemplary performance in ethical behavior, good governance, environmental management, employee practices, product development that improves quality of life, support for communities, honest marketing, and so on.

2. *Cutting costs raises compliance risk.* The more companies use traditional means to cut costs—finding low-wage producers in less developed countries, pressuring suppliers, downsizing, cutting corners, and so on—the more potential there is for crises related to noncompliant ethical practices. The risks involved in successfully complying with society's expectations for ethical behavior, safety, product liability, environmental practices, and good treatment of all stakeholders might well outweigh the benefits accrued from these kinds of cost savings.

3. *Strategy must involve society.* For forward-thinking companies, social and environmental problems represent the growth opportunities of the future. For example, GE is looking to solve challenges related to the scarcity of global natural resources and changing demographics, while IBM has made social innovation a priority alongside business product and process innovation.

4. *Reducing risks means building trust.* Classic risk management strategies must expand beyond financial and currency analysis to include destabilizing trends and events arising from society. Smart leaders realize that no company can manage these risks if it does not earn the trust of society's leaders and of its communities.

5. *Satisfying shareholders means satisfying stakeholders.* In the long-run, the company that pays attention to the business–society relationship ultimately serves its investors' interests because (a) its antennae are better tuned to identifying risk, (b) it is able to build trust with its stakeholders, and (c) it is well positioned to develop goods and services that society values.

6. *Global growth requires global gains.* Increasingly, growth requires a global perspective that recognizes the importance of strong communities that supply infrastructure; maintain

stable business climates; attract investment capital; supply healthy, educated workers; and support growth that generates consumers with greater purchasing power. But long-term growth also requires development. For example, by 2012, phone and calling costs will drop enough to permit 4 billion people to have access to a mobile phone. Visionaries in the industry realize that the companies that serve not just consumer demand for quality devices, but their demand for quality of life, will seize the greatest market share.

7. *Productivity requires sustainability.* Companies have seen that commitment to environmental management and safety in the workplace has been a driver of lower costs and greater productivity. In addition, companies that take on the challenge of constraining their behavior through commitments to corporate citizenship find new incentive to innovate to compete. The more companies innovate, the more productive and sustainable they become.

8. *Differentiation relies on reputation.* In the United States, an estimated 50 million people, representing over $225 billion a year in purchasing power, comprise the emerging "lifestyles of health and sustainability" consumer base. As the influence of these activist consumers grows, they will demand companies to demonstrate sterling reputations and commitment to society.

9. *Good governance needs good representation.* The recent wake of corporate scandals is generating strict controls and governance reforms. But behind these changes is a deeper revolution calling for companies to include stakeholders in formal governance.

These "laws" are likely to play a key role in strategy formulation in the years ahead. Companies that accept, understand, and embrace them will find that being a "good citizen" has significant strategic value and does not detract from but actually enhances business success. Although the late Milton Friedman might have trouble accepting this new reality, the "business of business is good citizenship."

NOTES

1. Mark P. Lagon, "Visions of Globalization: Pretexts for Prefabricated Prescriptions—and Some Antidotes," *World Affairs,* 01–01 (2003), p. 142.
2. As the noted economist Paul Krugman observes in *Geography and Trade*, Cambridge, MIT Press, 1993, the world in the nineteenth century was considerably more international in terms of capital and product flows than today's economy.
3. Alan M. Rugman, *The End of Globalization*, New York, Random House Business Books, 2001.
4. This section is substantially based on Fariborz Ghadar and Erik Peterson, *Global Tectonics—What Every Business Needs to Know*, Penn State Center for Global Business Studies, 2005.
5. Sven Behrendt and Parrag Khanna, "Risky Business: Geopolitics and the Global Corporation," *Strategy + Business,* Fall 2003, pp. 68–75.
6. Davis, S. and J. Botkin, "The Coming of Knowledge-Based Business," *Harvard Business Review,* September 1994, p. 65.
7. David J. Skyrme Associates, "The Knowledge Economy and its Implications for Markets," 1997.
8. "The Vanishing Mass Market," *BusinessWeek,* July 12, 2004.
9. The following description is based on P. J. H. Schoemaker and C. A. J. M. van de Heijden, "Integrating Scenarios into Strategic Planning at Royal Dutch/Shell," *Planning Review,* 20 (1992): pp. 41–46.
10. See www.gsg.org.
11. Steve Rochlin, "The New Laws for Business Success," *Corporate Citizen 2006,* A Publication by the Center for Corporate Citizenship, Carroll School of Management, Boston College, 2006.

Chapter 4

Analyzing an Industry

INTRODUCTION

We tend to think of an industry as a group of companies or organizations that compete directly with each other in the marketplace. Although intuitive, the simplicity of this definition masks a complex issue. In many instances, an industry can be reasonably defined in more than one way. Do makers of facsimile machines compete with each other, with manufacturers of personal computers and PDAs, with telephone companies, with the U.S. Postal Service and overnight delivery companies, or with all of them? Is competition primarily between products, companies, or networks of alliance partners? Should we analyze rivalry at the business unit level or at the corporate level? Should we distinguish between regional competition and global rivalry? As these questions suggest, deciding on industry boundaries is difficult. In addition, misspecification of an industry can be extremely costly. The use of too narrow a definition can lead to strategic myopia and cause executives to overlook important opportunities or threats, such as would occur if railroads were judged to be competing with other railroads. The use of too broad a definition, such as identifying a firm's industry simply as "high technology," could prevent a meaningful assessment of the competitive environment.

What Is an Industry?

An industry is best defined in terms of four dimensions: (1) *products*, (2) *customers*, (3) *geography*, and (4) *stages* in the *production-distribution pipeline*.[1] The first dimension—products—can be further broken down into two components: function and technology. *Function* refers to what the product or service does. Some cooking appliances bake. Others bake and roast. Still others fry or boil. Functionality can be actual or perceived. Some over-the-counter remedies for nasal congestion, for example, are positioned as cold relievers, whereas others with similar chemical formulations are promoted as allergy medicines. The difference is as much a matter of positioning and perception as of actual functionality. *Technology* is a second distinguishing factor: some cooking appliances use gas, whereas others are electric; some cold remedies are available in liquid form, whereas others are sold in gel capsules.

Defining an industry's boundaries requires the simultaneous consideration of all of these dimensions. In addition, it is important to distinguish between the *industry* in which a company competes and the *market(s) it serves*. For example, a company might compete in the large kitchen appliance *industry* but choose refrigerators as its *served market*. This can be depicted as a collection of (adjacent) three-dimensional cells, each characterized by a particular combination of functions/uses, technologies/materials, and types of customers. The task of defining an industry, therefore, consists of identifying the group of market cells that are most relevant to the firm's strategic analysis.

In the process of generating strategic alternatives, it is often helpful to use multiple industry definitions. Assessing a company's growth potential, for example, might require the use of a different industry/market definition than assessing its current relative cost position.

Industry Structure and Porter's Five Forces Model

Michael Porter's *five forces* model is a useful tool for industry and competitive analysis.[2] It holds that an industry's profit potential

Figure 4-1 Porter's Five Forces Model

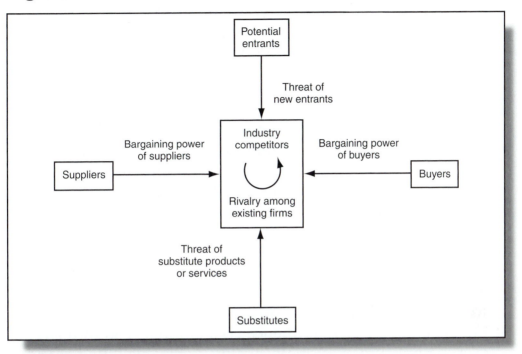

Source: Reprinted with the permission of *The Free Press*, an imprint of Simon & Schuster Adult Publishing Group, from *Competitive Strategy: Techniques for Analyzing Industries and Competitors* by Michael E. Porter. Copyright © 1980, 1998 by *The Free Press.*

is largely determined by the intensity of the *competitive rivalry* within that industry, and that rivalry, in turn, is explained in terms of five forces: (1) the *threat of new entrants*, (2) the *bargaining power of customers*, (3) the *bargaining power of suppliers*, (4) the *threat of substitute products* or *services*, and (5) the *jockeying among current rivals* (Figure 4-1).

The Threat of Entry

When it is relatively easy to enter a market, an industry can be expected to be highly competitive. Potential new entrants threaten to increase the industry's capacity, to intensify the fight for market share, and to upset the balance between demand and supply. The likelihood of new entrants depends on (1) what barriers to entry exist and (2) how entrenched competitors are likely to react.

There are six major barriers to market entry: (1) economies of scale, (2) product differentiation (brand equity), (3) capital requirements, (4) cost disadvantages that are independent of size, (5) access to distribution channels, and (6) government regulations. Consider, for example, the difficulty of entering the soft drink industry and competing with advertising giants such as Coca-Cola and Pepsi Cola or the plight of microbrewers trying to gain distribution for their brands of beer against major companies such as Anheuser-Busch. In high-technology industries, capital requirements and accumulated experience serve as major barriers. Industry conditions can change, however, and cause strategic windows of opportunity to open up. A prime example is deregulation. When airlines were deregulated in the 1980s, new carriers were able to enter the industries.

Powerful Suppliers and Buyers

Buyers and suppliers influence competition in an industry by exerting pressure over prices, quality, or the quantity demanded or sold. Soft drink bottlers, for example, suffered a damaging erosion of their profit margins when concentrate producers dramatically raised prices in the late 1980s and bottlers could not pass the increases on to consumers because of fierce competition at the retail level.

Generally, suppliers are more powerful when (1) there are a few dominant companies and they are more concentrated than the industry they serve; (2) the component supplied is differentiated, making switching among suppliers difficult; (3) there are few substitutes; (4) suppliers can integrate forward; and (5) the industry generates but a small portion of the suppliers' revenue base.

Buyers have substantial power when (1) there are few of them and/or they buy in large volume; (2) the product is relatively undifferentiated, making it easy to switch to other suppliers; (3) the buyers' purchases represent a sizable portion of the sellers' total revenues; and (4) buyers can integrate backward.

Substitute Products and Services

Substitute products and services continually threaten most industries and, in effect, place a lid on prices and profitability. HBO and pay-per-view are substitutes to the movie rental business and effectively limit what the industry can charge for its services. Moreover, when cost structures can be changed, for example, by employing new technology, substitutes can take substantial market share from existing businesses. The increased availability of pay-per-view entertainment over cable networks, for example, erodes the competitive position of movie rental companies. From a strategic perspective, therefore, substitute products or services that deserve the closest scrutiny are those that (1) show improvements in price performance relative to the industry average and (2) are produced by companies with deep pockets.

Rivalry Among Participants

The intensity of competition in an industry also depends on the number, relative size, and competitive prowess of its participants; the industry's growth rate; and related characteristics. Intense rivalry can be expected when (1) competitors are numerous and relatively equal in size and power; (2) industry growth is slow and the competitive battle is more about existing customers than about creating new customers; (3) fixed costs are high or the product or service is perishable; (4) capacity increases are secured in large increments; and (5) exit barriers are high, making it prohibitively expensive to discontinue operations.

Andrew Grove, founder of Intel, has suggested adding a sixth force to Porter's model: the influence of *complementary products.* Computers need software, and software needs hardware; cars need gasoline, and gasoline needs cars. When the interests of the industry are aligned with those of complementors, the status quo is preserved. However, new technologies or approaches can upset the existing order and cause complementors' paths to diverge.[3] An example is a change in technological standards, which renders *previously* compatible products and services incompatible.

The influence of these forces continues to shift as industry structures and business models change. For example, companies are increasingly using the Internet to streamline their procurement of raw materials, components, and ancillary services. To the extent this enhances access to information about products and services and facilitates the valuation of alternate sources of supply, it increases the bargaining power of manufacturers over suppliers. However, the same technology might reduce barriers to entry for new suppliers and provide them with a direct channel to end users, thereby reducing the leverage of intermediaries. The effect of the Internet on the possible threat of substitute products and services is equally ambiguous. On the one hand, by increasing efficiency, it can expand markets. On the other hand, as new uses of the Internet are pioneered, the threat of substitutes increases. At the same time, the Internet's rapid spread has reduced barriers to entry and increased rivalry among existing competitors in many industries. This has occurred because Internet-based business models generally are hard to protect from imitation and, because they often are focused on reducing variable costs, they create an unwanted focus on price. Thus, although the Internet does not fundamentally alter the nature of the forces affecting industry rivalry, it changes their relative influence on industry profitability and attractiveness.[4]

INDUSTRY EVOLUTION

Industry structures change over time. Entry barriers can fall, as in the case of deregulation, or rise considerably, as has happened in a number of industries where brand identity became an important competitive weapon. Sometimes industries become more concentrated as real or perceived benefits of scale and scope cause businesses to consolidate. Models of *industry evolution* can help us understand how and why industries change over time. Perhaps the word *evolution* is somewhat deceptive; it suggests a process of slow, gradual change. Structural change can occur with remarkable rapidity, as in the case when a major technological breakthrough enhances the prospects of some companies at the expense of others.

Four Trajectories of Change[5]

A recent study suggests that industries evolve according to one of four distinct trajectories of change: radical, progressive, creative, and intermediating. Two types of obsolescence define these paths of change: (1) a threat to an industry's *core activities*, which account for a significant portion of an industry's profits: and (2) a threat to the industry's *core assets*, which are valued as differentiators. The steady decrease in importance of a dealer's traditional sales activities as online shopping has increased is a good example of the first type of obsolescence. The eroding brand value of many prescription drugs in the face of generic competition illustrates the second.

Figure 4-2 shows the relationship between these two types of obsolescence and the four trajectories of industry change. *Radical* change occurs when an industry is threatened with obsolescence

Figure 4-2 Trajectories of Industry Change

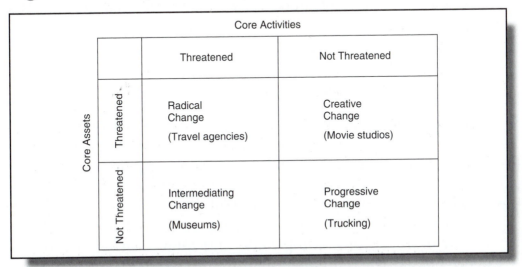

Source: Reprinted by Permission of *Harvard Business Review*. From "How Industries Change" by A. M. McGahan, 10/04. Copyright © 2004 by the Harvard Business School Publishing Corporation; all rights reserved.

of both its core activities and core assets at the same time. McGahan cites the major changes in the travel business as an example. As airlines modernized and began to compete more directly with enhanced reservation systems, and corporate travel clients turned to Internet-based service providers such as Expedia and Travelocity, many traditional travel agents had to reinvent themselves as a matter of survival.

Progressive change can be expected when neither form of obsolescence is imminent. This is the most common form of industry change. The long-haul trucking industry has seen changes, but its fundamental value proposition has remained the same. In such environments, competitive strategies and innovation often are targeted at increased efficiencies through scale and cost reduction.

Creative and *intermediating* change paths are defined by the dominance of one of the two forms of obsolescence. Under creative change, the core assets are threatened, but the core activities retain their value. Strategically, this scenario calls for the renewal of asset values; think of a movie studio having to produce another blockbuster. Under intermediating change, the core assets remain valuable, but the core activities are threatened. Museums are highly valuable as repositories of art, for example, but modern communication methods have reduced their power as educators.

Industry Structure, Concentration, and Product Differentiation

It is often useful to analyze changes in industry structure in terms of the movement from a primarily *vertical* to a more *horizontal* structure, or vice versa; changes in the degree of industry *concentration;* and increases or decreases in the degree of *product differentiation.*

These dimensions are illustrated by the convergence of three industries that originated some 50 years apart— telecommunications, computers, and television. This convergence has spawned an integrated multimedia industry in which traditional industry boundaries have all but disappeared. Instead of consisting of three distinct businesses in which being vertically integrated was key to success, the industry has evolved into five primarily horizontal segments in which businesses can successfully compete: content (products and services), packaging (bundling of content and additional functionality), the network (physical infrastructure), transmission (distribution), and display devices. In this new structure, strategic advantage for many companies is primarily determined by their relative positions within one of the five segments. However, vertical integration is likely to become an important business strategy once again when economics of scale and scope become more critical to competitive success and a principal driver behind another round of industry consolidation.

When economies of scale are important and market share and total unit costs are inversely related, industry structures often are *concentrated*. In such industries, the size distribution of business firms is often highly skewed and the so-called "Rule of Three and Four" might apply. This rule states that many stable markets will have only three significant competitors and that the market shares of these competitors will roughly be proportioned as four-to-two-to-one, reflecting a concentration level of approximately 70 percent of total industry sales for the three companies.

Studies have also shown that, as markets mature, they sometimes become less concentrated, suggesting that the relationship between relative share and cost position is less pronounced for *mature* markets than it is for *immature* markets. This explains why larger companies often lose market share as the industry matures: Their cost advantage diminishes over time. In contrast, in *fragmented* industries, characterized by a relatively *low* degree of *concentration*, no single player has a major market share. Such industries are found in many areas of the economy. Some are highly *differentiated*, such as application software; others tend to *commodity* status, as in the case of lumber. In the absence of major forces for change, fragmented industries can remain fragmented for a long time.

Product Life Cycle Analysis

The *product life cycle model*—based on the theory of diffusion of innovations and its logical counterpart, the pattern of acceptance of new ideas—is perhaps the best known model of industry evolution. It holds that an industry passes through a number of stages: introduction, growth, maturity, and decline. The different stages are defined by changes in the rate of growth of industry sales, generally thought to follow an S-shaped curve, reflecting the cumulative result of first and repeat adoptions of a product or service over time.

The product life cycle can be a useful analytic tool for strategy development. Research has shown that the evolution of an industry or product class depends on the interaction of a number of factors, including the competitive strategies of rival firms, changes in customer behavior, and legal and social influences. Figure 4-3 shows typical competitive responses to the changes that accompany the transition from a market's introduction stage to growth to maturity and, ultimately, to decline.

A high level of uncertainty characterizes the introductory or emerging stage of a product or industry life cycle. Competitors often are unsure which segments to target and how. Potential customers are unfamiliar with the new product or service, the benefits it offers, where to buy it, or how much to pay. Consequently, a substantial amount of experimentation is a hallmark of emerging industries. *Growth* environments are less uncertain and competitively more intense. At this stage of an industry's evolution, the number of rivals is usually largest. Therefore, competitive shakeouts are common toward the end of the growth phase. *Mature* industries, although the most competitively stable, are relatively stagnant in terms of sales growth. However, product development can give rise to new spurts of growth in specific segments, technological breakthroughs can alter the course of market development and upset the competitive order, and global opportunities can open avenues for further growth. *Declining* industries are typically regarded as unattractive, but clever strategies can produce substantial profits. We will return to these different scenarios in Chapter 7 when we consider specific strategies for each life cycle stage.

Although useful as a general construct for understanding how the principle of diffusion can shape industry sales over time, the product life cycle concept has little predictive value. Empirical studies have shown that industry growth does not

Figure 4-3 Strategic Choices over the Product Life Cycle

Characteristic	Emerging	Growth	Maturity	Decline
Concentration of competitors	High; few pioneers	Declining as more competition enters	Increasing after shakeout	High; few remaining harvesters
Product differentiation	Low, if any	Increasing; imitations and variations	High; increasing market segmentation	Decreasing as competitors leave market
Barriers to entry	High, if product can be protected	Decreasing; growing technology transfer	Increasing as capital intensity increases	High capital intensity, low returns
Barriers to exit	Low; little investment	Low, but increasing	High for large company	Decreasing; endgame
Price elasticity of demand	Inelastic, few customers	Increasingly elastic	Inelastic only in segments	Very elastic; bargaining power of buyers high
Ratio of fixed to variable cost	Generally low	Increasing	High	Decreasing
Economies of scale	Few, generally unimportant	Increasing capital intensity	High	High
Experience curve effects	Large early gains	Very high; large production volume	Decreasing magnitude	Few
Vertical integration of competitors	Low	Increasing	High	High
Risk involved in business	Low	Increasing	Increasing	Declining barriers exit

Source: A. J. Rowe, R. O. Mason, K. E. Dickel, and N. A. Snyder, *Strategic Management: A Methodological Approach*, 3rd edition, Addison-Wesley Longman, Glenview, IL, 1989. Used with permission of Dr. Alan J. Rowe.

always follow an S-shaped pattern. In some instances, stages are very brief. More important, the product life cycle concept does not explicitly acknowledge the possibility that companies can *affect* the shape of the growth curve through strategic actions such as increasing the pace of innovation or repositioning their offerings. Taking an industry growth curve as a given, therefore, can unnecessarily become a self-fulfilling prophecy.

New Patterns

Many new industries, such as cellular telephone or high-definition television, evolve through some convergence in *technological standards*. Competition for standards or formats is frequently waged within a group of companies between the developer of one standard and another group of companies favoring a different standard. Competition for standard or format share is important, because the winning standard will garner for its adopters a substantial share of future profits. Battles for cell phone technologies and set-top box standards, for example, decide the winners in market share.

For industries in which competition for standards is an important determinant of strategic success, C. K. Prahalad has proposed a model that describes industry evolution in three phases.[6] In the first phase, competition is mostly focused on *ideas, product concepts, technology choices, and the building of a competency base.* The primary goal at this stage is to learn more about the future potential of the industry and about the key factors that will determine future success or failure. In the second phase, competition is more *about building a viable coalition of partners that will support a standard against competing formats.* Companies cooperating at this stage may compete vigorously in phase three of the process—*the battle for market share for end products and profits.*

As competition becomes more global, industries consolidate, technology becomes more pervasive, and the lines between customers, suppliers, competitors, and partners are increasingly becoming blurred. With greater frequency, companies that compete in one market collaborate in others. At times, they can be each other's customers or suppliers. This complex juxtaposition of roles makes accurately forecasting an industry's future structure extremely difficult and relying on simple, stylized models of industry evolution very dangerous. As industry boundaries become more permeable, structural changes in *adjacent* industries (industries serving the same customer base with different products or services, or industries using similar technologies and production processes) or *related* industries (industries supplying components, technologies, or complementary services) increasingly influence an industry's outlook for the future. Finally, change sometimes is simply a function of experience. Buyers generally become more discriminating as they become more familiar with a product and its substitutes and, as a consequence, they are likely to be more explicit in their demands for improvements.

METHODS FOR ANALYZING AN INDUSTRY

Analyzing an industry is typically done based on a method of strategic segmentation that focuses on a subset of the total customer market, a competitor analysis that concentrates on individual corporations or their major units, or a strategic group analysis of all firms that face similar threats and opportunities.

Segmentation

Strategic segmentation is the process of dividing an industry or market into relatively homogeneous, minimally overlapping segments that benefit from distinct competitive strategies. Strategic segmentation is linked in a six-step process with *strategic targeting* of a particular segment and the act of *positioning* the firm for competitive advantage within the targeted segment(s) (Figure 4-4). Strategic segmentation is the process of identifying segments that offer the best prospects for long-term, sustainable results. It considers the long-term defensibility of different segments by analyzing barriers to entry such as capital investment intensity, proprietary technologies and patents, geographical location, tariffs, and other trade barriers.

Segmentation is complex because there are many ways to divide an industry or market. The most widely used categories of segmentation variables are *customer characteristics* and *product- or*

Figure 4-4 Strategic Segmentation, Targeting, and Positioning

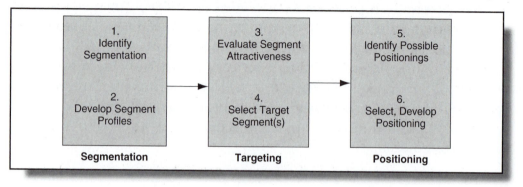

service-related variables. Customer descriptors range from geography, size of customer firm, customer type, and customer lifestyle to personal descriptive variables, such as age, income, or sex. Product- or service-related segmentation schemes divide the market on the basis of variables such as user type, level of use, benefits sought, competing offerings, purchase frequency and loyalty, and price sensitivity.

Competitor Analysis

Because industry structures and patterns of evolution are becoming more complex, traditional business assumptions often are not tenable. Many markets are no longer distinct nor are their boundaries well defined; competition is not mainly about capturing market share; customer and competitor profiles are constantly shifting; and competition occurs simultaneously at the business unit and corporate levels. These new realities call for executives to adopt a broader perspective on strategy and for them to ask new questions. Do consumer companies compete at the business unit level, at the corporate level, or both? Do companies compete as stand-alone entities or as extended families that include their supplier bases? When a firm defines its competition, should executives focus on the corporate portfolio of which the Strategic Business Unit (SBU) is a part? What are the competitive advantages of a portfolio of businesses against stand-alone businesses? Which is more important to sustainable competitive advantage: access to money or information technology?

As these questions suggest, competitive analysis must be paired with an analysis of the drivers of industry evolution. Consequently, strategies cannot be neatly compartmentalized at the SBU or corporate level. A principal rationale behind the concept of the diversified corporation is that the benefits of a portfolio transcend financial strength. A portfolio of related businesses reflects an integrated set of resources—core competencies that transcend business units—and has the potential for developing a sustainable corporate advantage that must be considered along with competitive factors at the business unit level.

To analyze *immediate competitors*, five key questions are useful:

1. Who are our firm's direct competitors now and in the near term?
2. What are their major strengths and weaknesses?
3. How have they behaved in the past?
4. How might they behave in the future?
5. How will our competitors' actions affect our industry and company?

Developing a solid understanding of who a firm's immediate competitors are and what motivates their competitive behavior is important for strategy formulation. An analysis of key competitors' major strengths and weaknesses and their past behavior, for example, may suggest attractive competitive opportunities or imminent threats. Understanding why a competitor behaves a certain way helps to make a determination of how likely it is to expect a major strategic or retaliatory initiative. Assessing competitors' successes and failures assists in predicting their future behavior. Finally, an analysis of a competitor's organizational structure and culture can be insightful; a cost-driven, highly structured competitor is unlikely to mount a successful challenge with an innovation-driven, market-oriented strategy.

In analyzing competitive patterns, it is often useful to assign roles to particular competitors. In many markets, it is possible to identify a *leader*, one or more *challengers*, and a number of *followers* and *nichers*. Although labeling competitors can be dangerously simplistic, such an analysis can provide insight into the competitive dynamics of the industry.

Leaders tend to focus on expanding total demand by attracting new users, developing new uses for their products or services, and by encouraging more use of existing products and services. Defending market share is important to them, but they might not want to aggressively take share from their immediate rivals because to do so can be more costly than expanding the market, or because they want to avoid scrutiny by regulatory agencies. Coca-Cola, for example, is focused more on developing new markets overseas than it is on taking market share from Pepsi Cola in the domestic market.

Challengers typically concentrate on a single target—the leader. Sometimes they do so directly, as in the case of Fuji's challenge to Kodak. At other times, they use indirect strategies. Computer Associates, for example, acquired a number of smaller competitors before embarking on directly competitive attacks against larger rivals.

Followers and *nichers* compete with more modest strategic objectives. Some followers use a strategy of innovative imitation, whereas others elect to compete selectively in a few segments or with a more limited product or service offering. Nichers typically focus on a narrow slice of the market by concentrating, for example, on specific end users, geographic areas, or by offering specialty products or services.

The identification of *potential* competitors is more difficult. Firms that are currently not in the industry but that can enter at relatively low cost should be considered. So should companies for whom there is obvious synergy by being in the industry. Customers or suppliers who can integrate backward or forward comprise another category of potential competitors.

Strategic Groups

Many industries have numerous competitors, far more than can be analyzed individually. In such cases, the application of the concept of *strategic groups* makes the task of competitor analysis more manageable. A strategic group is a set of firms that face similar threats and opportunities, which are different from the threats and opportunities faced by other sets of companies in the same industry. Rivalry is usually more intense within strategic groups than between them, because members of the same strategic group focus on the same market segments with similar strategies and resources. In the fast food industry, for example, hamburger chains tend to compete more directly with other hamburger chains than with chicken or pizza restaurants. Similarly, in pharmaceuticals, strategic groups can be defined in terms of the disease categories on which companies focus. Analysis of strategic groups helps to reveal how competition evolves between competitors with a similar strategic focus. Strategic groups can be mapped by using price, product-line breadth, the degree of vertical integration, and other variables that differentiate competitors within an industry.

ANALYZING PRODUCT/MARKET SCOPE

Insights into the competitive attractiveness of a company's product/market scope can be achieved through the use of four different analytical techniques: market analysis, growth vector analysis, gap analysis, and profit pool analysis.

Market Analysis

Segmentation and competitor analysis are useful for identifying competitive opportunities and threats. To quantify the attractiveness of a particular industry or segment, a *market analysis* must be performed. Market analysis also is useful for developing a better understanding of the key success factors and the core competencies a company will need to develop to succeed in achieving its strategic objectives.

A *market analysis* includes an assessment of (1) the actual and potential size of the market, (2) market and segment growth, (3) market and segment profitability, (4) the underlying cost structure and trends, (5) current and emerging distribution systems, (6) the importance of regulatory issues, and (7) technological changes.

Growth Vector Analysis

A company can increase its strategic scope within an industry by offering more products/technologies/services to tap more customer segments. The group of product–market combinations that a firm serves defines its product/market scope (Figure 4-5). Growth *within* the current market scope is called *concentration,* growth enjoyed by moving into related or new customer segments is referred to as *market development,* and growth into related or new products is *product/technology development.* A change in both customer segments served and products/technologies offered is called *diversification,* which is discussed in greater detail in Chapter 9.

When analyzing alternative directions for growth, it is useful to perform a similar analysis on key competitors. The combined analysis allows executives to determine whether the original assumptions about growth, the business's competitive position, and the potential for improvement are still tenable, as well as to gain insight into competitors' intentions, and the way the specific product markets are evolving. Companies that stay close to their core competencies and

Figure 4-5   Product and Market Combination Analysis

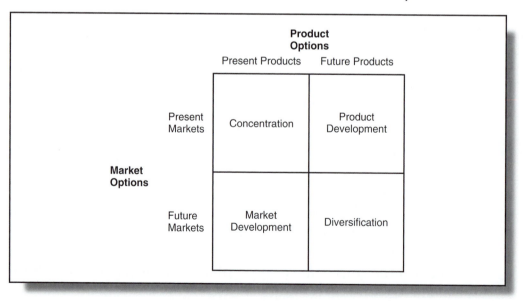

concentrate their growth in related markets and products are more successful than companies that diversify widely.

Gap Analysis

Plotting growth vectors for a company and its primary competitors often reveals *gaps* in the way a market is served, where industry sales are below their potential. *Gap analysis*—the process of comparing an industry's market potential to the combined current market penetration by all competitors—can lead to the identification of additional avenues for growth. Figure 4-6 depicts this process. Gaps between a market's potential and current sales levels can be the result of (1) product line gaps—the unavailability of product versions for specific applications or usage occasions, (2) distribution gaps—overlooked customer segments that have difficulty accessing the product, (3) usage gaps—underdeveloped applications for the product, and (4) competitive gaps—opportunities to displace competitors that offer weak product entries or questionable performance.

Figure 4-6   Gap Analysis

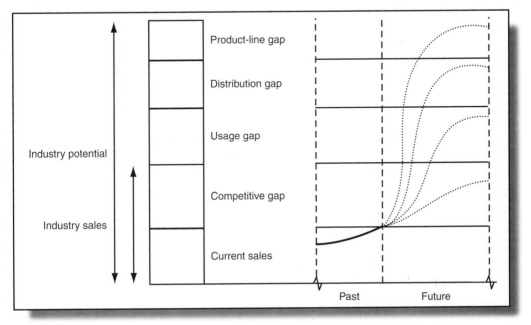

Profit Pool Analysis

An industry's *profit pool* is the total amount of profit earned at all points along the industry's value chain.[7] In analyzing companies in an industry that make profits, and at what stages in the value chain their profits are earned, it is important to understand industry economics. Profitability typically varies by customer group, product category, geographic area, and distribution channel. In addition, the pattern of profit distribution often is quite different from that of revenue concentration. In the automobile industry, for example, car manufacturing and distribution generate the highest revenues, but auto leasing, insurance, and auto loans are the most profitable activities.

"Mapping" the industry's profit pool provides important insight into profit potential. It also helps executives to understand how the industry is evolving, why profit pools form where they have, and how the profit distribution is likely to change. Mapping a profit pool consists of four steps: (1) defining the pool's boundaries, (2) estimating its overall size, (3) allocating profits to the different value chain activities, and (4) verifying the results.

NOTES

1. D. Abell and J. Hammond, *Strategic Market Planning: Problems and Analytical Approaches,* Englewood Cliffs, NJ, Prentice Hall, 1979.
2. M. E. Porter, *Competitive Strategy,* New York, Free Press, 1980.
3. A. S. Grove, *Only the Paranoid Survive,* New York, Doubleday, 1996.
4. M. E. Porter, "Strategy and the Internet," *Harvard Business Review,* March 2001, pp. 63–78.
5. This section is based on A. M. McGahan, "How Industries Change," *Harvard Business Review,* October 2004, pp. 87–94.
6. C. K. Prahalad, "Weak Signals Versus Strong Paradigms," *Journal of Marketing Research,* 1995, 32: iii–ix.
7. O. Gadiesh and J. L. Gilbert, "Profit Pools: A Fresh Look at Strategy," *Harvard Business Review,* May–June 1998, pp. 139–147; O. Gadiesh and J. L. Gilbert, "How to Map Your Industry's Profit Pool," *Harvard Business Review,* May–June 1998, pp. 149–162.

Chapter 5

Analyzing an Organization's Strategic Resource Base

INTRODUCTION

An assessment of strategic resources and capabilities—and of pressures for and against change—is critical when determining what strategies a company successfully can pursue. An organization's strategic resources include its physical assets; relative financial position; market position, brands, and the capabilities of its people; and specific knowledge, competencies, processes, skills, and cultural aspects of the organization.

Analyzing a company's internal strategic environment has two principal components: (1) cataloging and valuing current resources and core competencies that can be used to create a competitive advantage and (2) identifying internal pressures for change and forces of resistance.

In this chapter, we characterize a company's strategic resource base in terms of physical, financial, human resource, and organizational assets and describe techniques for analyzing a company's strategic resource base. In the second section, we look at internal organizational change drivers and counterforces that have a major influence on the feasibility of exercising particular strategic options and introduce the company life cycle model.

STRATEGIC RESOURCES

A company's strategic resource base consists of its *physical, financial, human resource,* and *organizational* assets. Physical assets such as state-of-the-art manufacturing facilities or plant or service locations near important customers can materially affect a company's competitiveness. Financial strength—excellent cash flow, a strong balance sheet, and a strong financial track record—is a measure of a company's competitive position, market success, and ability to invest in its future. The quality of a company's human resources—strong leadership at the top, experienced managers, and well-trained, motivated employees—may well be a firm's most important strategic resource. Finally, strategic organizational resources are the specific competencies, processes, skills, and knowledge under the control of a corporation. They include qualities such as a firm's manufacturing experience, brand equity, innovativeness, relative cost position, and ability to adapt and learn as circumstances change.

To evaluate the relative worth of a company's strategic resources, four specific questions should be asked: (1) How valuable is a resource; does it help build and sustain competitive advantage? (2) Is this a unique resource or do other competitors have similar resources? If competitors have substantially similar resources or capabilities or can obtain them with relative ease, their strategic value is diminished. (3) Is the strategic resource easy to imitate? This is related to uniqueness. Ultimately, most strategic resources, with some exceptions for patents and trademarks, can be duplicated. The question is—at what cost? The more expensive it is for rivals to duplicate a strategic resource, the more valuable it is to a company. (4) Is the company positioned to exploit the resource? Possessing a strategic resource is one thing; being able to exploit it is quite another. A strategic resource that has little value to one company might be an important strategic asset for another. The issue is whether a resource can be leveraged for competitive advantage.

Physical Assets

A company's physical assets, such as state-of-the-art manufacturing facilities and plant or service locations near important customers, can materially affect a company's competitiveness. For airline companies, the average age of their fleet of aircraft is an important concern. It affects customer perceptions, routing flexibility, and operating and maintenance costs. Infrastructure is a key issue for telecommunications companies. It determines their geographical reach and defines the types of customer service they can provide. In retailing and real estate, the old adage "location, location, location" still applies.

Physical assets do not necessarily need to be owned. Judicious use of outsourcing, leasing, franchising, and partnering can substantially enhance a company's reach with a relatively modest commitment of resources.

Analyzing a Company's Financial Resource Base

At the corporate level, an evaluation of a company's financial performance and position involves a thorough analysis of the company's current and *pro forma* income statement and cash flows at the divisional or business unit level, with additional consideration of the balance sheet at the corporate level.

Financial ratio analysis can provide a quick overview of a company's or business unit's current or past profitability, liquidity, leverage, and activity. *Profitability ratios* measure how well a company is allocating its resources. *Liquidity ratios* focus on cash flow generation and a company's ability to meet its financial obligations. *Leverage ratios* may suggest potential improvements in the financing of operations. *Activity ratios* measure productivity and efficiency. These ratios (Figure 5-1) can be used to assess (1) the business's position in the industry, (2) the degree to which certain strategic objectives are being achieved, (3) the business's vulnerability to revenue and cost swings, and (4) the level of financial risk associated with the current or proposed strategy.

The *DuPont* formula for analyzing a company or business unit's return on assets directly links operating variables to financial

Figure 5-1   Ratio Analysis

Ratio		Definition
1. *Profitability*		
a. Gross profit margin	$\dfrac{\text{sales} - \text{cost of goods sold}}{\text{sales}}$	Total margin available to cover operating expenses and yield a profit
b. Net profit margin	$\dfrac{\text{profits after taxes}}{\text{sales}}$	Return on sales
c. Return on assets	$\dfrac{\text{earnings before interest and taxes (EBIT)}}{\text{Total assets}}$	Return on the total investment from both stockholders and creditors
d. Return on equity	$\dfrac{\text{profits after taxes}}{\text{total equity}}$	Rate of return on stockholders' investment in the firm
2. *Liquidity*		
a. Current ratio	$\dfrac{\text{current assets}}{\text{current liabilites}}$	The extent to which the claims of short-term creditors are covered by short-term assets
b. Quick ratio	$\dfrac{\text{current assets} - \text{inventory}}{\text{current liabilites}}$	Acid-test ratio; the firm's ability to pay off short-term obligations without having to sell its inventory
c. Inventory to net working capital	$\dfrac{\text{inventory}}{\text{current assest} - \text{current liabilies}}$	The extent to which the firm's working capital is tied up in inventory
3. *Leverage*		
a. Debt-to-assets ratio	$\dfrac{\text{total debt}}{\text{total assets}}$	The extent to which borrowed funds are used to finance the firm's operations
b. Debt-to-equity ratio	$\dfrac{\text{total debt}}{\text{total equity}}$	Ratio of funds from creditors to funds from stockholders
c. Long-term debt-to-equity ratio	$\dfrac{\text{long-term debt}}{\text{total equity}}$	The balance between debt and equity
4. *Activity*		
a. Inventory turnover	$\dfrac{\text{sales}}{\text{inventory}}$	The amount of inventory used by the company to generate its sales
b. Fixed-asset turnover	$\dfrac{\text{sales}}{\text{fixed assets}}$	Sales productivity and plant use
c. Average collection	$\dfrac{\text{accounts receivable}}{\text{average daily sales}}$	The average length of time required to receive payment

performance. For example, as shown in Figure 5-2, return on assets is computed by multiplying earnings, expressed as a percentage of sales, by asset turnover. Asset turnover, in turn, is the ratio of sales to total assets used. A careful analysis of such relationships allows pointed questions about a strategy's effectiveness and the quality of its execution.

Accounting-based measures have generally been found to be inadequate indicators of a business unit's economic value. *Shareholder value analysis*, in contrast, focuses on cash flow generation, which is the principal determinant of shareholder wealth.

Figure 5-2 The *DuPont* Formula for Computing Return on Assets

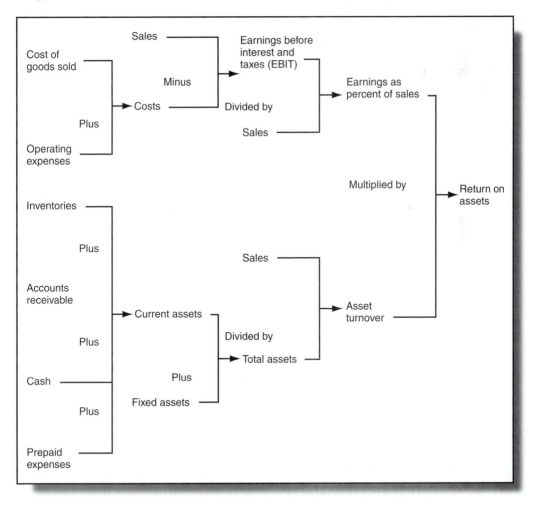

It is helpful in answering the following questions: (1) Does the current strategic plan create shareholder value, and, if so, how much? (2) How does the business unit's performance compare with the performance of others in the corporation? (3) Would an alternative strategy increase shareholder value more than the current strategy?

The use of accounting-based financial measures to assess current performance, such as return on investment (ROI), have been supplanted by the broader shareholder value-based measures of *economic value added* (EVA) and *market value added* (MVA). EVA is a value-based financial performance measure that focuses on economic value creation. Unlike traditional measures based on accounting profit, EVA recognizes that capital has two components: the cost of debt and the cost of equity. Most traditional measures, including return on assets (ROA) and return on equity (ROE), focus on the cost of debt but ignore the cost of equity. The premise of EVA is that executives cannot know whether an operation is really creating value until they assess the complete cost of capital.

In mathematical terms, EVA = Profit − [(Cost of Capital)(Total Capital)], where *profit* is after-tax operating profit, *cost of capital* is the weighted cost of debt and equity, and *total capital* is book value plus interest-bearing debt. Consider the following example. When buying an asset, executives invest capital from their company and borrowed funds from a lender. Both the stockholders and the lender require a return on their capital. This return is the "cost of capital" and includes both the cost of equity (the company's investment) and the cost of debt (the lender's investment). The company does not generate any meaningful profits until returns generated by the investment exceed the weighted capital charge. Once this occurs, the assets are contributing a positive EVA. If, however, the returns continue to lag the weighted cost of capital, EVA is negative, and change may be needed.

Varity, Inc. used EVA as a basis for reinvigorating its corporate culture and reestablishing its financial health. The company focused employees' attention on its negative $150 million EVA. It established clear objectives to turn EVA positive within a 5-year time frame. These objectives included revising the firm's capital structure by initiating a stock buyback program, considering strategic opportunities with high EVA prospects, and efficiently managing working capital. By establishing a 20 percent internal cost of capital, managers found attractive strategic opportunities, including the construction of a new manufacturing facility, establishing an Asian presence through a joint venture, and divesting its door-lock actuator business.[1]

Two additional benefits of EVA are that (1) it can help align employee and owner interests through employee compensation plans and (2) it can be the basis for a single competitive performance measure called market value added (MVA). Under EVA-based incentive programs, employees are rewarded for contributing to profits through the efficient use of capital. As employees become conscious of the results of their capital use decisions, they become more selective in the ways they spend shareholder investment. MVA is equal to market value less capital invested. Thus, EVA can be used as a metric for various internal functions, such as capital budgeting, employee performance evaluation, and operational assessment. In contrast, external shareholder value is measured through MVA, which is equal to future discounted EVA streams.

Although EVA offers attractive features, effective implementation has proven difficult. In addition, several independent studies have produced mixed results regarding a relationship between EVA and superior firm performance.[2] *Fortune* reported that companies that used EVA posted average annual returns of 22 percent, versus 13 percent for competitors that did not.[3] The *Wall Street Journal*, however, referenced a study conducted at the University of Washington, which concluded that "earnings per share is still a more reliable guide to stock performance than EVA and other 'residual-income' measures."[4] Another study of 88 companies concluded that EVA adopters tend to emphasize financial measures over quality and customer service.[5] The findings further suggest that although initial performance gains are realized by EVA adopters, these improvements tend to stall shortly after EVA is implemented.

These reservations notwithstanding, EVA portrays the true results of a company's strength by considering the cost of debt and equity. Tools, such as ROE, ROA, and EPS (earnings per share), measure financial performance, but ignore the cost of equity component of cost of capital. Therefore, it is possible to have positive earnings and positive returns but a negative EVA. By encouraging an operation to manage indebtedness, a firm that uses EVA maximizes capital efficiency and allocation. If, for example, a business can conserve its assets by improving collections of receivables and inventory turnover, EVA will rise.

Cost analysis deals with the identification of strategic cost drivers—those cost factors in the value chain that determine long-term competitiveness in the industry. Strategic cost drivers include variables such as product design, factor costs, scale, scope of operations, and capacity use. To assist in strategy development, cost analysis focuses on those costs and cost drivers that are of strategic importance because they can be influenced by strategic choice.

Cost benchmarking is useful in assessing a firm's costs relative to those of competing firms, or for comparing a company's performance against best-in-class competitors. The process involves five steps: (1) selecting areas or operations to benchmark, (2) identifying key performance measures and practices, (3) identifying best-in-class companies or key competitors, (4) collecting cost and performance data, and (5) analyzing and interpreting the results. This technique is extremely practical and versatile. It allows for direct comparisons of the efficiencies with which different tasks in the value chain are performed. It is dangerous, however, to rely heavily on benchmarking for guidance, because it focuses on similarities rather than differences between rival firms' strategic designs and on proven, versus prospective, bases of competitive advantage.

A complete evaluation of a company's financial resources should include a *financial risk* analysis. Most financial models are deterministic. That is, managers specify a single estimate for each key variable. Yet, many of these estimates are made with the recognition that there is a great deal of uncertainty about their true value. Together, such uncertainties can mask high levels of risk. It is important, therefore, that risk be explicitly considered. This involves determining the variables that have the greatest effect on revenues and costs as a basis for assessing different risk scenarios. Some of the variables that are commonly considered are market growth rate, market share, price trends, the cost of capital, and the useful life of the underlying technology.

Human Capital: A Company's Most Valuable Strategic Resource

Companies are run by and for people. Although some strategic resources can be duplicated, the people who comprise an organization or its immediate stakeholders are unique. Understanding their concerns, aspirations, and capabilities is, therefore, key to determining a company's strategic position and options.

A survey by *Chief Executive* demonstrates that more and more focus is being put on attracting, developing, and retaining *human capital*. Of the CEOs surveyed, 43 percent believe that finding and retaining good people is their greatest challenge, and 84 percent believe that "people issues" are far more important than before. A study conducted by the American Society for Training and Development examined 500 U.S.–based publicly traded firms. By looking at annual training expenditures and stockholder returns, it concluded that the top half of firms in terms of spending on training had higher stockholder returns than did the bottom half.[6]

Continuous employee development, through on-the-job training and other programs, is critical to the growth of human capital. FedEx develops its homegrown talent through a commitment to continuous learning. The company puts 3 percent of its total expenses into training—six times the proportion of the average company. All line and staff managers attend 11 weeks of mandatory training in their first year. More than 10,000 employees have been to the "Leadership Institute" and have attended weeklong courses on the company's culture and operations.[7] Many other companies are adopting similar strategies and reaping the benefits. Motorola executives report that their company receives $33 for every $1 invested in employee education.

Organizational Strategic Resources

A firm's organizational resources include its *knowledge and intellectual capital base;* its *reputation* with customers, partners, suppliers, and the financial community; specific *competencies, processes,* and *skill sets;* and its *corporate culture.*

Knowledge and *intellectual capital* are major drivers of competitive advantage. A firm's competitive advantage comes from the value it delivers to customers. Competitive advantage is created and sustained when a company continues to mobilize new knowledge faster and more efficiently than its competitors. Recognizing the importance of knowledge as a strategic asset, Skandia, NASDAQ, Chevron, and Dow Chemical have established director-level positions in charge of intellectual capital.

Additional evidence of the growing importance of knowledge and intellectual capital as strategic resources is provided by the financial markets. Although intellectual capital is difficult to measure and not formally represented on the balance sheet, a company's market capitalization increasingly reflects the value of such resources and the effectiveness with which they are managed. Netscape, before being acquired, had a $4 billion market capitalization based on its stock price, even though the company's sales were only a few million dollars per year. Investors based the high stock price on their assessment of the company's intangibles—its knowledge base and quality of management.

The number of *patents* issued in the United States each year has doubled in the last decade. Increasingly, patents are global. Through a new international patent system organized by the United Nations World Intellectual Property Organization, through the World Trade Organization, and through growing demand from inventors for patents that are protected throughout the world, patenting systems are converging. Landmark court decisions also have made new areas of technology patentable in the United States. A 1980 case opened biotechnology and gene-related findings for patenting, a 1981 case allowed the patenting of software, and a 1998 case spawned more business method patents.

Strong patent protection can be of great strategic value. For example, to protect its intellectual property and preserve its competitive advantage in the manufacturing and testing processes involved in its build-to-order system, Dell secured 77 patents protecting different parts of the building and testing process. Such protection pays. IBM collected $30 million in a patent infringement suit from Microsoft—after which Bill Gates sent a memo to employees with the directive to "patent as much as we can."

Increasingly, patents are exploited strategically to generate additional revenue. Licensing patents has helped build the market for IBM technology and boosted its licensing revenues. An increasing number of firms practice "strategic patenting"—using patent applications to colonize entire new areas of technology even before tangible products are created.

The largest part of a company's intellectual capital base, however, is not patentable. It represents the total *knowledge* accumulated by individuals, groups, and units within an organization about customers, suppliers, products, and processes and is made up of a mixture of past experiences, values, education, and insights. As an organization learns, it makes better decisions. Better decisions, in turn, improve performance and enhance learning.

Knowledge becomes an asset when it is managed and transferred. *Explicit knowledge* is formal and objective and can be codified and stored in books, archives, and databases. *Implicit* or *tacit knowledge* is informal and subjective. It is gained through experience and transferred through personal interaction and collaboration.

A study about how Xerox repair technicians refined their knowledge illustrates the difference.[8] The company's assumption had been that the technicians serviced companies' copying machines by following the documented diagnostic road maps that Xerox provided. Research, however, revealed that technicians often went to breakfast together, and while eating, talked about their work. They exchanged stories, posed problems, offered solutions, constructed answers, and discussed the machines, thereby keeping one another up-to-date about what they had learned. Thus, the approaches that the technicians used to repair the Xerox machines were actually based as much on their informal exchanges as on their formal training. What was thought to be a process based on explicit knowledge was, in fact, based on tacit knowledge, experience, and collaboration.[9]

The Importance of Brands

A firm's *reputation* with customers, partners, suppliers, and regulatory agencies can be a powerful strategic asset. Physical distance between customers, distributors, and manufacturers created the need for *brands*. They provided a guarantee of reliability and quality. In a global and Internet-based economy, they build trust and reinforce value. Consumers might be reluctant to use their credit cards to purchase products over the Internet if it were not for the trust they accord to companies such as Amazon, Dell, and eBay. Because consumer trust is the basis of all brand values, companies that own the brands have an immense incentive to work to retain that trust.

Thus, *brands* are strategic assets that assist companies in building and retaining customer loyalty. A strong brand can help maintain profit margins and erect barriers to entry. Because a brand is so valuable to a company, it must constantly be nourished, sustained, and protected. Doing so is becoming harder and more expensive. Consumers are busier, more distracted, and have more media options than ever before. Coca-Cola, Gillette, and Nike struggle to increase volumes, raise prices, and boost margins. In addition, failure in support of a brand can be catastrophic. A mistargeted advertising campaign, a drop-off in quality, or a corporate scandal can quickly reduce the value of a brand and the reputation of the company that owns it.

Every year, *BusinessWeek*, in cooperation with *Interbrand*, a leading brand consultancy, publishes a ranking of the 100 Best Global Brands by dollar value. Brand value is calculated as the net present value of the earnings that the brand is expected to generate and secure in the future. Brands are selected according to two criteria: (1) The brands have to be global, generating significant earnings in the main global markets, and (2) there must be sufficient marketing and financial data publicly available for preparing a reasonable valuation.

Although every company wants to grow its brand, executives must find a way to produce growth while remaining faithful to the company mission. The *BusinessWeek*/Interbrand rankings of global firms recognize companies that succeed in this task as the best global brands.[10]

The *BusinessWeek*/Interbrand study found that companies that succeed in growing their brands while pursuing their missions build customer loyalty that enables the company to attempt risky expansions. Such companies tend to exhibit certain identifiable qualities, which include three strong recommendations for executives:

1. *Do not fear public flops.* In 2006, Google gained 46 percent in brand value—the biggest year-over-year rise of any company ever. The company has succeeded in leveraging its universally recognizable brand to launch a variety of new products, even though its target success rate for these new ventures is lower than 40 percent.

2. *Face your weaknesses.* From 1998 to 2003, McDonald's market capitalization fell by $12.2 billion. Its nearly 100 percent brand awareness in global markets was associated with tired or troubled images: Ronald McDonald, junk food, and obesity. Worse, opinion studies showed a growing distrust by mothers about taking their children to McDonald's. In response, the company added premium-priced salads, chicken meals, and fruit offerings. In 2006, McDonald's global brand increased by 6 percent, and its market capitalization grew by $2 billion.

3. *Protect your culture.* The *BusinessWeek*/Interbrand study found that Starbucks vigorously protects its image by prohibiting other brands from being sold in its retail stores, while parlaying its brand value by coproducing a series of music CDs, books, and films.

Core Competencies

Core competencies represent world class capabilities that enable a company to build a competitive advantage. 3M has developed a core competency in coatings. Canon has core competencies in optics, imaging, and microprocessor controls. Procter & Gamble's marketing prowess allows it to adapt more quickly than its rivals to changing opportunities. The development of core competencies has become a key element in building a long-term strategic advantage. An evaluation of strategic resources and capabilities, therefore, must include assessments of the core competencies a company has or is developing, how they are nurtured, and how they can be leveraged.

Core competencies evolve as a firm develops its business processes and incorporates its intellectual assets. Core competencies are not just things a company does particularly well; rather, they are sets of skills or systems that create a uniquely high value for customers at best-in-class levels. To qualify, such skills or systems should contribute to perceived customer benefits, be difficult for competitors to imitate, and allow for leverage across markets. Honda's use of small-engine technology in a variety of products—including motorcycles, jet skis, and lawn mowers—is a good example.

Core competencies should be focused on creating value and be adapted as customer requirements change. Targeting a carefully selected set of core competencies also benefits innovation. Charles Schwab, for example, successfully leveraged its core competency in brokerage services by expanding its client communication methods to include the Internet, the telephone, branch offices, and financial advisors.

Hamel and Prahalad suggest three tests for identifying core competencies. First, core competencies should provide access to a broad array of markets. Second, they should help differentiate core products and services. Third, core competencies should be hard to imitate because they represent multiple skills, technologies, and organizational elements.[11]

Experience shows that only a few companies have the resources to develop more than a handful of core competencies. Picking the right ones, therefore, is the key. "Which resources or capabilities should we keep in-house and develop into core competencies and which ones should we outsource?" is a key question to ask. Pharmaceutical companies, for example, increasingly outsource clinical testing in an effort to focus their resource base on drug development. Generally, the development of core competencies should focus on long-term platforms capable of adapting to new market circumstances; on unique sources of leverage in the value chain where the firm thinks it can dominate; on elements that are important to customers in the long run; and on key skills and knowledge, not on products.

FORCES FOR CHANGE

Internal Forces for Change

In Chapter 3, we discussed change forces that emanate from a company's external strategic environment. A second set of drivers for strategic change comes from within the organization or from its immediate stakeholders. Disappointing financial performance, new owners or executives, limitations on growth with current strategies, scarcity of critical resources, and internal cultural changes are examples of drivers that give rise to pressures for change.

Because internal resistance can reduce a company's capacity to adapt and chart a new course, it deserves a strategist's careful attention. Organizational resistance to change can take four basic forms: (1) structural, organizational rigidities; (2) closed mind-sets reflecting support for obsolete business beliefs and strategies; (3) entrenched cultures reflecting values, behaviors, and skills that are not conducive to change; and (4) counterproductive change momentum that is not in tune with current strategic requirements.[12]

The four forms of resistance represent very different strategic challenges. Internal structures and systems, including technology, can be changed relatively quickly in most companies. Converting closed minds to the need for change, or changing a corporate culture, is considerably harder. Counterproductive change is especially difficult to remedy because it typically involves altering all three forms of resistance—structures and systems have to be rethought, mind-sets must change, and new behaviors and skills have to be learned.

Company Life Cycle Forces for Change

The forms and strengths of organizational resistance that develop highly depend on a company's history, performance, and culture. Nevertheless, some patterns can be anticipated. Companies go through life cycles. A cycle begins when a founder or founding team organizes a start-up. At this time, a vision or purpose is established, the initial direction for the company is set, and the necessary resources are marshaled to transform this vision into reality. In these early stages, the identities of the founders and that of their company are difficult to separate.

As companies grow, more-formal systems are needed to handle a widening variety of functions. The transition from informality to a more-formal organizational structure can stimulate or hinder strategic change. This passage to organizational maturity, often described as the "entrepreneurial-managerial" transition, poses a dilemma familiar to many companies: how to maintain an entrepreneurial spirit while moving toward an organizational structure increasingly focused on control.

Growth makes organizational learning a requirement for continued success. The evolution of management processes, such as delegation of authority, coordination of effort, and collaboration among organizational units, can have an increasing influence on a company's effectiveness in responding to environmental and internal challenges. In younger companies, the internal operating environment is frequently characterized by greater ambiguity than in established organizations. Often, the ambiguity that encouraged entrepreneurship and innovation also results in a lack of control in a rapidly growing company, which can cause the firm to lose its strategic focus.

Evolving and established companies share the pervasive challenge of finding strategies to manage growth. For some evolving companies, uncontrolled growth is a major concern. As they try to cope with rapid growth, they find that success masks a host of development problems. Dilemmas of leadership can develop, loss of focus becomes an issue, communication becomes harder, skill development falls behind, and stress becomes evident. In established companies, the pressure to grow faster can skew strategic thinking. Ill-considered acquisitions or market expansions, forays into unproven technologies, deviations from developing core skills, and frequent exhortations for more entrepreneurial thinking are indicative of the challenges experienced in more mature companies.

Strategic Forces for Change

The increased importance of a firm's capacity to effectively deal with change has made a strategic perspective on this issue essential. As we have seen, a host of internal factors can reduce a company's capacity for change. Sometimes structural rigidities, a lack of adequate resources, or an adherence to dysfunctional processes inhibit change. Most often, however, resistance to change can be traced to cultural factors.

One of the early arguments in favor of analyzing the interactive nature of organizational factors such as structure, systems, and style with strategy is the so-called 7-S model, developed at McKinsey & Company.[13] Its central idea is that organizational effectiveness stems from the interaction of a number of factors, of which strategy is just one.

The model includes seven different variables: strategy, structure, systems, shared values, skills, staff, and style. Intentionally, its design is not hierarchical; it depicts a situation in which it is not clear which factor is the driving force for change or the biggest obstacle to change. The different variables are interconnected—change in one will force change in another, or, put differently, progress in one area must be accompanied by progress in another to effect meaningful change. As a consequence, the model holds that solutions to organizational problems that invoke just one or a few of these variables are doomed to fail. Therefore, an emphasis on "structural" solutions ("Let's reorganize") without attention to strategy, systems, and all the other variables, can be counterproductive. Style, skills, and superordinate goals—the main values around which a business is built—are observable, even measurable, and can be at least as important as strategy and structure in bringing about fundamental change in an organization. The key to orchestrating change, therefore, is to assess the potential impact of each factor, align the different variables in the model in the desired direction, and then act decisively on all dimensions.

STAKEHOLDER ANALYSIS

In assessing a company's strategic position, it is important to identify key stakeholders inside and outside the organization, the roles they play in fulfilling the organization's mission, and the values they bring to the process. External stakeholders—key customers, suppliers, alliance partners, and regulatory agencies—have a major influence on a firm's strategic options. A firm's internal stakeholders—its owners, board of directors, CEO, executives, managers, and employees—are the shapers and implementers of strategy.

In determining the company's objectives and strategies, executives must recognize the legitimate rights of the firm's stakeholders. Each of these interested parties has justifiable reasons for expecting—and often for demanding—that the company satisfy its claim. In general, stockholders claim competitive returns on their investment; employees seek job satisfaction; customers want what they pay for; suppliers seek dependable buyers; governments want adherence to legislation; unions seek member benefits; competitors want fair competition; local communities want the firm to be a responsible citizen; and the general public expects the firm's existence to improve their nation's quality of life.

The general claims of stakeholders are reflected in thousands of specific demands on every firm—high wages, pure air, job security, product quality, community service, taxes, occupational health and safety regulations, equal employment opportunity regulations, product variety, wide markets, career opportunities, company growth, investment security, high ROI, and many, many more. Although most, perhaps all, of these claims represent desirable ends, they cannot be pursued with equal emphasis. They must be assigned priorities in accordance with the relative emphasis that the firm will give them. That emphasis is a consequence of the criteria that the firm uses in its strategic decision making.

NOTES

1. V. A. Rice, "Why EVA Works for Varity," *Chief Executive*, 1996, 110: 40–44.
2. K. Lehn and A. K. Makhija, "EVA & MVA: As Performance Measures and Signals for Strategic Change," *Strategy & Leadership*, 1996, 24 (3): 34–41.
3. S. Tully, "The EVA Advantage," *Fortune*, 1999, 139 (6): 210.
4. J. B. White, "Value-Based Pay Systems Are Gaining Popularity," *The Wall Street Journal*, April 10, 1997, p. B8.
5. J. L. Dodd and J. Johns, "EVA Reconsidered," *Business and Economic Review*, 1999, 45 (3): 13–18.
6. R. Oliver, "The Return on Human Capital," *Journal of Business Strategy*, July/August 2001, pp. 7–10.
7. J. Byrne, A. Reinhardt, and R. D. Hof, "The Search for the Young and Gifted: Why Talent Counts," *BusinessWeek*, October 4, 1999.
8. J. S. Brown and P. Duguid, "Balancing Act: How to Capture Knowledge Without Killing It," *Harvard Business Review*, 2000, 78: 73–80.
9. R. Cross and L. Baird, "Technology Is Not Enough: Improving Performance by Building Organizational Memory," *Sloan Management Review*, 2000, 41: 69–78.
10. D. Kiley, "Best Global Brands," *BusinessWeek*, August 7, 2006, p. 54.
11. C. K. Prahalad and G. Hamel, "The Core Competence of the Corporation," *Harvard Business Review*, May–June 1990, pp. 79–93.
12. P. Strebel, "Choosing the Right Change Path," *California Management Review*, 1994, 36: 30.
13. R. H. Waterman, Jr., T. J. Peters, and J. R. Phillips, "Structure Is Not Organization," *Business Horizons*, June 1980, pp. 14–26.

Chapter **6**

Formulating Business Unit Strategy

INTRODUCTION

Business unit strategy involves creating a profitable competitive position for a business within a specific industry or market segment. Sometimes called *competitive strategy*, its principal focus is on *how* a firm should compete in a given competitive setting. In contrast, an overarching corporate strategy is concerned with the identification of market arenas *where* a corporation can compete successfully and *how*, as a parent company, it can add value to its strategic business units (SBUs).

Deciding how to compete in a specific market is a complex issue for a business. Optimal strategies depend on many factors, including the *nature of the industry*; the company's *mission*, *goals* and *objectives*; its *current position* and *core competencies*; and major *competitors' strategic choices*.

We begin our discussion by examining the *logic* behind strategic thinking at the business unit level. We first address the basic question: What determines relative profitability at the business unit level? We look at the relative importance of the industry in which a company competes and the competitive position of the firm within its industry, and we identify the drivers that determine sustainable competitive advantage. This logic naturally suggests a number of *generic strategy choices*—broad strategy prescriptions that define the principal dimensions of competition at the business unit level. The generic strategy that is most attractive, and the form that it should take, depends on the specific opportunities and challenges. The chapter next deals with the question of how to assess a strategic challenge. A variety of useful techniques are introduced for generating and evaluating strategic alternatives. The final section addresses the issue of designing a profitable business model.

FOUNDATIONS

Strategic Logic at the Business Unit Level

What are the principal factors behind a business unit's relative profitability? How important are product superiority, cost, marketing and distribution effectiveness, and other factors? How important is the nature of the industry?

Although there are no simple answers to such questions, and the attractiveness of different strategic options depends on the competitive situation analyzed, much has been learned about what drives competitive success at the business unit level.

We begin with the observation that, at the broadest level, firm success is explained by two factors: the *attractiveness of the industry* in which a firm competes and its *relative position* within that industry. For example, the seemingly insatiable demand for new products in the early days of the software industry guaranteed big profits for the industry leaders and for many of their smaller rivals. In the fiercely competitive beer industry, however, relative positioning is a far more important determinant of profitability, as Budweiser's unprecedented performance has shown.

How Much Does Industry Matter?

In a comprehensive study of business performance in four-digit SIC industry categories, Anita McGahan and Michael Porter provided an answer to the question: How much does industry matter? They found that industry, industry segment, and corporate parent accounted for 32 percent, 4 percent, and 19 percent, respectively, of the aggregate variance in business profits, with the remaining variance spread among many other less consequential influences. These results support the conclusion that industry characteristics are an important determinant of profit potential. Industry directly accounted for 36 percent of the explained total variation in profitability.[1]

Relative Position

The relative profitability of rival firms depends on the *nature of their competitive position* (i.e., on their ability to create a *sustainable competitive advantage* vis-à-vis their competitors). The two generic forms of sustainable competitive positioning are a competitive advantage based on *lower delivered cost* and one based on the ability to *differentiate* products or services from those of competitors and command a price premium relative to the cost incurred.

Whether lowest cost or differentiation is most effective depends, among other factors, on a firm's choice of *competitive scope*. The scope of a competitive strategy includes such elements as the number of product and buyer segments served, the number of different geographic locations in which the firm competes, the extent to which it is vertically integrated, and the degree to which it must coordinate its positioning with related businesses in which the firm is invested.

Decisions about scope and how to create a competitive advantage are made on the basis of a detailed understanding of what customers value and what capabilities and opportunities a company has relative to its competitors. In this sense, strategy reflects a firm's configuration and how the different elements interrelate. Competitive advantage results when a company has a better understanding of what customers desire and when it learns to meet those customer needs at a lower cost than its rivals or when it creates buyer value in unique ways that allow it to charge a premium.

The Importance of Market Share

The relative importance of market share as a strategic goal at the business unit level has been the subject of considerable controversy.

Arguing that profitability should be the primary goal of strategy, some analysts believe that executives have been led astray by the principal pursuit of market share.[2] Many failed companies have achieved high market shares, including A&P in grocery sales, Intel in memory products, and WordPerfect in word processors. Thus, executives must ask themselves: Are we managing for volume growth or value growth?

The PIMS Project

Although no manager should pursue growth for growth's sake, evidence suggests that in some industries market share is an important determinant of long-term profitability. Bradley Gale and Robert Buzzell, in reviewing the evidence on this subject, put it succinctly:

> Large market share is both a reward for providing better value and a means of realizing lower costs. Under most circumstances, enterprises that have achieved a large share of the markets they serve are considerably more profitable than their smaller-share rivals. This connection between market share and profitability has been recognized by corporate executives and consultants . . .[3]

However, in trying to relate this conclusion of a quarter of a century ago to present competitive dynamics, it is critically important to realize that the researchers were referring principally to heavy manufacturing industries when they reached their conclusions.

The Marketing Science Institute at the Harvard Business School undertook research into the relative profitability of different market strategies. The PIMS (Profit Impact of Market Strategy) project involved more than 600 businesses over a period of more than 15 years.[4]

The major findings of the PIMS study were as follows:

1. Absolute and relative market share are strongly correlated with ROI. Businesses with higher market shares were generally more profitable because of economies of scale, experience effects, market power, and the quality of management.

2. Product quality is key to market leadership and allows companies with larger market shares to charge higher prices and, therefore, achieve higher margins.
3. ROI is positively correlated with market growth.
4. Vertical integration can be beneficial later in the product life cycle. Forward integration is more profitable than backward integration.
5. High investment intensity tends to depress ROI, as do high inventory levels.
6. Capacity use is critical for businesses with a high level of capital intensity; companies with small market shares are particularly vulnerable.

The PIMS findings help to explain many business success stories through the 1980s and many business performance declines of the 1990s. However, the dynamic, technology-driven experiences of the past 20 years bear little resemblance to the marketplace where successful competitors followed the PIMS model. Thus, although the lessons from the PIMS research were beneficial at the time that they were first taught, the number of business settings in which they have enduring relevance is decreasing rapidly. This observation highlights the need for executives to continually update their assumptions about key strategic relationships.

FORMULATING A COMPETITIVE STRATEGY

Key Challenges

Managers face four key challenges in formulating competitive strategy at the business unit level: (1) analyzing the competitive environment, (2) anticipating key competitors' actions, (3) generating strategic options, and (4) choosing among alternatives.

The first challenge, "analyzing the competitive environment," deals with two questions: With whom will we compete, now and in the future? and What relative strengths will we have as a basis for creating a sustainable competitive advantage? Answering these questions requires an analysis of the remote external environment, the industry environment, and internal capabilities. The second challenge, "anticipating key competitors' actions," focuses on understanding how competitors are likely to react to different strategic moves. Industry leaders tend to behave differently from challengers or followers. A detailed competitor analysis is helpful in gaining an understanding of how competitors are likely to respond and why. The third challenge, "identifying strategic options," requires a balancing of opportunities and constraints to craft a diverse array of strategic options ranging from defensive to preemptive moves. The fourth challenge, "choosing among alternatives," requires an analysis of the long-term impact of different strategy options as a basis for a final choice.

What Is Competitive Advantage?

A firm has a *competitive advantage* when it is successful in designing and implementing a value-creating strategy that competitors are not currently using. The competitive advantage is *sustainable* when current or new competitors are not able to imitate or supplant it.

A competitive advantage often is created by combining strengths. Firms look for ways to exploit competencies and advantages at different points in the value chain to add value in different ways. Southwest Airlines' industry-best 15-minute turnaround time for getting airplanes back into the air, for example, is a competitive advantage that saves the firm $175 million annually in capital expenditures and differentiates the firm by allowing it to offer more flights per plane per day. Use of value analysis helps a firm to focus on areas in which it enjoys competitive advantages and to outsource functions in which it does not. To enhance its cost leadership position, Taco Bell outsources many food preparation functions, thereby allowing it to cut prices, reduce employees, and free up 40 percent of its kitchen space.

It is important for executives to understand the nature and sources of a firm's competitive advantages. They should also make sure that middle managers understand the competitive advantages, because the managers' awareness allows for a more effective exploitation of such advantages and leads to increased firm performance. Building a competitive advantage is, therefore, rooted in identifying, practicing, strengthening, and instilling throughout the organization those leadership traits that improve the firm's reputation among its stakeholders. As a consequence, a focus on organizational learning and on creating, retaining, and motivating a skilled and knowledgeable workforce may be the best way for executives to foster competitive advantages in a rapidly changing business environment.

Value Chain Analysis

In competitive terms, *value* is the perceived benefit that a buyer is willing to pay a firm for what a firm provides. Customers derive value from product differentiation, product cost, and the ability of the firm to meet their needs. Value-creating activities are, therefore, the discrete building blocks of competitive advantage.

A *value chain* is a model of a business process. It depicts the value creation process as a series of activities, beginning with processing raw materials and ending with sales and service to end users. *Value chain analysis* involves the study of costs and elements of product or service differentiation throughout the chain of activities and linkages to determine present and potential sources of competitive advantage.

The value chain divides a firm's business process into component activities that add value: primary activities that contribute to the physical creation of the product and support activities that assist the primary activities and each other, as shown in Figure 6-1. Charles Schwab successfully used its expertise in a support activity to create value in a primary activity. The firm offers a broad range of distribution channels (primary activity) for its brokerage services and holds extensive expertise in information technology and brokerage systems (support activities). Schwab uses its IT knowledge to create two new distribution channels for brokerage services—E-Schwab on the Internet and the Telebroker touch-tone telephone brokering service—both of which provide value by delivering low-cost services.[5]

Once a firm's primary, support, and activity types are defined, value chain analysis assigns assets and operating costs to all

Figure 6-1 The Value Chain

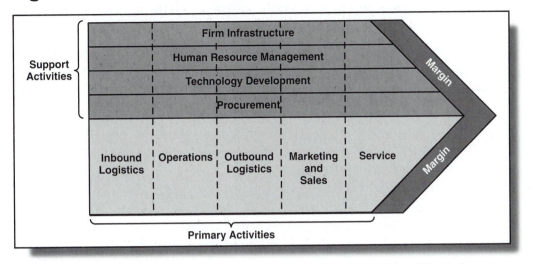

Source: Reprinted by permission of *Harvard Business Review.* The Value Chain. "How Information Gives You Competitive Advantage; the Information Revolution Is Transforming the Nature of Competition," by M. E. Porter and V. E. Miller, *63* (4) 1985. Copyright © 1985 by the Harvard Business School Publishing Corporation; all rights reserved.

value-creating activities. Activity-based cost accounting often is used to determine whether a competitive advantage exists.

A firm *differentiates* itself from its competitors when it provides something unique that is valuable to buyers beyond a low price. Dell's ability to sell, build-to-order, and ship a computer to the customer within a few days is a unique differentiator of its value chain. Benetton, the Italian casual wear company, reconfigured its traditional outsourced manufacturing and distribution network to achieve differentiation.[6] Its executives reasoned that the company could improve its flexibility by directly overseeing key business processes throughout the supply chain. If specific activities reduce a buyer's cost or provide a higher level of buyer satisfaction, customers are willing to pay a premium price. Sources of differentiation of primary activities that provide a higher level of buyer satisfaction include build-to-order manufacturing, efficient and on-time delivery of goods, promptness in responding to customer service requests, and high quality.

It is important to identify the value that individual primary and support activities contribute beyond their costs. Different segments of the value chain represent potential sources of profit and, therefore, define *profit pools.*[7] Value chain analysis showed Nike and Reebok how their core competencies in product design (a support activity) and marketing and sales (primary activities) created value for customers. This conclusion led Nike to outsource almost all other activities. In a second case, after completing a detailed value chain analysis, Millennium Pharmaceuticals opted to shift from drug research in the upstream portion of the industry to drug manufacturing downstream, to improve its profitability. This strategy was derived from the firm's clearer understanding of the entire pharmaceutical value chain and its newly recognized ability to better exploit different profit pools.[8]

Analyzing the value chains of competitors, customers, and suppliers can help a firm add value by focusing on the needs of downstream customers or the weaknesses of upstream suppliers.[9] Dow Chemical captures value from downstream rubber glove producers, to whom it used to sell chemicals, by making the gloves itself. BASF adds value by leveraging its core competencies in the paint-coating process by painting car doors for auto manufacturers, instead of just selling them the paint.

Value chain analysis can also be used to shape responses to changing upstream and downstream market conditions through collaboration with customers and suppliers to improve speed, cut costs, and enhance the end customer's perception of value. This is especially true as intercompany links such as electronic data integration systems, strategic alliances, just-in-time manufacturing, electronic markets, and networked companies blur the boundaries of many organizations.

Approaching value chain analysis as a shared process involving the different members of the chain can optimize a firm's value creation by minimizing collective costs. Dell, for example, shares information about its customers with its suppliers. This improves its suppliers' ability to forecast demand, which results in reduced inventory and logistics costs for Dell and the suppliers. Home Depot and General Electric established an alliance between their value chains that reduces direct and indirect costs for each firm. A Web-based application links Home Depot's point-of-purchase data to GE's e-business system and enables Home Depot to ship directly to its customers from GE. The value chain to value chain connection enables Home Depot to sell more GE products and to reduce the inventory in its own warehouses. In addition, GE can use the real-time demand information from Home Depot to adjust the production rate of appliances.

With advances in information technology and the Internet, companies can monitor value creation across many activities and linkages. For purposes of monitoring, it is useful to distinguish between the physical and virtual components of the value chain. The *physical value chain* represents the use of raw materials and labor to deliver a tangible product. The *virtual value chain* represents the information flows underlying the physical activities evident within a firm. Engineering teams at Ford Motor Company optimize the physical design process of a vehicle using real-time collaboration in a virtual workplace. Oracle Corporation is a front-runner in adding virtual value for the customer by using the Internet to directly test and distribute their software products.

PORTER'S GENERIC BUSINESS UNIT STRATEGIES

Differentiation or Low Cost?

Earlier, we distinguished between two *generic* competitive strategic postures: *low cost* and *differentiation.* They are called *generic* because in principle they apply to any business and any industry. However, the relative attractiveness of different generic strategies is related to choices about competitive scope. If a company chooses a relatively broad target market (e.g., Wal-Mart), a low-cost strategy is aimed at *cost leadership.* Such a strategy aggressively exploits opportunities for cost reduction through economies of scale and cumulative learning (experience effects) in purchasing and manufacturing and generally calls for proportionately low expenditures on R&D, marketing, and overhead.

Cost leaders generally charge less for their products and services than rivals and aim for a substantial share of the market by appealing primarily to budget-sensitive customers. Their low prices serve as an entry barrier to potential competitors. As long as they maintain their relative cost advantage, cost leaders can maintain a defensible position in the marketplace.

With a more narrow scope, a low-cost strategy is based on *cost focus*. As with any focus strategy, a small, well-defined market niche—a particular group of customers or geographic region—is selected to the exclusion of others. Then, in the case of cost focus, only activities directly relevant to serving that niche are undertaken, at the lowest possible cost.

Southwest Airlines is renowned for its cost-focus strategy. A low-fare carrier that has the highest profit margins in the airline industry, Southwest Airlines grew 4,048 percent in the 1990s. Its low-cost, no-frills strategy has been highly successful in the U.S. domestic market.

The cost-focus strategy is based on a narrow scope, with a small, well-defined market niche. Southwest concentrates on short-haul routes with high traffic densities and offers frequent flights throughout the day. Efficiency has been improved by eliminating costs associated with "hub" routes involving large major U.S. airports. Operating in only 57 cities in 28 states, Southwest targets secondary airports because of their lower cost structures.

Southwest's fundamentally different operating structure allows it to charge lower fares than more established airlines. A typical flight, which lasts 1 hour on average, has no assigned seats; in-flight service consists of drinks and snacks only, and the company does not offer transfer of luggage to other airlines.

Southwest's fleet consists of 284 Boeing 737s, which make more than 2,400 flights per day. Having one type of aircraft allows for greater efficiency and easier turnarounds. All Southwest 737s use the same equipment, thereby keeping training and maintenance costs down. Finally, high-asset use, reflected in a turnaround time averaging 20 minutes, which is less than half the industry average, reduces its operating expenses by 25 percent.

Differentiation postures can similarly be tied to decisions of scope. A *differentiation* strategy aimed at a broad, mass market seeks to create uniqueness on an industry-wide basis. Walt Disney Productions and Nike are examples. Broad-scale differentiation can be achieved through product design, brand image, technology, distribution, service, or a combination of these elements. Finally, like cost focus, a *differentiated focus* strategy is aimed at a well-defined segment of the market and targets customers willing to pay for value added, as depicted in Figure 6-2.

Requirements for Success

The two generic routes—*low cost* and *differentiation*—are fundamentally different. Achieving *cost leadership* requires a ruthless devotion to minimizing costs through continuous improvement in manufacturing, process engineering, and other cost-reducing strategies. Scale and scope effects must be leveraged in all aspects

Figure 6-2   Generic Strategy Choices

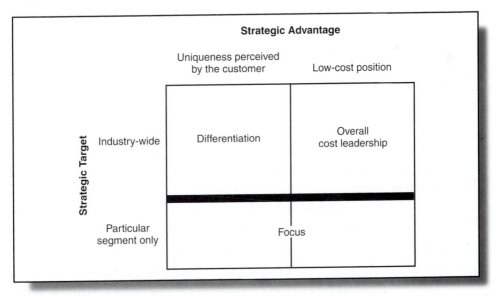

Source: Reprinted with the permission of *The Free Press*, an imprint of Simon & Schuster Adult Publishing Group, from *Competitive Strategy: Techniques for Analyzing Industries and Competitors* by Michael E. Porter. Copyright © 1980, 1998 by The Free Press.

of the value creation process—in the design of products and services, purchasing practices, and distribution. In addition, achieving and sustaining cost leadership requires tight control and an organizational structure and incentive system supportive of a cost-focused discipline.

Differentiation requires an altogether different approach. Here, the concern is for value added. Differentiation has multiple objectives. The primary objective is to redefine the rules by which customers arrive at their purchase decisions by offering something unique that is valuable. In doing so, companies also seek to erect barriers to imitation. Differentiation strategies are often misunderstood; "spray painting the product green" is *not* differentiation. Differentiation is a strategic choice to provide something of value to the customer other than a low price. One way to differentiate a product or service is to add functionality. However, many other, sometimes more effective, ways to differentiate are possible. R&D aimed at enhancing product quality and durability (Maytag) is a viable element of a differentiation strategy. Investing in brand equity (Coca-Cola) and pioneering new ways of distribution (Avon Cosmetics) are others.

Considerable evidence suggests that the most successful differentiation strategies involve multiple sources of differentiation. Higher quality raw materials, unique product design, more reliable manufacture, superior marketing and distribution programs, and quicker service all contribute to set a company's offering apart from rival products. The use of more than one source of differentiation makes it harder for competitors to effectively imitate. In addition to using multiple sources, integrating the different dimensions of value added—functionality, economic, and psychological value—is critical. Effective differentiation thus requires explicit decisions about how much value to add, where to add such value, and how to communicate such added value to the customer. Critically for the firm, customers must be willing to pay a premium relative to the cost of achieving the differentiation. Successful differentiation, therefore, requires a thorough understanding of what customers value, what relative importance they attach to the satisfaction of different needs and wants, and how much they are willing to pay.

Risks

Each generic posture carries unique risks. Cost leaders must concern themselves with technological change that can nullify past investments in scale economics or accumulated learning. In an increasingly global economy, firms that rely on cost leadership are particularly vulnerable to new entrants from other parts of the world that can take advantage of even lower factor costs. The biggest challenge to differentiators is *imitation*. Imitation narrows actual and perceived differentiation. If this occurs, buyers might change their minds about what constitutes differentiation and then change their loyalties and preferences.

The goal of each strategic generic posture is to create sustainability. For cost leaders, sustainability requires continually improving efficiency, looking for less expensive sources of supply, and seeking ways to reduce manufacturing and distribution costs. For differentiators, sustainability requires the firm to erect barriers to entry around their dimensions of uniqueness, to use multiple sources of differentiation, and to create switching costs for customers. Organizationally, a differentiation strategy calls for strong coordination among R&D, product development and marketing, and incentives aimed at value creation and creativity.

The Saga of Dell

The story of Dell's rise in the PC industry illustrates how a relentless pursuit of cost leadership and a close alignment between strategy and business structure can pay off. Convinced that he had a winning formula for selling personal computers, Michael S. Dell, the company's founder, turned a low-margin mail-order operation into a high-profit, high-service business by challenging every aspect of PC selling and manufacturing. The company successfully applied its just-in-time manufacturing philosophy to the rest of its supply chain—requiring, for example, that critical components be warehoused within 15 minutes' travel time of a Dell factory. In addition, by marrying this low-cost, speed-based business model to the new principles of electronic commerce, Dell created a sustainable competitive advantage.

In relatively short order, Dell moved from a challenger to the number one seller of PCs over the Web. Many corporations that were willing to buy over the telephone preferred electronic purchasing. Consequently, Dell stock became one of the best high-technology growth investments, and its business model became the envy of the industry.

In mid-2005, Michael Dell retired. On January 31, 2007, he returned to the role of CEO after 18 months of faltering financials. In Dell's absence, if not before, his company had fallen victim to complacency, believing that its highly successful business model would remain defensible and productive: "We make PCs cheap. This is what we do, and we do it a lot." Although Dell had broadened its product line to include storage, printers, and TVs, it never countered the innovative and aggressive moves of its competitors, nor did it invest in new competitive advantages for its base or expanded business lines. One moral to this story is that each generic strategy has limitations as well as upside potential. Cost leadership produced great sales at Dell when market demand was high, but it kept Dell from maintaining its growth path when sufficient sales could only be found in new product-market segments where differentiation was demanded.

Critique of Porter's Generic Strategies

Most research on the efficacy of Porter's framework indicates that generic strategies are not always viable. Low-cost strategies are less effective when low cost is the industry norm. Furthermore, evidence suggests that executives reject Porter's generic strategies in favor of strategies that combine elements of cost leadership, differentiation, and flexibility to meet customer needs.[10]

The most common arguments against Porter's generic strategies are that low-cost production and differentiation are not mutually exclusive and that when they can exist together in a firm's strategy, they result in sustained profitability.[11] The preconditions for a cost leadership strategy stem from the industry's structure, whereas the preconditions for differentiation stem from customer tastes. Because these two factors are independent, the opportunity of a firm's pursuing both cost leadership and differentiation strategies should always be considered.

In fact, differentiation can permit a firm to attain a low-cost position. For example, expenditures to differentiate a product can increase demand by creating loyalty, which decreases the price elasticity for the product. Such actions also can broaden product appeal, enabling the firm to increase market share at a given price, and it increases volume sold. Differentiation initially increases unit cost. However, the firm can reduce unit cost in the long run if costs fall due to learning economies, economies of scale, and economies of scope. Conversely, the savings generated from low-cost production permit a firm to increase spending on marketing, service, and product enhancement, thereby producing differentiation.

Finally, the possibility of providing both improved quality and lower costs exists within the total quality management framework. High quality and high productivity are complementary, and low quality is associated with higher costs.

There are dangers associated with pursuing a single strategy. Caterpillar, Inc. differentiated itself by manufacturing the highest-quality earthmoving equipment. However, the company was so preoccupied with precision and durability that it was undercut on price by 30 percent by Japanese firms that emphasized efficiency and economy. In addition, if companies pursue specialized strategies, competitors can imitate them more easily than if they used mixed strategies. For example, a pure cost leadership strategy can accelerate the move toward commodity markets, in which case no competitor benefits.

Another concern arises because of evidence that the pursuit of a pure generic strategy will not sustain a competitive advantage in hypercompetitive environments. When the competitive environment changes rapidly, successful organizations must maintain flexibility. Pursuing a generic strategy within the arena of hypercompetition will only provide the firm with a temporary competitive advantage, the sustainability of which is dependent on a combination of customer needs, firm resources, and capabilities, and the existence of isolating mechanisms.

VALUE DISCIPLINES

Michael Treacy and Fred Wiersema coined the term *"value disciplines"* to describe different ways companies can create value for customers (Figure 6-3). Specifically, they identify three generic strategies: *product leadership, operational excellence,* and *customer intimacy.*[12]

Product Leadership

Companies pursuing *product leadership* produce a continuous stream of state-of-the-art products and services. Such companies are innovation driven, and they constantly raise the bar for competitors by offering more value and better solutions.

Figure 6-3 Value Disciplines

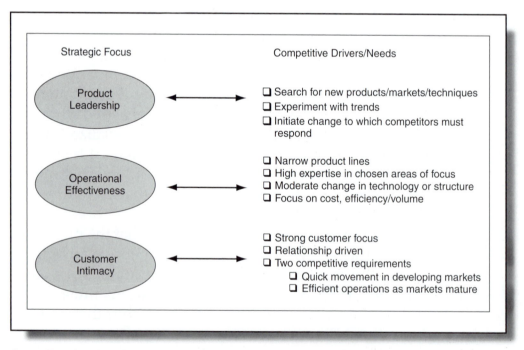

Source: Based on M. Treacy and F. Wiersema, "Customer Intimacy and Other Value Disciplines," *Harvard Business Review,* Jan.–Feb. 1993, pp. 84–93.

The product leadership discipline is based on the following four principles:

1. **The encouragement of innovation.** Through small ad hoc working groups, an "experimentation is good" mind-set, and compensation systems that reward success, constant product innovation is encouraged.
2. **A risk-oriented management style.** Product leadership companies are necessarily innovators, which requires a recognition that there are risks (as well as rewards) inherent in new ventures.
3. **A recognition** that the company's current success and future prospects lie in its talented product design people and those who support them.
4. **A recognition** of the need to educate and lead the market regarding the use and benefits of new products.

Examples of companies that use product leadership as a cornerstone of their strategies include Intel, Apple, and Nike.

Operational Excellence

Operational excellence—the second value discipline—describes a strategic approach aimed at better production and delivery mechanisms. Wal-Mart, American Airlines, FedEx, and Starwood Hotels & Resorts Worldwide all pursue operational excellence.

Starwood is one of the largest hotel chains in the world with 742 establishments in 80 countries, including famous brands such as Sheraton, Westin, Four Points, and St. Regis. Following an extended period of subpar performance, the company decided to stylishly renovate its underperforming hotels and focus on doing and presenting everything it already did, much better.

The firm's biggest changes were made to the Sheraton hotel chain, which underwent a $750 million makeover. This renovation was undertaken to restore a reputation for reliability, value, and consistency. The revamping did away with flowered bedspreads in favor of a Ralph Lauren style. Amenities such as ergonomic desk chairs and two-line telephones became standard.

Much of Starwood's Four Points brand underwent renovations with as much as 80 percent of the original hotel structure torn down. Every room was redesigned and redecorated. Twenty-four-hour fitness facilities were opened. Olympic-sized heated swimming pools with outdoor reception areas became standard. Business centers were expanded to include ballrooms and meeting rooms to accommodate groups of all sizes. Management expanded dining options to range from restaurants to pubs. Guestroom hallways and lobbies were brightened and dramatically redesigned in a subtle, Mediterranean style. Wallpaper borders, sconce lighting, and artful signage were added to present the hotel with a bright fresh look.

Starwood's focus on operational excellence was immediately successful. For the four straight quarters following the activation of the changes, Starwood led Marriott and Hilton in North American revenue per available room. Operating income increased 26 percent.

Customer Intimacy

A strategy based on *customer intimacy* concentrates on building customer loyalty. Nordstrom and Home Depot continually tailor their products and services to changing customer needs. Pursuing customer intimacy can be expensive, but the long-term benefits of a loyal clientele can pay off handsomely.

Because the vast majority of companies worldwide now claim to give top priority to customer concerns, it might be hard to imagine how a firm distinguishes itself through customer intimacy. Home Depot provides an excellent example of a firm that succeeds. Home Depot uses customer intimacy initiatives to marginalize competitors. The company's plan began with the creation of its "Service Performance Initiative," which emphasizes changing daily operations to provide a more shopper-friendly store atmosphere. Home Depot added off-hour stocking, which moves merchandise in and out of inventory during late evening hours or after closing for those stores that have not expanded their operating hours to 24 hours per day.

The main benefit of the new stocking method is the ability of employees to focus on customer service and sales. Before the implementation of the initiative, salespeople spent 40 percent of their time with customers and 60 percent on other work-related duties. After the customer-intimacy initiatives, salespeople were able to spend 70 percent of their time with customers on sales-oriented tasks and 30 percent on other duties.

Home Depot undertook two additional customer-intimacy initiatives. The first was the installation of Linux Info for point-of-sale support systems. With the new system, customers can place orders from home over the Internet and have the purchase processed at the store's register. This process allows customers to enter the store simply for pickup, having already purchased their merchandise. The second initiative involves home improvement classes taught at its stores. Customer intimacy is enhanced when professionals teach customers how to buy and install the proper materials and construction equipment. Home Depot sells products and receives customer feedback as a result of the courses.

Each value discipline calls for a different set of competencies and has its own requirements for success (Figure 6-4). Most companies

Figure 6-4 Different Value Disciplines Call for Different Competencies

Strategic Focus	Work Environment	Employee Competencies
Customer intimacy	Values-driven, dynamic, challenging, informal, service-oriented, qualitative, employee as customer, "whatever it takes"	Relationship-building, listening, rapid problem-solving, independent action, initiative, collaboration, quality-focused
Operational excellence	Predictable, measurable, hierarchical, cost-conscious, team-based, formal	Process control, continuous improvement, teamwork, analysis, financial/operational understanding
Product leadership	Experimental, learning-focused, technical, informal, fast-paced, resource-rich	Information sharing, creativity, group problem solving, breakthrough thinking, artistic, visionary

Source: Based on M. Treacy and F. Wiersema, "Customer Intimacy and Other Value Disciplines," *Harvard Business Review,* Jan.–Feb. 1993, pp. 84–93.

try to excel in one of the three value disciplines and be competitive in the others. Explicitly choosing a value discipline and focusing available resources on creating a gap between the company and its immediate competitors sharpens a company's strategic focus.

DESIGNING A PROFITABLE BUSINESS MODEL[13]

Designing a profitable business model is a critical part of formulating a business unit strategy. Creating an effective model requires a clear understanding of how the firm will generate profits and the strategic actions it must take to succeed over the long term.

Adrian Slywotzky and David Morrison have identified 22 business models—designs that generate profits in a unique way. They present these models as examples, believing that others do or can exist. The authors also confirm that in some instances profitability depends on the interplay of two or more business models.

What is our business model? How do we make a profit? Slywotzky and Morrison suggest that these are the two most productive questions asked of executives. The classic strategy rule suggested: "Gain market share and profits will follow." This approach once worked for most industries. However, as a consequence of competitive turbulence caused by globalization and rapid technological advancements, the once popular belief in a strong correlation between market share and profitability has collapsed in many industries.

How can businesses earn sustainable profits? The answer is found by analyzing the following questions: Where will the firm be able to make a profit in this industry? How should the business model be designed so that the firm will be profitable? Slywotzky and Morrison describe the following profitability business models as ways to answer these questions:

1. *Customer Development/Customer Solutions Profit model.* Companies that use this business model make money by finding ways to

improve their customers' economics and investing in ways for customers to improve their processes.

2. *Product Pyramid Profit model.* This model is effective in markets where customers have strong preferences for product characteristics, including variety, style, color, and price. By offering a number of variations, companies can build so-called product pyramids. At the base are low-priced, high-volume products, and at the top are high-priced, low-volume products. Profit is concentrated at the top of the pyramid, but the base is the strategic firewall (i.e., a strong, low-priced brand that deters competitor entry), thereby protecting the margins at the top. Consumer goods companies and automobile companies use this model.

3. *Multicomponent System Profit model.* Some businesses are characterized by a production/marketing system that consists of components that generate substantially different levels of profitability. In hotels, for example, there is a substantial difference between the profitability of room rentals and that of bar operations. In such instances, it often is useful to maximize the use of the highest-profit components to maximize the profitability of the whole system.

4. *Switchboard Profit model.* Some markets function by connecting multiple sellers to multiple buyers. The switchboard profit model creates a high-value intermediary that concentrates these multiple communication pathways through one point, or "switchboard," and thereby reduces costs for both parties in exchange for a fee. As volume increases, so, too, do profits.

5. *Time Profit model.* Sometimes, speed is the key to profitability. This business model takes advantage of first-mover advantage. To sustain this model, constant innovation is essential.

6. *Blockbuster Profit model.* In some industries, profitability is driven by a few great product successes. This business model is representative of movie studios, pharmaceutical firms, and software companies, which have high R&D and launch costs and finite product cycles. In this type of environment, it pays to concentrate resource investments in a few projects rather than to take positions in a variety of products.

7. *Profit Multiplier model.* This business model reaps gains, again and again, from the same product, character, trademark capability, or service. Think of the value that Michael Jordan, Inc. creates with the image of the great basketball legend. This model can be a powerful engine for businesses with strong consumer brands.

8. *Entrepreneurial Profit model.* Small can be beautiful. This business model stresses that diseconomies of scale can exist in companies. They attack companies that have become comfortable with their profit levels, with formal, bureaucratic systems that are remote from customers. As their expenses grow and customer relevance declines, such companies are vulnerable to entrepreneurs who are in direct contact with their customers.

9. *Specialization Profit model.* This business model stresses growth through sequenced specialization. Consulting companies have used this design successfully.

10. *Installed Base Profit model.* A company that pursues this model profits because its established user base subsequently buys the company's brand of consumables or follow-on products. Installed base profits provide a protected annuity stream. Examples include razors and blades, software and upgrades, copiers and toner cartridges, and cameras and film.

11. *De Facto Standard Profit model.* A variant of the Installed Base Profit model, this model is appropriate when the Installed Base model becomes the de facto standard that governs competitive behavior in the industry, as is the case with Oracle.

NOTES

1. A. M. McGahan and M. E. Porter, "How Much Does Industry Matter, Really?" *Strategic Management Journal,* 1997, 18: 15–30.

2. A. J. Slywotzky and D. J. Morrison, with B. Andelman, *The Profit Zone; How Strategic Business Design Will Lead You To Tomorrow's Profits,* New York, Times Books, 1997.

3. B. T. Gale and R. D. Buzzell, "Market Position and Competitive Strategy," in *The Interface of Marketing and Strategy,* G. Day, B. Weitz, and R. Wensley (eds.), Greenwich, CT, JAI Press, Inc., 1993.

4. R. D. Buzzell and B. T. Gale, The PIMS Principles; *Linking Strategy To Performance*, New York, The Free Press, 1987.

5. J. Webb and C. Gile, "Reversing the Value Chain," *The Journal of Business Strategy*, 2001, 22 (2): 13–17.

6. A. Camuffo, P. Romano, and A. Vinelli, "Back to the Future: Benetton Transforms Its Global Network," *Sloan Management Review*, 2001, 43: 46–52.

7. O. Gadiesh and J. L. Gilbert, "Profit Pools: A Fresh Look at Strategy." *Harvard Business Review*, 1998, 76 (3): 139–147.

8. D. Champion, "Mastering the Value Chain," *Harvard Business Review*, 2001, 79 (6): 109–115.

9. F. Budde, B. R. Elliott, G. Farha, C. R. Palmer, and R. Steffen, "The Chemistry of Knowledge," *The McKinsey Quarterly*, 2000, (4): 98–107.

10. R. B. Robinson, Jr. and J. A. Pearce II, "Planned Patterns of Strategic Behavior and Their Relationship to Business-Unit Performance." *Strategic Management Journal*, 1988, 9 (1): 43–60; Murray, A. I., "A Contingency View of Porter's Generic Strategies," Academy of Management Review, 1988, 13 (3): 390–400.

11. C. W. L. Hill, "Differentiation versus Low Cost or Differentiation and Low Cost: A Contingency Framework," *Academy of Management Review*, 1988, 13 (3): 401–412.

12. M. Treacy and F. Wiersema, "Customer Intimacy and Other Value Disciplines," *Harvard Business Review*, Jan.–Feb. 1993, pp. 84–93.

13. A. J. Slywotzki, et al., op. cit., 1997.

Chapter 7

Business Unit Strategy: Contexts and Special Dimensions

INTRODUCTION

Generic strategies are useful for identifying broad frameworks within which a competitive advantage can be developed and exploited. However, to forecast the relative effectiveness of different options, strategists consider the *context* in which a strategy is to be implemented. To see how such analysis is done, in this chapter we examine six types of industry settings. First, we look at three contexts that relate to the various evolutionary stages of an industry: *emerging, growth*, and *mature and declining*. Next, we discuss three industry environments that pose unique strategic challenges: *fragmented, deregulating*, and *hypercompetitive* industries. Because hypercompetition is increasingly characteristic of business-level competition in many industries, we then discuss two critical attributes of successful firms in dynamic industries: speed and innovation.

EMERGING, GROWTH, MATURE, AND DECLINING INDUSTRIES

Strategy in Emerging Industries

New industries or industry segments emerge in a variety of ways. Technological breakthroughs can launch entirely new industries or reform old ones, as in the case of changes to the telephone industry with the advent of cellular technology. Sometimes changes in the macro environment spawn new industries. Examples are solar energy and Internet technology.

From a strategic perspective, new industries present new opportunities. Their technologies are typically immature. This means that competitors will actively try to improve existing designs and processes or leapfrog them altogether with next-generation technology. A battle for standards might ensue. Costs are typically high and unpredictable, entry barriers are low, supplier relationships are underdeveloped, and distribution channels are just emerging.

Timing can be critical in determining strategic success in an emerging market. The first company to come out with a new product or service often has a *first mover advantage*. First movers have the opportunity to shape customer expectations and define the competitive rules of the game. In high-technology industries, first movers can sometimes set standards for all subsequent products. Microsoft was able to accomplish this with its Windows operating system. In general, first movers have a relatively brief window of opportunity to establish themselves as industry leaders in technology, cost, or service.

Exercising strategic leadership in the emerging market can be an effective way to reduce risk. In addition to the ability to shape the industry structure based on timing, method of entry, and experience in similar situations, leadership opportunities include the ability to control product and process development through superior technology, quality, or customer knowledge; the ability to leverage existing relationships with suppliers and distributors; and the ability the leverage access to a core group of early, loyal customers.

Strategy in Growth Industries

Growth presents a host of challenges. Competitors tend to focus on expanding their market shares. Over time, buyers become knowledgeable and can better distinguish between competitive offerings. As a result, increased segmentation often accompanies the transition to market maturity. Cost control becomes an important element of strategy as unit margins shrink and new products and applications are harder to find. In industries with global potential, international markets become more important. The globalization of competition also introduces new uncertainties as a second wave of global competitors enters the race.

During the early growth phase, companies tend to add more products, models, sizes, and flavors to appeal to an increasingly segmented market. Toward the end of the growth phase cost considerations become a priority. In addition, process innovation becomes an important dimension of cost control, as do the redefinitions of supplier and distributor relations. Finally, horizontal integration becomes attractive as a way of consolidating a company's market position or increasing a firm's international presence.

Competing companies that enter the market at this time, often labeled *followers*, have different advantages than early market leaders. Later entrants have the opportunity to evaluate alternative technologies, delay investment in risky projects or plant capacity, and imitate or leapfrog superior product and technology offerings. Followers also tap into proven market segments rather than take the risks associated with trying to develop latent market demand into ongoing revenue streams.

Firms that consider entry into a growing industry must also face the strategic decision of whether to enter through internal development or acquisition. Entry into a new segment or industry through *internal development* involves creating a new business, often in a somewhat unfamiliar competitive environment. It also is likely to be slow and expensive. Developing new products, processes, partnerships, and systems takes time and requires substantial learning. For these reasons, companies increasingly are turning to *joint ventures*, *alliances*, and *acquisitions* of existing players as strategies for invading new product-market segments.

Two major issues must be analyzed as part of the decision process to enter a new market: (1) What are the structural barriers to entry? (2) How will incumbent firms react to the intrusion? Some of the most important structural impediments are the level of investment required, access to production or distribution facilities, and the threat of overcapacity.

Potential retaliation is more difficult to analyze. Incumbents will oppose a new player if resistance is likely to pay off. This is more likely to occur in mature markets if growth is low, products or services are not highly differentiated, fixed costs are high, capacity is ample, and the market is of great strategic importance to incumbents. However, the likelihood of competitor resistance at any stage of the life cycle suggests that the search for new markets should focus on industries that are experiencing some disequilibria, where incumbents are likely to be slow to react, in which the firm can influence the industry structure, and where the benefits of entry exceed the costs, including the costs of dealing with possible retaliation by incumbents.

Strategy in Mature and Declining Industries

Carefully choosing a balance between differentiation and low-cost postures and deciding whether to compete in multiple- or single-industry segments are critically important issues as maturity sets in and decline threatens. Growth tends to mask strategic errors and let companies survive; a low- or no-growth environment is far less benevolent.

Firms earn attractive profits during the long maturity stage of an industry's growth when they do the following: (1) concentrate on segments that offer chances for higher growth or higher return; (2) manage product and process innovation aimed at further differentiation, cost reduction, or rejuvenating segment growth; (3) streamline production and delivery to cut costs; and (4) gradually "harvest" the business in preparation for a strategic shift to more promising products or industries.

Counterbalancing these opportunities, mature and declining industries contain a number of strategic pitfalls that companies should avoid: (1) an overly optimistic view of the industry or the company's position within it, (2) a lack of strategic clarity shown by a failure to choose between a broad-based and a focused competitive approach, (3) investing too much for too little return—the so-called "cash trap," (4) trading market share for profitability in response to short-term performance pressures, (5) unwillingness to compete on price, (6) resistance to industry structural changes or new practices, (7) placing too much emphasis on new product development compared with improving existing ones, and (8) retaining excess capacity.[1]

Exit decisions often are extremely difficult, in part because exiting might be actively opposed in the marketplace. Possible exit barriers include government restrictions, labor and pension obligations, and contractual obligations to other parties. Even if a business can be sold, in part or as a whole, a host of issues must be addressed. The negative effects of an exit on customer, supplier, and distributor relations, for example, can ripple throughout the entire corporate structure if the firm is an SBU of a larger corporation. In this case, shared cost arrangements can produce cost increases in other parts of the business, and labor relations can become strained, thereby diminishing the strategic outlook for the corporation as a whole.

Industry Evolution and Functional Priorities

The requirements for success in industry segments change over time. Strategists need to use these changing requirements as a basis for identifying and evaluating a firm's strengths and weaknesses. Figure 7-1 depicts four stages of industry evolution and the changes in functional capabilities that often are associated with business success at each stage.[2] At a minimum, it suggests dimensions that are particularly deserving of in-depth consideration when a strategic assessment is undertaken.

The early development of a product market typically entails slow growth in sales, major R&D emphasis, rapid technological change in the product, operating losses, and a need for sufficient resources or slack to support a temporarily unprofitable operation. Success at this emerging stage often is associated with technical skill, with being first in new markets, and with having a marketing advantage that creates widespread awareness.

Figure 7-1 Stages of Industry Evolution and Functional Priorities of Business Strategy

Functional area				
	Introduction	*Growth*	*Maturity*	*Decline*
			Stage of Industry Evolution	
Marketing	Resources/skills to create widespread awareness and find acceptance from customers; advantageous access to distribution	Ability to establish brand recognition, find niche, reduce price, solidify strong distribution relations, and develop new channels	Skills in aggressively promoting products to new markets and holding existing markets; pricing flexibility; skills in differentiating products and holding customer loyalty	Cost-effective means of efficient access to selected channels and markets; strong customer loyalty or dependence; strong company image
Production, operations	Ability to expand capacity effectively, limit number of designs, develop standards	Ability to add product variants, centralize production, or otherwise lower costs; ability to improve product quality; seasonal subcontracting capacity	Ability to improve product and reduce costs; ability to share or reduce capacity; advantageous supplier relationships; subcontracting	Ability to prune product line; cost advantage in production, location, or distribution; simplified inventory control; subcontracting or long production runs
Finance	Resources to support high net cash overflow and initial losses; ability to use leverage effectively	Ability to finance rapid expansion, to have net cash outflows but increasing profits; resources to support product improvements	Ability to generate and redistribute increasing net cash inflows; effective cost control systems	Ability to reuse or liquidate unneeded equipment; advantage in cost of facilities; control system accuracy; streamlined management control

(Continued)

145

Figure 7-1. Continued

	Stage of Industry Evolution			
	Introduction	*Growth*	*Maturity*	*Decline*
Personnel	Flexibility in staffing and training new management; existence of employees with key skills in new products or markets	Existence of an ability to add skilled personnel; motivated and loyal workforce	Ability to cost effectively reduce workforce, increase efficiency	Capacity to reduce and reallocate personnel; cost advantage
Engineering and research and development	Ability to make engineering changes, have technical bugs in product and process resolved	Skills in quality and new feature development; ability to start developing successor product	Ability to reduce costs, develop variants, differentiate products	Ability to support other grown areas or to apply product to unique customer needs
Key functional area and strategy focus recovery	Engineering: market penetration	Sales: consumer loyalty; market share	Production efficiency; successor products	Finance; maximum investment

Source: From J. A. Pearce II and R. B. Robinson, Jr., *Strategic Management: Strategy Formulation, Implementation, and Control*, 11th ed., R. D. Irwin, Inc., Chicago, IL, 2009, chap. 5.

146

Rapid growth brings new competitors and reorders the strengths necessary for success. Brand recognition, product differentiation, and financial resources to support both heavy marketing expenses and price competition become key strengths.

As the industry moves through a shakeout phase and into the maturity stage, sales growth continues, but at a decreasing rate. The number of industry segments increases, but technological change in product design slows considerably. As a result, competition usually becomes more intense, and promotional or pricing advantages and differentiation become key internal strengths. The rate of technological change in process design accelerates as the many competitors seek to provide the product in the most efficient manner. Although R&D is critical in the emerging stage, efficient production is now crucial.

When the industry moves into the decline stage, strengths center on cost advantages, superior supplier and customer relationships, and financial control. Competitive advantage can exist at this stage if a firm serves gradually shrinking markets that competitors choose to leave.

FRAGMENTED, DEREGULATING, AND HYPERCOMPETITIVE INDUSTRIES

Strategy in Fragmented Industries

Fragmented industries are those in which no single company or small group of firms has a large enough market share to strongly affect the industry structure or outcomes. Many areas of the economy share this trait, including retail sectors, distribution businesses, professional services, and small manufacturing. Fragmentation seems to be most prevalent when entry and exit barriers are low; there are few economies of scale or scope; cost structures make consolidation unattractive; products or services are highly diverse or need to be customized; and close, local control is essential.

Thriving in fragmented markets requires creative strategizing. Focus strategies that creatively segment the market based on product, customer, type of order/service, or geographic area, combined with a "no frills" posture, can be effective. Sometimes, scale and scope economies are hidden, await new technological breakthroughs, or are not well recognized because the attention of the players has been elsewhere. In such instances, creative strategy can unlock these hidden sources of advantage and dramatically change the dynamics of the industry. The entrepreneurial ventures of H. Wayne Huizinga are prime examples.

Wall Street was distinctly skeptical when Huizinga took Waste Management Corporation public in 1971 and explained that he would acquire hundreds of mom-and-pop garbage companies using stock as his principal currency. He planned to exploit differences in public and private valuation and, by placing these smaller entities under a single management, unlock hidden value. At the time of its initial public offering, Waste Management had a capitalization of $5 million. When Huizinga departed in 1984, its market value was $3 billion.

Huizinga got the same initial reception when he took control of Blockbuster in 1987. By taking a similar strategic approach to the one that had transformed the waste disposal industry, Huizinga grew Blockbuster's market capitalization from $32 million initially to $8.4 billion in 1994 when he sold the company to cable giant Viacom.[3]

Strategy in Deregulating Industries

Deregulation has reshaped a number of industries. Some interesting competitive dynamics take place when artificial constraints are lifted and new players are allowed to enter. Perhaps the most important dynamic has to do with the timing of strategic moves. U.S. experience shows that deregulating environments tend to undergo considerable change twice: once when the market is opened and again about 5 years later.[4]

Deregulation in the United States became a major issue in 1975 when the Securities and Exchange Commission abolished fixed rates for U.S. securities brokers. Deregulation in airlines, trucking, railroads, banking, and telecommunications quickly followed. In each instance, a more or less similar pattern developed:

1. Immediately following the opening of the market, a large number of new entrants rushed in—most failing within a relatively short period of time.
2. Industry profitability deteriorated rapidly as new entrants, often operating from a lower cost basis, destroyed industry pricing for all competitors.
3. The pattern of segment profitability altered significantly. Segments that once were attractive became unattractive because too many competitors entered, whereas previously unattractive segments suddenly became more interesting from a strategic perspective.
4. The variance in profitability between the best and worst players increased substantially, reflecting a wider quality range of competitors.
5. Two waves of merger and acquisition activity ensued. A first wave focused on consolidating weaker players, and a second wave among larger players aimed at market dominance.
6. After consolidation, only a few players remained as broad-based competitors; most were forced to narrow their focus to specific segments or products in a much more segmented industry.

Deregulation of energy markets in the United States provides excellent examples of how competitors face both loss and opportunity. Deregulation of the energy industry in 1996 caused economic hardship for many of California's electric power companies. In 2001, Pacific Gas and Electric, California's largest investor-owned utility, reported $9 billion of debt and filed for bankruptcy. Two primary reasons account for the bankruptcy of the once-leading retail electricity company. First, PG&E incurred billions of dollars of debt that it was not able to pass along to its customers. Utility companies, including PG&E, were forced to pay high rates to wholesalers. However, because of deregulatory measures, they were not allowed to charge higher retail prices to consumers. Second, a provision of the deregulation disallowed the company from expanding its power generators to other regions of the state.

Therefore, power had to travel farther distances and accrue added costs for the utility company along the way.

PG&E filed for Chapter 11 bankruptcy, arguing that government regulators did not move swiftly to resolve the crisis that had caused multiple blackouts and cost the state billions of dollars. By taking its case to court, PG&E hoped to erase some of the $9 billion debt that it owed wholesalers and to try to reverse regulations that do not allow the company to increase retail rates.

Strategically, deregulation poses a host of challenges for companies. Joel Bleeke identifies four distinct strategic postures that prove successful in coping with the turmoil associated with deregulation: (1) broad-based distributors that offer a wide range of products and services over a large geographic area; (2) low-cost entrants that develop into niche players; (3) focused segment marketers that emphasize the company's value added to specific, loyal customer groups; and (4) shared utilities that focused on making economies of scale available to smaller competitors.[5]

Broad-based distribution companies that understand the challenges associated with fending off a flood of low-cost upstarts take early pricing actions, eliminate cross subsidies between products or segments, and conserve resources for protracted battles in a deteriorating environment. For example, following deregulation, AT&T quickly reduced prices to high-volume business customers to counter MCI and Sprint's aggressive marketing efforts. It also cut about 20 percent of its workforce to match the cost structure of the new entrants. AT&T conserved capital by cutting back on new market development and acquisitions to prepare for the inevitable future rainy day.

Low-cost entrants are typically catalysts for change in a deregulating environment. Few such entrants, however, can successfully stake out a sustainable position based on low cost alone. Most survivors tend to become specialty or niche players over time. The key strategic choices they have to make are deciding the segments to target—taking on broad-based competitors in their core markets may not be the best choice—and deciding on a migration route toward their specialty or niche status.

Focused segment marketers target value-added segments from the outset. Their staying power often depends on the strength of their relationships with their customers. Accordingly, the principal strategic challenges facing focused segment marketers include (1) identifying new approaches for strengthening relationships with customers (e.g., by developing customer information systems and databases), (2) leveraging segment strength into entry into related segments or product categories, and (3) upgrading products and services to lock in existing customers.

Shared utilities define a fourth strategic group in a deregulated environment. Their profit strategy is to provide low-cost entrants with economies of scale by sharing costs among many companies. Telerate, for example, provides worldwide, instant government bond and foreign exchange quotations to a range of small and medium-size traders, allowing them to compete more effectively with their larger rivals.

Shared utilities are essential to the evolution of the industry, but a shakeout among competing utilities often is unavoidable. The battle among different airline reservations systems is a good illustration. At most, a few will ultimately survive and, likely, one will become the de facto industry standard.

Pricing in Newly Deregulated Industries

Deregulation often scares incumbents into making self-destructive price cuts. The widespread but untested assumption is that monopoly firms are inefficient and that they overprice their products and services. However, experience shows that the case against established firms often is overstated. When new competitors enter, the market demands reduced prices, which can result from efficiencies and competitive effects. However, startups are inherently inefficient and shared markets reduce efficiencies of scale and scope.

Research by Florissen, Maurer, Schmidt, and Vahlenkamp identifies four factors that incumbents should use to adjust their prices correctly after deregulation takes effect:[6]

1. **Competitors' prices.** Rather than being tempted to match the lowest price offered by any new competitor, incumbent firms should plan to measure up again the most relevant competitor. Competitors with well-known brands, for example, often

have the best chance of luring away an incumbent's customers and should be matched or bettered on price.

2. **Switching rates.** Some customers will leave an incumbent as soon as the opportunity exists. Their reasons vary from dissatisfaction with service, price, product features, and interpersonal dynamics to an anticipation that new will mean better. However, most customers in regulated markets see the products or services as commodities and fairly few will consider switching to a new provider unless it offers some exceptional benefit. Therefore, although incumbents need to adjust prices downward as necessary to stay competitive and not allow a price gap to encourage customers to switch providers, they do not have to become price leaders to retain the bulk of their customers.

3. **Customer value.** Not all customers are of equal value to an incumbent. Some are willing to pay greater premiums, were acquired at higher costs, and produce more revenue from cross-selling initiatives. Unlike fickle customers whose defection may result in small profits losses because of their extreme price conscientiousness, high-margin customers are usually less price sensitive and are more concerned with quality and service. Lowering prices for these preferred customers is costly and does little good.

4. **Cost to serve.** New competitors are often ill prepared to price services effectively, meaning simultaneously competitively and profitably. Incumbents are in a far better position because they understand the true cost of their service. Therefore, rather than reducing their prices to levels that cannot be maintained, incumbents can moderate their profit margins but refrain from running in the red out of fear of losing customers to competitors who cannot maintain their initial pricing structure.

Strategy in Hypercompetitive Industries

Hypercompetitive industries are characterized by intense rivalry. Successful strategies often are based on taking the competitor by surprise (e.g., by introducing a product when least expected) and then moving on as the competition tries to recover. *Hypercompetitive strategies*, therefore, are designed to enable the company to gain an advantage over competitors by disrupting the market with quick and innovative change. The goal is to neutralize previous competitive advantages and create an unbalanced industry segment.[7]

The intense rivalry in a hypercompetitive environment often results in short product life cycles, the emergence of new technologies, competition from unexpected players, repositioning by current players, and major shifts in market boundaries. Personal computers, microprocessors, and software all frequently experience the effects of hypercompetition. The telecommunications industry also provides many examples. Commonly, hypercompetitive strategies involve the bundling of services (e.g., local calling, long-distance calling, Internet access, and even television transmission) to retain current customers and acquire new ones.

In a hypercompetitive market, successful companies are able to manipulate competitive conditions to create advantage for themselves and destroy the advantages enjoyed by others. Within their dynamic and ever-changing environment, firms that stand to benefit are those possessing three major qualities: rapid innovation and speed, superior short-term strategic focus, and market awareness.

Speed and innovation are the foremost requirements for success in a hypercompetitive environment. The focus of companies is on gaining temporary advantage, achieving short-term profitability, and then quickly shifting their strategic focus before competition can react effectively. It is crucial that hypercompetitive companies be able to innovate rapidly and then follow up on that innovation with equally quick manufacturing, marketing, and distribution of their products. In this manner, they are able to rapidly shift the industry dynamics and gain market share at a pace that exceeds that of the competition. Without speed, a company is at a severe disadvantage because competitors will capitalize on market opportunities first, costing it valuable market share.

The second characteristic of successful firms in hypercompetition is superior short-term strategic focus. Firms that have the ability to manipulate the competition into making long-term commitments will find the hypercompetitive marketplace beneficial.

The final requirement for success in a hypercompetitive environment is strong market awareness. Firms must be able to understand consumer markets to deliver high-impact products and provide superior standards of customer support. Having strong customer focus allows firms to identify a customer's needs while uncovering new and previously untapped markets for their products. Once the needs of the customer are identified, firms win temporary market share through a redefinition of quality.

The traditional concept of sustainable competitive advantage is centered on the belief that long-term profitability can be achieved through segmented markets and low to moderate levels of competition. However, strategists now recognize another requirement: Over the long term, sustainable profits are possible only when entry barriers restrict competition. Evidence from the current business environment is that business models that are dependent on these conditions have a sharply declining rate of success, principally because of hypercompetition. Continuous erosion and re-creation of competitive advantage have come to characterize many industries with companies seeking to disrupt the status quo and gain a temporary profitable advantage over larger competitors.

Competitive Reactions Under Extreme Competition

The pace of competitive change continues to quicken with increasing globalization, technological advancement, and economic liberalization. The consequences include high rivalry in mature undifferentiated industries that results in shrinking profits; shaky dominance by dominant market share firms that are pressured by smaller, more flexible and often more innovative competitors; and shrinking industries with endangered leaders and struggling niche players.

This characterization of extreme competition led Huyett and Viguerie to suggest six actions that established companies can consider to counter the fresh, aggressive, and innovative moves of competitors:[8]

1. *Retool strategy and restore its importance.* Strategic planning can be given short shrift when daily pressures for performance are high and the pace of change is so great that the number of possible outcomes seems to defy the logic of

planning for them. Therefore, corporate executives are advised to challenge SBU managers to adopt a portfolio view in strategic planning to increase their responsiveness to radical opportunities.

2. *Manage transition economics.* In trying to strike a balance between profit margins and market share, planners should be aware of the importance of building low-cost positions to free funds for innovation efforts that will help fend off aggressive competitors.

3. **Fight aggregation with disaggregation.** Although scale advantages will make some large firms inclined toward aggregation of markets, others will find small, high-profit opportunities by creating differentiated value propositions through disaggregation.

4. *Seek out new demand and new growth.* Hypercompetition does not preclude the use of traditional strategies. Particularly when competing with firms that rely on organic growth, external growth through mergers and acquisitions, licensing, joint ventures, and strategic alliances can be successful, even as late entrants work to accelerate the pace of innovation and organizational change.

5. *Use a portfolio of initiatives to increase speed and flexibility.* Strategic managers and planners are encouraged to think of organizational assets as resources that enable the company to launch new products and services, innovate to reduce costs, and provide the basis for price competitiveness in varied markets worldwide. Such a resource-based view is superior to a fixed-commitment approach in extreme competition that places a premium on market responsiveness and innovation.

6. *Count on strategic risk.* Strategists need to be mindful that extreme competition is characterized by volatile corporate earnings and stock prices. Huyett and Viguerie specifically warn of four types of risks that are of particular concern in extremely competitive environments:

   - Value proposition risks, which warn of negative consequences if competitors introduce lower-priced products or services

- Cost-curve risks, which warn of negative consequences if competitors are able to become the low-cost provider
- Bad-conduct risks, which warn of negative consequences if a price war occurs
- Bad-bet risks, which warn of negative consequences from overly optimistic assumptions

BUSINESS UNIT STRATEGY: SPECIAL DIMENSIONS

Speed

Speed in innovation, manufacturing, distribution, and a host of other areas is emerging as a key success factor in a growing number of industries, especially those characterized by transitional or habitual hypercompetition.[9] Coupled with trends toward globalization, the multiplying business applications of the Internet have led to the elevation of speed as a strategic priority. The unprecedented growth in business-to-consumer and business-to-business Internet connections has made speed almost as important as quality and a customer orientation in some markets. Yet, it is the newest and least understood of the critical success factors.

In a competitive context, *speed* is the pace of progress that a company displays in responding to current or anticipated business needs. It is gauged by a firm's response times in meeting customer expectations, in innovating and commercializing new products and services, in changing strategy to benefit from emerging market and technological realities, and in continuously upgrading its transformation processes to improve customer satisfaction and financial returns.

Responding to industry challenges to increase their customer responsiveness are *speed merchants* who built their strategies on the rapid pace of their operations. Their accelerated change activities become a hallmark for the progress of the industry. Speed merchants modify their environments to convert their core competencies into competitive advantages. As a consequence, competitive landscapes are altered in their favor. The public images of a growing number of firms are synonymous with the speed that they exhibit: AAA with fast emergency road service, Dell with fast computer assembly, Domino's with fast pizza delivery, and CyberGate with fast Internet access. A critical assessment of the strategies of these high-profile companies provides three important insights: (1) distinct and identifiable sources of pressure that create the demand on a company to accelerate its speed; (2) an emphasis on speed places new cost, cultural, and change process requirements on a company; and (3) several implementation methods to accelerate a firm's speed of operations.

Figure 7-2 presents a model to guide executives in the acceleration of their companies' speed. It reminds us that pressures to increase company speed can be generated both externally and internally. Firms can assume a reactive posture and await an increase in speed by competitors before making their own investment, or they can gamble on a payoff from a proactive "move to improve."

Pressures to Speed

Speed is almost universally popular. Customers in nearly every product-market segment seek immediate need satisfaction, and they reward quick-acting companies with market share growth. Because employees of speed-oriented companies enjoy the job

Figure 7-2 Model for Accelerating Speed

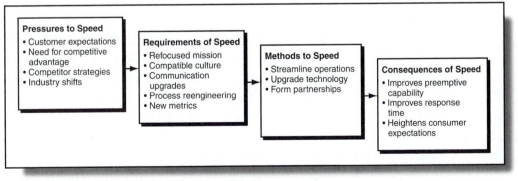

Source: Reprinted from *Organizational Dynamics*, 2002, 30 (3), John A. Pearce II, "Speed Merchants," pp. 1–16. Copyright © 2002, with permission from Elsevier Science.

flexibility and heightened individual responsibility that are required to maintain the strategy, they reward their employers with the loyalty and commitment that is so highly prized in competitive environments. Suppliers to fast-moving companies are willing to bear extra costs and responsibilities to earn partnerships with firms that seem destined to overtake competitors that conduct business in time-tested rather than time-conscious ways.

Pressures for speed come from customers' expectations, from competitors who accelerate their own pace, from the company itself when it seeks to establish a new competitive advantage, and from the adjusting priorities of a changing industry. These pressures for speed often seem to blend into a seamless force. However, different sources of pressure can be most effectively addressed with a specifically targeted company strategy. Therefore, strategic planners' correct anticipation or recognition of the specific source of pressure helps to ensure that their investments in new speed will provide maximum returns.

Experience has shown that there are four principal sources of pressure for increasing speed:

1. *Customers.* Customers demand responsiveness. The consumer quality movement of the past two decades has been trumped by a new emphasis on getting quality products and services quickly.
2. *Need for creating a new basis for competitive advantage.* Increasing the speed with which products are innovated, developed, manufactured, and distributed has been associated with the success of firms in establishing a new competitive advantage and important cost benefits.
3. *Competitive pressures.* Competitive viability often mandates changes for the acceleration of speed. When facing intense competitive pressures, speed is often one of the few options for a company to choose to differentiate its offering.
4. *Industry shifts.* Speed is particularly important to survival in industries characterized by short product life cycles. Global competition, exponential advancements in technology, and shifting customer demands combine to produce shorter life cycles and the need for faster product development.

Requirements of Speed

As a strategic weapon, a speed initiative requires that every aspect of an organization be focused on the pace at which work is accomplished. Executives must foster a "fast" culture within their organizations. The agility that comes from a speed orientation and carefully tailored resource investments provides the prerequisite competitive means to change and accelerate a firm's strategic course. Specifically, action must be taken on the following issues: refocusing the business mission, creating a speed-compatible culture, upgrading communications within the business, focusing business process reengineering, and committing to new performance metrics.

Refocusing the Business Mission

When the board and officers articulate a long-term vision for a speed-oriented company, they provide a basis for shared expectations, planning, and performance evaluation regarding the increase in speed throughout the organization.

Creating a Speed-Compatible Culture

A company can facilitate speed by nurturing an organizational culture that is conducive to speed and by adopting an evaluation system that rewards those who can increase aspects of organizational speed. Change management techniques, including TQM, benchmarking, time-based competition, outsourcing, and partnering, can each play a role in focusing an organization on increasing facets of its overall speed.

Upgrading Communication

The increase in speed requires dramatically upgraded methods for clear and timely communication. Increasingly, all parties expect instantaneous communication between customers, manufacturers, suppliers, and service providers.

Refocusing Business Process Reengineering

Business process reengineering (BPR) is undertaken to reorganize a company to eliminate barriers that create distance between employees and customers. It involves fundamentally rethinking and redesigning a process to enable a customer focus to permeate all phases of business activity. The deployment of employees is evaluated to determine how they can best contribute. Upgrading employee contributions not eliminating employees, is the true intent of BPR.

Committing to New Performance Metrics

A specific set of metrics has proven valuable in gauging a firm's progress in improving performance from its investments in speed. The metrics include sales volume, innovation rate, customer satisfaction, processing time, cost controls, and marketing specifics, such as innovation support, learning, and initiatives.

Methods to Speed

The development of speed as a competitive advantage begins with an internal analysis by a firm to determine where speed exists and where it does not. Companies then look to quickly eliminate any "speed gaps." Three categories of methods dominate corporate option lists: streamlining operations, upgrading technology, and forming partnerships.

Streamlining Operations

Many companies enter new markets with a level of competitive information that would have traditionally been labeled as insufficient to support investment. However, most of these firms are not marginalizing quality; they have adopted a new strategic schema. With a speed-enhanced ability to obtain quick postimplementation feedback from the marketplace and to respond with unparalleled speed in making adjustments, successful innovations no longer need to be flawless at introduction.

Upgrading Technology

Using the latest informational technologies to create speed, companies are able to roll out new product information faster. The common goal of speed-focused IT is to connect manufacturers with retailers to enhance information sharing and to streamline and accelerate product distribution. In turn, shortening pipelines speeds products to shelves and satisfies customers with less costly inventories. Doubling back, technology enables companies to learn customers' buying patterns to better anticipate their preferences.

Forming Partnerships

Sharing business burdens is a proven way to shorten the time needed to improve market responsiveness (i.e., "partners collapse time"). Ford Motor Company's partnership with General Motors and DaimlerChrysler provides a front-page example. The three major auto manufacturers joined to develop an Internet portal that links their purchasing organizations with 30,000 raw material suppliers. These Web-based exchanges also increase the speed with which the automobile companies respond to customer inquiries at every stage along the supply chain.

The evidence from business practice supports the emergence of speed as a critical success factor as a primary element in business unit strategy. The company goal of accelerating speed to satisfy consumer needs is becoming less of an option and more of a mandate for financial survival. Fortunately, businesses can be systematic in evaluating the pressures and requirements for change that they face in accelerating their speed. Methods available for implementing upgrades are becoming quickly established and are backed by the records of success faster firms enjoy.

Creating Value Through Innovation

Value creation greatly depends on innovation. Sustained profitable growth requires more than judicious acquisitions or careful "subtraction" by shedding unprofitable operations or downsizing. Many companies recognize they need to generate more value from core businesses and leverage their core competencies more effectively. These strategic initiatives, in turn, increase the demand for innovation.[10]

Innovation is a major strategic challenge for most companies. Clayton M. Christensen coined the concepts of *disruptive* and *sustaining innovation* to describe what he calls the "Innovators' Dilemma"—how successful companies with established products can keep from being pushed aside by competitors with newer, cheaper products that will, over time, get better and become a serious threat.[11]

He notes that incumbent industry leaders and competitors mostly engage in *sustaining innovation*—innovation that focuses on "better" products. Some sustaining innovations are simple, incremental, year-to-year improvements; others are dramatic, breakthrough technologies, such as the transition from analog to digital and from digital to optical. Although they represent a real technological advance, their effect was to bring a better product into the market that could be sold for higher margins to the best customers served by the industry leaders.

New entrants and challengers have greater freedom to engage in *disruptive innovation*—launching products that may not be as good as the existing products and, therefore, not attractive to current customers, but that are simple, and often more affordable. These new entrants find acceptance in undemanding and underserved segments of the market and create a beachhead for competition for mainstream customers with improved products later. Christensen calls this *disruptive innovation* not because it defines a technological breakthrough, but because it disrupts the established basis of competition.

The computer hardware industry offers many examples of disruptive innovation. The introduction of the minicomputer disrupted the mainframe industry. The personal computer disrupted minicomputer sales. Wireless handheld devices, such as Blackberries and Palm Pilots, disrupted notebook computers.

Although industry leaders *can* survive a disruptive attack and retain their leadership position, strong evidence suggests that the only way to do so is by creating a separate unit. The reason is that the separate entity needs the freedom to create a business model that is tuned to the new disruptive way of doing business, which ultimately leads to the demise of the business model of the parent company. When the minicomputer disrupted the mainframe, IBM was late but survived by creating a separate business unit in Rochester, Minnesota. Later, when the personal computer disrupted the minicomputer, IBM set up a separate business unit in

Florida. Such adjustments to its business model helped IBM survive as the only major computer company from the 1960s.

General Electric is well known for its capacity to reinvent itself. In every major transformation in the last 30 years, GE succeeded by setting up or acquiring new disruptive business units and selling off or shutting down ones that had reached the end of their economic lives. It never attempted to transform the business model of an existing business unit as a way of "catching up" to the new basis for competition imposed by disruptive innovations.

Sustaining innovation can keep a company viable for many years; targeting current customers exclusively can be damaging in the long run. To start a new-growth business, noncustomers often are the most important customers to understand. Discovering why they are not customers encourages innovation and stimulates growth.

A focus by incumbents on profit rather than growth can impede innovation, thereby inhibiting growth.[12] Public companies, under pressure from Wall Street to produce steady returns, face a particularly strong challenge. Investors and industry analysts are likely to expect the company to generate more of its earnings growth from profitability, whereas company executives tend to prefer earnings to come from increasing revenue. However, there is empirical evidence that the more a company's earnings come from either profitability improvement or revenue growth at the expense of the other, the more likely it is that the company's strategy is inherently flawed.[13] The differing emphases between investors and executives suggests why private companies often have better opportunities to invest for the long term and pursue disruptive innovations, which require a long time to develop and mature and might produce short-term losses in the early stages of development.

Creating a culture of innovation eludes many companies because it transcends traditional strategic planning practices. Strategic planning too often centers on existing or closely related products and services rather than on opportunities to drive future demand. In contrast, innovation is a product of anticipating, assessing, and fulfilling potential customer needs in a creative manner. Sometimes innovation is technology based, but often it springs from the firm's recognition of explicit or latent customer needs. Innovation can be directed at any point in the customer or company value chain, from sourcing raw materials to value-added, after-sale services.

Although many businesses pursue innovation, for almost 100 years Minnesota Mining & Manufacturing (3M) has succeeded because its business model is based on a culture that is geared to producing innovative products. Best known for Post-it Notes, Scotch Guard, and Scotch Tape, 3M's business segments include industrial, transportation, graphics and safety, health care, consumer and office, electronics and communications, and specialty materials.

Because of the company's unparalleled success as an innovator, its approach deserves broader consideration. Fundamentally, six mandates drive innovation at 3M:

1. Support innovation from research and development to customer sales and support.
2. Understand the future by trying to anticipate and analyze future trends. 3M has developed a program called "Foresight" in which industry experts survey the remote and external environments for changes in technology and other trends to identify new market opportunities, called "Greenfields."
3. Establish stretch goals. This driver is important to 3M because it is a measure that encourages growth. One example of a stretch goal is the new-product sales target. This target is that 40 percent of sales will be from products introduced in the past 4 years. In addition, 10 percent of sales will be from products introduced in the current year.
4. Empower employees to meet goals. At 3M, this is accomplished through its 40-year-old "15 percent rule." This gives 3M researchers the opportunity to devote 15 percent of their time to any creative idea or project, and management approval is not required.
5. Support broad networking across the company. This driving force calls for the sharing of discoveries within the company. A 3M corporate policy states that technologies belong to the company, which signals that research results are to be shared across all of its six business segments.

6. Recognize and reward innovative people. An innovative program at 3M rewards innovative people through peer-nominated award programs and a corporate "hall of fame."

Fostering a culture of innovation takes time and effort. Although there is no universal model for creating an innovating environment, a look at successful companies reveals certain common characteristics. First, a business needs a *top-level commitment to innovation*. Commitment to innovation is evident in the attitudes of top executives, through their communication of their belief to all levels of the organization in the benefits of innovation, and in their willingness to sponsor and guide new-product activity.

Second, a business needs a *long-term focus*. "Quarteritis," the preoccupation with the next quarter's results, is one of the most common stumbling blocks to innovation. Innovation is an investment in the future, not a rescue mission for current top- or bottom-line problems.

Third, a business needs a *flexible organization structure*. Innovation rarely flourishes in a rigid structure, with complicated approval processes or with bureaucratic delays and bottlenecks.

Fourth, a business needs a combination of *loose and tight planning and control*. Allocating all direct, indirect, overhead, and other costs to a development project virtually guarantees its demise. Few innovative ideas can immediately be translated into commercial ventures that cover all of their own costs or meet conventional payback requirements.

Finally, to create an environment for innovation a business needs a system of *appropriate incentives*. Reward systems in many companies are oriented toward existing businesses, with short-term considerations outweighing longer-term innovation and market development objectives. Innovation can flourish only when risk taking is encouraged, occasional failure is accepted, and managers are held accountable for missing opportunities as well as exploiting them.

Relationship Between Innovation and Performance

Evidence on the relationship between research and development (R&D), innovation, and financial performance is inconsistent. Booz Allen Hamilton's *The Global Innovation 1000* study in 2006 found no significant statistical relationships between R&D spending and measures of financial success.[14] The study identified the 1,000 public companies around the world that spent the most on R&D. Spending was highly concentrated, with the 20 largest R&D spenders accounting for $116 billion, or 28 percent, of the total. The top 20 companies have a median R&D-to-sales ratio that is 1.8 times that of the remaining sample, but fail to achieve a corresponding financial gain.

Boston Consulting Group's (BCG) *Innovation 2006* global survey involved 1,070 executives, representing 63 countries and all major industries. In contrast to the Booz Allen Hamilton research, the BCG research found that innovation translates into superior long-term stock market performance. The 25 most innovative companies identified by survey respondents had a median annualized return of 14.3 percent from 1999 through 2005, a full 300 basis points better than that of the S&P Global 1200 median.[15] Similarly, *The Innovation Premium*, published in 1999 by the Monitor Group, demonstrated a strong positive correlation between a company's effective focus on innovation and organic growth, and its future shareholder returns.[16]

Innovation and Profitability

Research suggests that executives lack confidence in their companies' ability to use innovation to drive profits. In a Forrester Research study, 67 percent of respondents from manufacturing firms considered themselves more innovative than competitors, but only 7 percent identified themselves as very successful in meeting their innovation performance goals.[17] Respondents in the BCG *Innovation 2006* survey questioned the effectiveness of their R&D spending; 48 percent of those surveyed were unsatisfied with the financial returns on their companies' investments in innovation.

The reason for the lack of success in translating innovation into profitable performance surfaced in a study of the growth records of the *Fortune* 50 sponsored by HP and the Corporate Executive Board. The study concluded that the single biggest growth inhibitor for large companies was "mismanagement of the innovation process."[18]

Another explanation for the lack of success in innovation is a lack of measurement metrics or the failure to implement the metrics effectively. In conjunction with the *Innovation 2006* survey, BCG invited a group of senior executives to complete a separate survey on innovation metrics and measurement.[19] Of the 269 respondents, 63 percent said their companies track five or fewer metrics. Only 47 percent said they apply postlaunch metrics sporadically, and 8 percent said they do not apply them at all. Fully half of all companies do not closely track the efficiency of their innovation processes. Less than half of respondents indicated that their firms link employee incentives directly to innovation metrics consistently, if at all.

R&D investments fail to generate successful products and financial gains for three main reasons: failure to develop truly innovative products, failure to successfully commercialize innovative products once they are on the market, and failure to market innovative products in a timely manner. Many corporate projects are abandoned in development: One estimate is that it takes 125 to 150 new initiatives to generate one marketplace success.[20] Others report different statistics, but all research indicates that the probability of success with innovations is small:

- Koudal and Coleman find that more than 85 percent of new product ideas never make it to market, and of those that do make it to market, 50 to 70 percent fail.[21]
- In a global study of 360 industrial firms launching 576 new industrial products, Stevens and Burley found an overall success rate of 60 percent from launch.[22]
- Ogawa and Pillar have confirmed the problems of new product commercialization, with newly launched products suffering from failure rates often reaching 50 percent or greater.[23]
- Delays in getting a product to market can be extremely costly. McKinsey & Co. found that a product that is 6 months late to market will miss out on 33 percent of the potential profits over the product's lifetime.[24]

Recommendations for Improving Performance Through Innovation

An overall evaluation of the research on the impact of innovation investments on company financial performance leads to six recommendations for strategic managers:

1. *Plan synergy between strategy and innovation.* Firms that innovate toward achieving a specific strategic goal improve their chances of success.[25]

2. *Areas where new opportunities and competitive advantage exist provide a firm's best chances to profit from innovation.* Product and service offerings, customers served, processes employed, and core competencies must be considered in innovation decisions.[26]

3. *Profits from innovation in business systems can match those from product development.*[27] Firms relying on new products alone might exclude the investments required to strengthen business systems, which will leave them vulnerable to competitors who strengthen business processes in the areas of marketing, information, and financial systems. Benefits of broad-based innovation include a system-wide supporting infrastructure for product innovation, the development of an entry barrier to would-be competitors, and other opportunities for innovation in the functions and processes.

4. *Look outside of the company's internal environment to increase the likelihood of success and reduce the risks of innovation.* Open business models enable organizations to be more effective in creating value by leveraging many more ideas via the inclusion of external concepts and capture greater value through more effective utilization of firm assets in the organization's operations and in other companies' businesses.[28]

5. *Alliances and corporate venture capital programs allow a firm to share the risks associated with exploration investments.*[29] Corporate venturing has the potential to furnish reliable, practical, near-term solutions to the innovation challenge by providing the opportunity for sourcing complementary and strategic intellectual property, additional financial resources, and skills.[30]

6. *Involve customers early and often in the innovation process.*
Through co-development, the customer takes an active role in
the innovation process by helping to define product requirements, components, and materials.[31] It can help companies
avoid costly product failures by soliciting new product concepts
from existing customers, pursuing the most popular of those
ideas, and asking for commitments from customers to purchase
a new product before commencing final development and
production.[32] The use of co-development is particularly effective in testing innovative products and in developing products
for relatively small and heterogeneous market segments.

NOTES

1. M. E. Porter, *Competitive Strategy: Techniques for Analyzing Industries and Competitors,* New York, The Free Press, 1980, Chapters 11 and 12.

2. J. A. Pearce II and R. B. Robinson, Jr., *Formulation, Implementation, and Control of Competitive Strategy,* 11th ed., Chicago, IL, Irwin/McGraw-Hill, 2009, Chapter 5.

3. A. E. Serwer, "Huizinga's Third Act," *Fortune,* August 5, 1996; and T. Ferguson, "Off-the-shelf-autos: A chat with J. David Power III," *Forbes,* February 10, 1997.

4. J. E. Bleeke, "Strategic Choices for Newly Opened Markets," *Harvard Business Review,* Sept.–Oct. 1990.

5. Bleeke, 1990, op. cit.

6. A. Florissen, B. Maurer, B. Schmidt, and T. Vahlenkamp, "The Race to the Bottom," *The McKinsey Quarterly,* no. 3 (2001): 98–107.

7. R. A. D'Aveni, "Strategic Supremacy Through Disruption and Dominance," *Sloan Management Review,* 1999, 40 (3).

8. W. I. Huyett and S. P. Viguerie, "Extreme Competition," *McKinsey Quarterly,* no. 1 (2005): 47–57.

9. J. A. Pearce II, "Speed Merchants," *Organizational Dynamics,* 2002, 30 (3): 1–16.

10. C. A. de Kluyver, "Innovation: The Strategic Thrust of the Nineties," *A Cresap Insight,* July 1988.

11. C. M. Christensen and M. Raynor, *The Innovator's Dilemma: When New Technologies Cause Great Firms to Fail,* Boston, Harvard Business School Press, 1997.

12. C. M. Christensen and M. Raynor, *The Innovator's Solution: Creating and Sustaining Successful Growth*, Boston, Harvard Business School Press, 2003.

13. D. Dodd and K. Favaro, "Managing the Right Tension," *Harvard Business Review*, 2006, 84 (12): 62–74.

14. R. Bordia, K. Denhoff, and B. Jaruzelski. "Smart Spenders: The Booz Allen Hamilton Global Innovation 1000," *Strategy + Business*, 2006, 45: 46–61.

15. J. P. Andrew, "Innovation 2006," *BCG Senior Management Survey*, July 19, 2006, pp. 1–30.

16. R. S. Jonash, "Driving Sustainable Growth and Innovation: Pathways to High-Performance Leadership," *Handbook of Business Strategy*, 2005, 6 (1): 197–202.

17. N. Radjou, "Networked Innovation Drives Profits," *Industrial Management*, 2005, 47 (1): 14–21.

18. R. Stringer, "How to Manage Radical Innovation," *California Management Review*, 2000, 42 (4): 70–88.

19. J. P. Andrew, "Measuring Innovation 2006," *BCG Senior Management Survey*, July 19, 2006, pp. 1–17.

20. M. Amram, "Magnetic Intellectual Property: Accelerating Revenues from Innovation," *Journal of Business Strategy*, 2003, 24 (3): 24–30.

21. P. Koudal and G. C. Coleman, "Coordinating Operations to Enhance Innovation in the Global Corporation," *Strategy & Leadership*, 2005, 33 (4): 20–32.

22. G. Stevens and J. Burley, "Piloting the Rocket of Radical Innovation," *Research Technology Management*, 2003, 46 (2): 16–25.

23. S. Ogawa and F. P. Piller, "Reducing the Risks of New Product Development," *MIT Sloan Management Review*, 2006, 47 (2): 65–71.

24. T. Vesey, "Speed-To-Market Distinguishes the New Competitors." *Research Technology Management*, 1991, 34 (6): 33–38.

25. C. B. Dobni, "The Innovation Blueprint," *Business Horizons*, 2006, 49 (4): 329–339.

26. M. Sawhney, R. C. Wolcott, and I. Arroniz, "The 12 Different Ways for Companies to Innovate," *MIT Sloan Management Review*, 2006, 47 (3): 75–81.

27. T. Shervani and P. C. Zerillo, "The Albatross of Product Innovation," *Business Horizons*, 1997, 40 (1): 57–62.

28. H. W. Chesbrough, "Why Companies Should Have Open Business Models," *MIT Sloan Management Review*, 2007, 40 (2): 22–28.

29. R. D. Ireland and J. W. Webb, "Strategic Entrepreneurship: Creating Competitive Advantage Through Streams of Innovation," *Business Horizons,* 2007, 50 (1): 49–59.

30. M. O'Leary-Collins, "A Powerful Business Model for Capturing Innovation," *Management Services,* 2005, 49 (2): 37–39.

31. P. Koudal and G. C. Coleman, "Coordinating Operations to Enhance Innovation in the Global Corporation," *Strategy & Leadership,* 2005, 33 (4): 20–32.

32. S. Ogawa and F. P. Piller, "Reducing the Risks of New Product Development," *MIT Sloan Management Review,* 2006, 47 (2): 65–71.

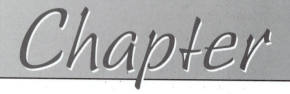

Chapter 8

Global Strategy Formulation

INTRODUCTION

"Going global" often is described as a gradual process starting with increased exports, followed by a modest international presence, growth into a multinational organization, and, ultimately, evolution into a transnational or global posture. This appearance of gradualism, however, is deceptive. It obscures key changes in a company's mission, core competencies, structure, processes, and culture, and, consequently, the enormous differences among managing international operations, a multinational enterprise, and a global corporation. Just as it is difficult to speak of a *global industry,* the term *global strategy*—although convenient for everyday use—is equally ambiguous. Specific *elements* of a strategy, such as market coverage or production, can be globalized. Truly global strategies—strategies that are global in all respects—are rare.

To create a global vision, a company must carefully define what globalization means for its particular businesses. This depends on the industry, the products or services, and the requirements for global success. For Coca-Cola, it meant duplicating a substantial part of its value-creation process—from product formulation to marketing and delivery—throughout the world. Intel's global competitive advantage is based on attaining technological leadership and preferred component supplier status on a global basis. For a midsize company, it may mean setting up a host of small foreign subsidiaries and forging numerous alliances. For others, it may mean something entirely different. Thus, although it is tempting to think of global strategy in universal terms, globalization is a highly company- and industry-specific issue. It forces a company to rethink its strategic intent, global architecture, core competencies, and entire current product and service mix. For many companies, the outcome demands dramatic changes in the way they do business—with whom, how, and why.

This chapter is organized into three parts. First, we take a macroeconomic perspective and consider why some countries and regions specialize in the manufacturing of particular products, focus on specific value-creating activities or host specific industries. As part of this discussion, we look at the key factors that drive industry globalization. Next, we focus on formulating global strategies at the microeconomic, corporate, level. This second section discusses the various dimensions of global strategy development, entry strategies, and region/country analysis and concludes with a detailed look at how Wal-Mart approached the globalization challenge. The final section of this chapter examines the unique risks associated with operating on a global scale and what a company can do to mitigate such risks.

GLOBALIZATION AND INDUSTRIAL CLUSTERING

The theory of comparative economic advantage holds that, as a result of natural endowments, some countries or regions of the world are more efficient than others in producing particular goods. Australia, for example, is naturally suited to the mining industry; the United States, with its vast temperate landmass, has a natural advantage in agriculture; whereas more-wooded parts of the world may have a natural advantage in producing timber-based products. This theory is persuasive for industries such as agriculture, mining, and timber. But what about industries such as electronics, entertainment, or fashion design?

To explain the clustering of these industries in particular countries and regions, a more comprehensive theory of the geography of competition is needed.

In the absence of natural comparative advantages, industrial clustering occurs as a result of a relative advantage that is created by the industry itself.[1] Producers tend to locate manufacturing facilities close to their primary customers. If transportation costs are not too high, and there are strong economies of scale in manufacturing, a large geographic area can be served from this single location. This, in turn, attracts suppliers to the industry. A labor market is likely to develop that begins to act like a magnate for "like" industries requiring similar skills. This co-location of "like" industries can lead to technological interdependencies, which further encourage clustering. Clustering, therefore, is the natural outcome of economic forces. A good example is provided by the semiconductor industry. Together, American and Asian firms supply most of the world's needs. The industry is capital intensive, research and development costs are high, the manufacturing process is highly complex, but transportation costs are minimal. Technology interdependencies encourage collocation with suppliers, whereas cost and learning curve effects point to scale efficiencies. Clustering, therefore, is mutually advantageous.

Only when transportation costs are prohibitive or scale economies are difficult to realize (i.e., when there are disincentives to clustering) do more decentralized patterns of industry location define the natural order. The appliance industry illustrates this. Companies such as General Electric and Whirlpool have globalized their operations in many respects, but the fundamental economics of the industry make clustering unattractive. The production of certain value-added components such as compressors or electronic parts can be concentrated to some extent, but the bulky nature of the product and high transportation costs make further concentration economically unattractive. In addition, advances in flexible manufacturing techniques are reducing the minimum scale needed for efficient production. This enables producers to tailor their product offerings more finely to local tastes and preferences, further thwarting the globalization of the industry.

Porter's National Diamond

Classical economic theory tells us why clustering occurs. However, it does not fully explain why *particular* regions attract certain global industries. Porter addressed this issue; using a framework he calls a "national diamond" shown in Figure 8-1.[2]

Factor Conditions

The answer begins with the degree to which a country or region's endowments match the characteristics and requirements of the industry. Such factor conditions include natural (climate, minerals) as well as created (skill levels, capital, infrastructure) endowments. But to the extent that such factors are mobile, or can be imitated by other countries or regions, factor conditions alone do not fully explain regional dominance. In fact, the opposite is true. When a particular industry is highly profitable and barriers to entry are low, the forces of imitation and diffusion cause such an industry to spread across international borders.[3] The Japanese compete in a number of industries that originated in the United States, Korean firms imitate Japanese strategies, and Central European nations are conquering industries that were founded in Western Europe. Industries that depend on such mobile factors as capital are particularly susceptible.

Figure 8-1 Determinants of National Competitive Advantage

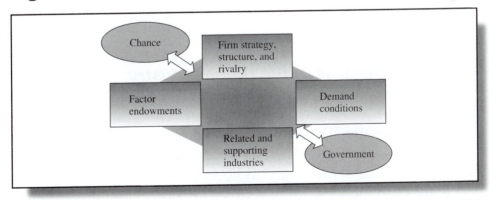

Source: Reprinted with the permission of *The Free Press*, a division of Simon & Schuster Adult Publishing Group, from *The Competitive Advantage of Nations* by Michael E. Porter. Copyright © 1990, 1998 by *The Free Press*.

Home Country Demand

A second factor is the nature and size of the demand in the home country. Large home markets act as a stimulus for industry development. And when a large home market develops before it takes hold elsewhere in the world, experienced firms have ample incentives to look for business abroad when saturation at home begins to set in. The motorcycle industry in Japan, for example, used its scale advantage to create a global presence following an early start at home.[4] Porter found that it is not just the *location* of early demand but its *composition* that matters. A product's fundamental or core design nearly always reflects home market needs. As such, the nature of the home market needs and the sophistication of the home market buyer are important determinants of the potential of the industry to stake out a future global position. It was helpful to the U.S. semiconductor industry, for example, that the government was an early, sophisticated, and relatively cost-insensitive buyer of chips. These conditions encouraged the industry to develop new technologies and provided early opportunities to manufacture on a substantial scale.

Related and Supporting Industries

The presence of related and supporting industries is the third element of Porter's framework. This is similar to our earlier observation about clustering. Hollywood is more than just a cluster of moviemakers. It encompasses a host of suppliers and service providers, and it has shaped the labor market in the Los Angeles area.

Competitiveness of the Home Industry

The structure and the rivalry in the home industry define the fourth element of the "national diamond" model. In essence, this element summarizes the "five forces" competitive framework described in Chapter 4. The more vigorous the domestic competition, the more successful firms are likely to be in competing on a global scale. Plenty of evidence supports this assertion. The fierce rivalry that exists among German pharmaceutical companies has made them a formidable force in the global market. And the intense battle for domestic market share has strengthened the competitive position of Japanese automobile manufacturers abroad.

Public Policy and Chance

The two final components of the model are public policy and chance. There can be no doubt that government policy can— through infrastructure, incentives, subsidies, or temporary protection—nurture global industries. Whether such policies are always effective is less clear. Picking "winners" in the global marketplace has never been the strong suit of governments. The chance element allows for the influence of random events, such as where and when fundamental scientific breakthroughs occur, the presence of entrepreneurial initiative, and sheer luck. For example, the early U.S. domination of the photography industry is as much attributable to the fact that George Eastman (of Eastman Kodak) and Edwin Land (of Polaroid) were born in the United States than to any other factor.

Industry Globalization Drivers

Figure 8-2 shows four sets of "industry globalization drivers"— underlying conditions that create the potential for an industry to

Figure 8-2   Industry Globalization Drivers

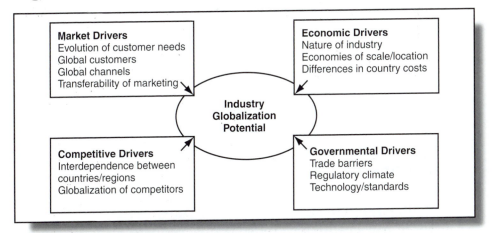

Source: Reprinted from *Columbia Journal of World Business,* Winter 1988, George S. Yip, Pierre M. Loene, and Michael E. Yoshino, "How to Take Your Company to the Global Market," pp. 14–26, copyright © 1998, with permission from Elsevier Science.

become more global and, as a consequence, for the potential viability of a global approach to strategy.[5] *Market drivers* are measures that define how customer behavior patterns evolve and converge. Market drivers are important because they indicate whether worldwide channels of distribution can develop, whether marketing platforms are transferable, and whether "lead" countries can be identified in which most innovation takes place. *Cost globalization drivers* are factors that define the opportunity for global scale or scope economics, experience effects, sourcing efficiencies reflecting differentials in costs between countries or regions, and technology advantages. They shape the economics of an industry. *Competitive drivers* are defined by the actions of competing firms—the extent to which competitors from different continents enter the fray, globalize their strategies and corporate capabilities, and create interdependence between geographical markets. *Government drivers* include such factors as favorable trade policies, a benign regulatory climate, and common product and technology standards.

Market Drivers

Many forces push companies to think more globally in order to meet foreign competition head on, to better serve an increasingly global customer base, to exploit diverse capabilities and cost advantages, and to take advantage of an easing global regulatory environment. *Meeting changing customer expectations*, however, is the primary reason many companies need to strengthen their global posture.

A high degree of regional or global similarity in product or service requirements and features calls for a *global product or service strategy*—implying substantial standardization. Marriott offers similar, but not identical, services around the world. Kentucky Fried Chicken, though adapting to local tastes and preferences, has standardized many elements of its operations. Software, oil products, and accounting services also increasingly look alike no matter where they are purchased.

In many countries, regulations require considerable local adaptation of products and services; insurance and financial services are illustrations. In such circumstances, similarity might be limited to benefits sought, and therefore a *global benefit strategy* would be more appropriate. When similarities are only confined to the underlying need for the product or service, such as for different types of medical equipment, the strategic focus should be on developing a *global product or service category*.[6]

As consumption patterns become more homogeneous around the world, global branding and marketing will become increasingly important to global success. Global distribution and Internet-based purchasing are causing further convergence. For some products, purchase behavior is still primarily *local*; for others, more *regional* procurement patterns have evolved. *Global sourcing*—selecting the best offer from anywhere around the world—is becoming the norm in a growing number of industries. General Electric sources from around the world for all of its businesses. Such global purchasing patterns can take different forms. Sometimes buyers merely seek global price transparency. At other times they desire supporting global logistics, purchasing agreements, or even account management.[7]

Cost Drivers

In a growing number of industries, the minimum sales volume required for cost efficiency is simply no longer available in a single country or region. The pharmaceutical industry provides a good example. The development of many new drugs can no longer be justified on the basis of the economic returns from a single country. As a consequence, economies of scale and scope; experience effects; and exploiting differences in factor costs for product development, manufacturing, and sourcing in different parts of the world have become critical to global success. This can create the need for *critical mass* in different parts of the value chain. For pharmaceutical companies, critical mass in R&D is key to nurturing a strong pipeline of new drugs and compounds; in the airline industry, logistics is a key scale variable. For soft drink markets, presence and global branding are key to creating global critical mass. Determining which parts of the value chain require critical mass also assists in assessing the need for mergers and acquisitions and guides the development of key alliances.

Competitive Drivers

The globalization potential of an industry also is influenced by competitive drivers such as (1) the degree to which total industry sales are made up by export or import volume, (2) the diversity of competitors in terms of their national origin, and (3) the extent to which major players have globalized their operations and created an interdependence between their competitive strategies in different parts of the world. High levels of trade, competitive diversity, and interdependence tend to increase competition and the potential for industry globalization.

An analysis of global competitive drivers should focus on whether competition is primarily waged at the local or regional level or whether it has evolved into a coordinated global pattern. Useful questions to ask include: How many competitive arenas does our company compete in? Do we mainly face the same principal competitors in different parts of the world? Do competitors employ similar strategies in the different arenas? How necessary is it to coordinate competitive responses on a global scale?

Government Drivers

Some industries are more regulated than others. In the steel industry, for example, the presence or absence of favorable trade policies, technical standards, policies and regulations, and government-operated or subsidized competitors or customers have a direct influence on a company's global strategic options. In the past, multinationals almost exclusively relied on governments to negotiate the rules of global competition. However, as the politics and economics of global competition have become more closely intertwined, companies are paying greater attention to the nonmarket dimensions of their global strategies in an attempt to shape the global competitive environment to their advantage. In the telecommunications industry, falling trade barriers and other deregulatory moves have encouraged companies to pursue more global approaches to their business. The threat of protectionism or reregulation in the steel industry, in contrast, inhibits industry globalization and causes companies to take a less global approach.

GLOBAL STRATEGY FORMULATION

At a generic level, we can distinguish between *multinational* (or *multidomestic*), *international, global,* and *transnational* strategies (Figure 8-3). As the name suggests, a *multinational* or *multidomestic* approach is applicable when customer needs and industry conditions vary considerably from country to country and a high degree of localization is required. One of world's best-known food companies—Nestlé—follows this type of strategy. It allows the company to adapt to differences in local taste preferences and distribution structures. Under this approach, most strategic and operating decisions are made at the local level; that is, they are decentralized to the business unit in each country.

In industries such as electronic appliances or computer chips in which global strategic advantage depends on (1) effectively

Figure 8-3 Generic Global Strategies

	Multinational	International	Global	Transnational
Strategic Orientation	Building flexibility to respond to national differences	Exploiting parent company knowledge and capabilities	Building cost advantages through global economies of scale	Developing global efficiency while maintaining flexibility and the capacity to learn
Assets and Capabilities Required	Strong, resourceful and entrepreneurial national operations	Effective mechanisms for diffusion and adaptation	Size and the ability to manage standardization	Strong culture of communication and transference. Arm's length management control system
Configuration of Assets and Capabilities	Decentralized and nationally self-sufficient	Sources of competency centralized. Operations decentralized	Centralized and globally scaled	Interdependent, dispersed, specialized and controlled

Source: Reprinted by permission of Harvard Business School Press. From *Managing Across Borders: The Transnational Solution,"* by C. A. Bartlett and S. Ghoshal, Boston 1989.

developing new products in the home market and (2) sequentially diffusing these innovations to foreign markets through affiliate organizations, an *international* strategic posture might be appropriate. The name reflects the importance of managing the international product life cycle through the transfer of technologies to foreign markets. This strategic posture is common in high-technology industries in which exploiting home country innovation is key to global value creation.

A *global* or *transnational* strategic posture is appropriate when some degree of standardization in products and services, in marketing, and in other aspects of strategy is possible. Coca-Cola and McDonald's, for example, have successfully standardized many of their value-creation activities around the world. In contrast, car manufacturers, including Ford, General Motors, and Toyota, have found that although parts of the vehicle production process can be standardized, differences in customer preferences, driving conditions, and related factors mandate a substantial amount of local adaptation. The objective of these approaches is to achieve global efficiencies while preserving local responsiveness.[8]

Global Strategy Dimensions

Global strategy formulation requires analysis of at least five additional dimensions: (1) market participation, (2) standardization/positioning, (3) activity concentration, (4) coordination of decision making, and (5) nonmarket factors. The objective of these assessments is to make thoughtful decisions about which strategy elements can and should be globalized and to what extent.

Market Participation

Few companies can afford to enter all markets open to them. Even the world's largest companies, such as General Electric, must exercise strategic discipline in choosing the markets they serve. They must weigh the relative advantages of a direct or indirect presence in different regions of the world. For midsize companies, the key to gaining global competitive advantage lies in creating a worldwide resource network through alliances with suppliers, customers, and sometimes competitors. A good strategy for one company, however, might have little chance of succeeding for another. Winning strategies are highly selective in terms of market participation, realistic market share and profit objectives, and current capabilities.

A global view of market opportunities requires a multidimensional perspective. In many industries, we can distinguish between "must" markets—markets in which a company must compete in order to realize its global ambitions—and "nice-to-be-in" markets in which participation is desirable but not critical. "Must" markets include those that are critical from a *volume* perspective, that define *technological leadership*, and in which key *competitive* battles are played out. In the cell phone industry, for example, Motorola looks to Europe as its primary competitive battleground, but it derives much of its technology from Japan and its sales volume from the United States.

Developing a global presence also takes time and requires substantial resources. Ideally, the pace of international expansion is dictated by customer demand. Companies have found, however, that it is sometimes necessary to expand ahead of direct opportunity in order to secure a long-term competitive advantage. China provides a good example. Nevertheless, many companies that entered China in anticipation of its membership in the World Trade Organization have found that early commitment to a promising market makes earning a satisfactory return on capital invested difficult. As a result, an increasing number of companies, particularly smaller and midsize corporations, favor global expansion strategies that minimize direct investment. Strategic alliances have made vertical or horizontal integration less important to profitability and shareholder value in many industries. Alliances boost contribution to fixed cost while expanding a company's global reach. At the same time, they can be powerful windows on technology and greatly expand opportunities to create the core competencies needed to effectively compete on a worldwide basis.

Standardization/Positioning

As globalization advances, many companies are seeking opportunities to standardize core products and services. Reducing cost and enhancing quality are primary motivations for standardization. With a few exceptions, however, the idea of an identical, fully standardized global product is a myth.[9] Even though substantial benefits can be achieved by standardizing key product or service components, some components must be customized. Sony, for example, standardizes substantial portions of its consumer electronics products except for the parts that must meet different national electric standards.

Adopting a more global market positioning is another form of standardization. This does not necessarily mean standardizing all elements of the marketing mix or the process by which marketing decisions are made. Rather, by applying a global, cost-benefit approach to formulating marketing strategy, companies seek to balance flexibility with uniformity. Companies such as Nestlé, Coca-Cola, Ford, Unilever, IBM, and Disney have found that a more-global marketing approach can derive important benefits. The use of global branding, for example, helps in building brand recognition, enhancing customer preference, and reducing worldwide marketing costs.

A useful construct for integrating the product/service and positioning dimensions is the *global branding strategy matrix* (Figure 8-4). It identifies four generic global strategies: (1) a *global (marketing) mix* strategy under which both the offer and the message are the same, (2) a *global offer* strategy characterized by an identical offer but different positioning around the world, (3) a *global message* strategy under which the offer might be different in various parts of the world but the message is the same, and (4) a *global change* strategy under which both the offer and the message are adapted to local market circumstances.[10]

Global mix strategies are relatively rare, reflecting the fact that only a few industries are truly global. They apply (1) when a product's usage patterns and brand potential are homogeneous on a global scale, (2) when scale and scope cost advantages substantially outweigh the benefits of partial or full adaptation, and (3) when competitive circumstances are such

Figure 8-4 The Global Branding Matrix

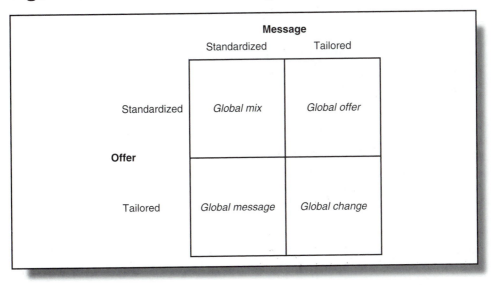

that a long-term, sustainable advantage can be secured using a standardized approach.

Global offer strategies apply when the same offer can advantageously be positioned differently in different parts of the world. Holiday Inns, for example, are positioned as first-class hotels in some parts of the Far East and in the value category in the United States. There are several reasons for considering a differential positioning in different parts of the world. When fixed costs associated with the offer are high, when key core benefits offered are identical, and when there are natural market boundaries, adapting the message for stronger local advantage is tempting. Although such strategies increase local promotional budgets, they give country managers a degree of flexibility in positioning the product or service for maximum local advantage. The primary disadvantage associated with this type of strategy is that it could be difficult to sustain or even dangerous in the long term as customers become increasingly global in their outlook and confused by the different messages in different parts of the world.

Global message strategies use the same message worldwide but allow for local adaptation of the offer. McDonald's, for example, is positioned virtually identically worldwide, but it serves vegetarian food in India and wine in France. The primary motivation behind this type of strategy is the enormous power behind creating a global brand. In industries in which customers increasingly develop similar expectations, aspirations, and values; in which customers are highly mobile; and in which the cost of product or service adaptation is fairly low, leveraging the global brand potential represented by one message worldwide often outweighs the possible disadvantages associated with factors such as higher local R&D costs. As with global offer strategies, however, global message strategies can be risky in the long run; global customers might not find elsewhere what they expect and regularly experience at home. This could lead to confusion or even alienation.

Global change strategies define a "best fit" approach and are by far the most common. For most products, some form of adaptation of both the offer and the message is necessary. Differences in a product's usage patterns, benefits sought, brand image, competitive structures, distribution channels, and governmental and other regulations all dictate some form of local adaptation. Corporate factors also play a role. Companies that have achieved a global reach through acquisition, for example, often prefer to leverage local brand names, distribution systems, and suppliers rather than embark on a risky global one-size-fits-all approach. As the markets they serve and the company become more global, selective standardization of the message and/or the offer itself can become more attractive.

Activity Concentration

To enhance global competitiveness, companies continuously reexamine (1) which parts of the value-creation process they should perform themselves and which to outsource, (2) whether they can eliminate duplicate operations in different parts of the world and reduce the number of manufacturing sites, and (3) whether they can relocate value-added activities to more cost-effective locations. Many factors must be considered in selecting the right level of participation and the location for key value-added activities. Factor conditions, the presence of supporting industrial activity, the nature and location of the demand for the product, and industry rivalry all should be considered. In addition, such issues as tax consequences, the ability to repatriate profits, currency and political risk, the ability to manage and coordinate in different locations, and synergies with other elements of the company's overall strategy should be factored in.

Making the right choices is complex. Consider the issues faced by the pharmaceutical industry. To cut costs and speed development, Eli Lilly outsources a substantial portion of its R&D—including clinical trials—to countries such as India and China. Lilly is not the only pharmaceutical company that has relocated R&D operations to the developing world; Pfizer tests drugs in Russia, and AstraZeneca conducts clinical trials in China. The main driver is rising development costs, estimated at some $1.1 billion per drug, including expenses on all the products that do not make it to the market; these costs are expected to increase to $1.5 billion by 2010.

More recently, Lilly and other drug makers have begun to expand their R&D efforts in India and China to include clinical trials. These are the late-stage experiments to prove that a drug can be used on humans. These tests are enormously expensive; Lilly estimates that each Phase III test costs at least $50 million a year. To reduce costs, Lilly plans to move 20 to 30 percent of this testing from the United States in the next few years. Although cost reduction is the main reason for the migration, this migration is made possible by the investments these nations have made in the necessary research labs, hospitals, and professional staffs to conduct studies that meet the stringent regulations of the U.S. Food & Drug Administration and drug regulators in the European Union.

Although these outsourcing initiatives are extremely successful, it is unlikely that Lilly will move its entire R&D portfolio abroad. It will likely keep a number of centers of excellence in the United States that are renowned for their path-breaking research on cancer and heart disease in order to maintain its leadership in these areas and to keep a research presence in the United States. Another reason that prevents pharmaceutical companies from outsourcing all of their research is that they might not be able to sell their newest products in countries such as India and China, because patients cannot afford them or because of worries about patent protection.[11]

Concentrating value-added activities and rationalizing operations on a global scale to focus on core skills and technologies can be risky. It can create organization and staffing problems and increase performance risk at a time when the dependence of one unit on others—within the company's own organization or within the organization of one or more of its strategic partners—is increased. Many companies, therefore, adopt a cautious, incremental approach to this aspect of globalizing their operations.

Increasing standardization or concentrating value-added components in key locations does not necessarily preclude being responsive to local demands. The overriding question is which parts of the value-creation process should be standardized or concentrated. A major engineering and construction firm, for example, found that less visible parts of its value-creation process—such as financing large projects—could best be handled globally, whereas customer-contact-intensive services, such as project management and building maintenance, were best managed locally. At the same time, the company globalized its entire estimating, project tracking, and programming services by constructing a state-of-the-art global information network using standardized software.

Coordination of Decision Making

Ultimately, the degree to which decision making—about which markets to participate in, how to allocate resources, and how to compete—is coordinated on a global scale defines the extent to which globalization has been implemented successfully. Many companies have found that integrating and coordinating activity on a global scale is at least as important as control. This can take the form of leveraging regional cost differentials, sharing key resources, cross-subsidizing national or regional battles for market share, or pursuing global brand and distribution positions. In the process, companies might have to reorganize their operations and adopt global corporate structures, characterized by production and distribution systems in key markets around the world—markets that enable cross-subsidization, competitive retaliation on a global basis, and world-scale volume.[12]

Nonmarket Dimensions

An essential difference between formulating strategy in a global and a primarily domestic context concerns the relative influence of nonmarket factors on the competitive environment and corporate performance. Increasingly, global corporate success is influenced by *nonmarket* factors that are governed by social, political, and legal arrangements. These arrangements directly affect the market environment but are primarily determined and intermediated by public institutions. This greater importance of nonmarket considerations in crafting a global strategy reflects the heterogeneity of the emerging global economy. Different countries have different political, economic, and legal systems and are at different stages of economic development. Cultures as well as educational and skill levels also can vary dramatically. These differences can have profound implications for the rules that shape global competition and, as a consequence, for crafting a global strategy. An effective global strategy addresses both elements; it has market dimensions that seek to create value through economic performance and nonmarket strategy dimensions aimed at unlocking competitive opportunity. The nonmarket environment often is nation or region specific; it is defined by the institutions, the culture, and the organization of political and economic interests in individual countries or regions. Nonmarket elements, therefore, tend to be less global than the market dimensions of a global strategy.

Entry Strategies

Getting started on the road toward a more global strategic posture poses a set of unique challenges. Should a company first establish an export base or license its products to gain experience in a newly targeted country or region? Or does the potential associated with first-mover status justify a bolder move, such as entering an alliance, making an acquisition, or even starting a new subsidiary? Many companies move from exporting to licensing to a higher investment strategy, in effect treating these choices as a learning curve. Figure 8-5 depicts these choices. Each has distinct advantages and disadvantages.

Exporting, although relatively low risk, also entails substantial costs and limited control. Exporters typically have little control over the marketing and distribution of their products, face high transportation charges and possible tariffs, and must pay distributors for a variety of services. What is more, exporting does not give a company firsthand experience in staking out a competitive position abroad, and it makes it difficult to customize products and services to local tastes and preferences.

Licensing reduces costs and also involves limited risk. However, it does not mitigate the substantial disadvantages associated with operating from a distance. As a rule, licensing strategies inhibit control and produce only moderate returns.

Strategic alliances and *joint ventures* have become increasingly popular in recent years. They allow companies to share the risks and resources required to enter international markets. Although returns also might have to be shared, they give a company a degree of flexibility not afforded by going it alone through direct investment.

Figure 8-5 International Entry Strategies

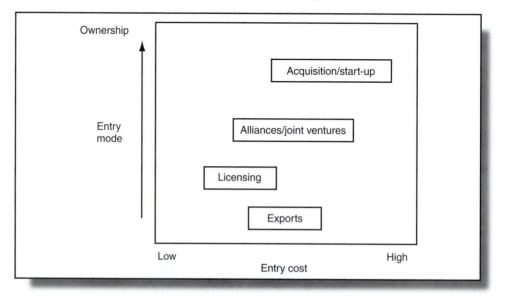

Ultimately, most companies will aim at building their own presence through company-owned facilities in important international markets. *Acquisitions* or *greenfield* startups represent this ultimate commitment. Acquisition is faster, but starting a new, wholly owned subsidiary might be the preferred option if no suitable acquisition candidates can be found.

Region/Country Analysis[13]

To assist companies in thinking through their globalization strategies, Khanna et al. suggest a five-dimensional framework to map a particular country or region's institutional contexts. Specifically, they suggest careful analysis of the following as they pertain to a particular country or region:

1. *Political and social systems.* A country's political system affects its product, labor, and capital markets. In socialist societies such as China, for instance, workers cannot form independent trade unions in the labor market, which affects wage levels. A country's social environment also is important. In South Africa, for example, the government's support for the transfer of assets to the historically disenfranchised native African community has affected the development of the capital market.

2. *Openness.* The more open a country's economy, the more likely it is that global intermediaries can freely operate there, which helps multinationals function more effectively. From a strategic perspective, however, openness can be a double-edged sword: A government that allows local companies to access the global capital market neutralizes a key advantage of foreign companies.

3. *Product markets.* Even though developing countries have opened up their markets and grown rapidly during the past decade, multinational companies struggle to get reliable information about consumers. Market research and advertising often are less sophisticated and, because there are no well-developed consumer courts and advocacy groups in these countries, people can feel that they are at the mercy of big companies.

4. *Labor markets.* Recruiting local managers and other skilled workers in developing countries can be difficult. The quality of local credentials can be hard to verify, there are relatively few search firms and recruiting agencies, and the high-quality firms that do exist focus on top-level searches, so companies must scramble to identify middle-level managers, engineers, or floor supervisors.

5. *Capital markets.* Capital and financial markets in developing countries often lack sophistication. Reliable intermediaries such as credit-rating agencies, investment analysts, merchant bankers, or venture capital firms might not exist, and multi-nationals cannot count on raising debt or equity capital locally to finance their operations.

How Wal-Mart Went Global[14]

One of the best examples of a company's evolution from a domestic company into a major global player is Wal-Mart Stores Inc., the largest retailer in the world. Wal-Mart operates three types of outlets: (1) Wal-Mart stores, which offer clothing, linens, small appliances, hardware, sporting goods, and similar items; (2) Sam's Clubs, which offer bulk items to customers who purchase warehouse memberships; and (3) Supercenters, which combine the inventories of a discount store with a full-line supermarket. The company has aggressively pursued globalization since 1991. Today, almost a quarter of its stores are located outside the United States, and a considerable percentage of its revenue and profit growth are derived from international operations.

Global Opportunity

Wal-Mart's decision to "go global" was driven by the need to grow. By confining itself to the domestic market, Wal-Mart would miss out on 96 percent of the world's potential customers. Emerging markets, despite their lower levels of disposable income, offered huge platforms for growth. Revenue and profit growth was also needed to satisfy the expectations of the capital markets and of its own employees. One of the key factors in

Wal-Mart's success is its dedicated and committed workforce. The wealth of its employees is directly tied to the market value of the company's stock. As a consequence, there is a direct link between growth and its effect on stock price and company morale.

In planning its global expansion, Wal-Mart leveraged two key resources originally developed in the United States. It exploited its tremendous buying power with such giant domestic suppliers as Procter & Gamble, Hallmark, Kellogg, Nestlé, Coke, Pfizer, Revlon, and 3M to procure goods cost-effectively for its foreign stores. It also took advantage of domestically developed knowledge and competencies in such areas as store management, the use of technology with suppliers, merchandising skills, and logistics.

Target Markets

In venturing outside the United States, Wal-Mart had the option of entering Europe, Asia, or other countries in the Western hemisphere. It realized that it did not have the resources—financial, organizational, or managerial—to enter them all simultaneously. It opted instead for a carefully considered, learning-based approach to market entry. During the first 5 years of its globalization (1991 to 1995), Wal-Mart concentrated heavily on establishing a presence in the Americas: Mexico, Brazil, Argentina, and Canada. This choice was motivated by the fact that the European market was less attractive to Wal-Mart as a first point of entry. The European retail industry was already mature, which meant that a new entrant would have to take market share away from an existing player. Well-entrenched European competitors, such as Carrefour in France and Metro A.G. in Germany, would have retaliated vigorously. Moreover, European retailers had formats similar to Wal-Mart's, reducing Wal-Mart's competitive advantage. Wal-Mart might have overcome these difficulties by entering Europe through an acquisition, but the higher growth rates of the Latin American and Asian markets would have made a delayed entry into those markets extremely costly in terms of lost opportunities. In contrast, the opportunity costs of delaying acquisition-based entries into European markets were relatively small. Asian markets also presented major opportunities, but they were geographically and culturally more distant. For these reasons, Wal-Mart chose as its first global points of entry Mexico (1991), Brazil (1994), and Argentina (1995)—the countries with the three largest populations in Latin and South America.

By 1996, Wal-Mart felt ready to take on the Asian challenge. It targeted China, with a population of more than 1.2 billion inhabitants in 640 cities, as the growth vehicle. This choice made sense in that the lower purchasing power of the Chinese consumer offered huge potential to a low-price retailer like Wal-Mart. Still, China's cultural, linguistic, and geographical distance from the United States presented relatively high entry barriers, so Wal-Mart established two beachheads as learning vehicles for establishing an Asian presence. During 1992–1993, Wal-Mart agreed to sell low-priced products to two Japanese retailers, Ito-Yokado and Yaohan, that would then market these products in Japan, Singapore, Hong Kong, Malaysia, Thailand, Indonesia, and the Philippines. Then, in 1994, Wal-Mart formed a joint venture with the C.P. Pokphand Company, a Thailand–based conglomerate, to open three Value Club membership discount stores in Hong Kong.

Mode of Entry

Once Wal-Mart had chosen its target markets, it had to select a mode of entry. It entered Canada through an acquisition. This was rational because Canada was a mature market—adding new retail capacity was unattractive—and because the strong economic and cultural similarities between the U.S. and Canadian markets minimized the need for much learning.

For its entry into Mexico, Wal-Mart took a different route. Because there were significant income and cultural differences between the U.S. and Mexican markets about which the company needed to learn and to which it needed to tailor its operations, a greenfield startup would be problematic. Instead, the company chose to form a 50-50 joint venture with Cifra, Mexico's largest retailer, counting on Cifra to provide operational expertise in the Mexican market.

In South America, Wal-Mart targeted the region's two largest markets: Brazil and Argentina. The company entered Brazil through a joint venture with Lojas Americana, a local retailer. Wal-Mart was able to leverage its learning from the Mexican experience and chose to establish a 60-40 joint venture in which it had the controlling stake. The successful entry into Brazil gave Wal-Mart even greater experience in South America, and it chose to enter Argentina through a wholly owned subsidiary. This decision was reinforced by the fact that there are only two major markets in Argentina.

Global Transfer of Skills

Wal-Mart acquired Woolco (Canada) at a time when high costs and low productivity had driven the Canadian company into the red. Wal-Mart quickly reconfigured Woolco along the lines of its successful U.S. model, a strategy made possible by the similarity between the U.S. and Canadian markets. The reconfiguration included the following:

- Sending a transition team to familiarize Woolco's 15,000 employees with the Wal-Mart way of doing business and to instill its core beliefs and practices
- Bringing every outlet up to Wal-Mart standards and renovating each plant within the first 4 months
- Immediately leveraging its high brand recognition into customer acceptance and loyalty by introducing its "everyday low prices" strategy to a market accustomed to high/low retail pricing
- Focusing on providing a broad merchandise mix, excellent customer service, and a high in-stock position
- Implementing employee rewards for diminished pilferage

All of these practices could be transplanted quickly and had proven successful in the United States. Wal-Mart's Canadian operation turned profitable in 1996—only 2 years after the acquisition. By 1997, it had become the leading discount retailer in the country.

Local Adaptation

Wal-Mart's entry into China provides insights into the challenges associated with the need to adapt to local preferences, as well as to regulatory and competitive requirements. Between 1990 and

1995, retail sales in China grew at an annual rate of 11 percent, fueled by economic liberalization and a large pent-up demand for consumer goods. These statistics mask the unique challenges faced by Wal-Mart. In China, regulations and government policies often were unpredictable, infrastructure was not well developed, and low levels of disposable income and language differences required tailored marketing approaches to product selection, labeling, and branding.

Wal-Mart experimented with different store formats, including a hybrid store, combining a supercenter and a warehouse club where memberships were sold but nonmembers could also shop, and smaller satellite stores that seemed to fit better with local needs. In addition to varied formats, Wal-Mart tested merchandise to determine what would have the greatest consumer appeal and fit best with the Chinese culture. As a result, Wal-Mart began to carry a wider range of products, particularly perishable goods that appealed to the Chinese palate. Product sourcing was another area requiring adaptation. Wal-Mart decided to purchase more than three-quarters of its merchandise targeted for the Chinese market in China. This strategy sought to balance the desire of local customers for high-status U.S.–made consumer goods with the pressure brought by local governments to purchase domestic goods.

Local Competition

In implementing its global strategy, Wal-Mart used several approaches to take on local competitors in different markets:

- *Acquiring a dominant player*. In Germany, Wal-Mart acquired the Wertkauf hypermarket chain of 21 stores, one of the most profitable hypermarket chains in the country, after deciding that building new hypermarkets in Germany would be ill advised because of the mature European market. Also, strict zoning laws precluded greenfield operations.
- *Acquiring a weak player*. Acquiring a weak player in the local market is an effective approach, provided the global company has the ability to quickly transform the weak player. This is what Wal-Mart did in Canada in acquiring Woolco.

- *Launching a frontal attack on the incumbent.* Attacking dominant and entrenched local competitors head-on is feasible only when the global company can bring a significant competitive advantage to the host country. Wal-Mart's entry into Brazil illustrates the potential—and the limitations—of a frontal attack. Carrefour, the French retailer, had been operating in Brazil since 1975. When Wal-Mart entered Brazil in 1996, it decided to challenge competitors through aggressive pricing. This strategy backfired when Carrefour and other local competitors retaliated and initiated a price war. Wal-Mart also realized that its global sourcing did not provide any built-in price advantage because the leading sales category in Brazilian supercenters was food, which was primarily sourced locally. Competitors such as Carrefour had an advantage in local sourcing because of their long relationships with local vendors. Wal-Mart therefore chose to focus on two dimensions where it could differentiate itself: (1) customer service, targeted at neutralizing Carrefour, and (2) merchandise mix, targeted at overwhelming smaller local competitors.

Gains and Setbacks

Not all of Wal-Mart's global moves have been successful, and this is a continuing source of frustration to investors. In 1999, the company spent $10.8 billion to buy the British grocery chain Asda. Not only was Asda healthy and profitable, it was already positioned as "Wal-Mart lite." Today, Asda is lagging well behind its number one rival, Tesco. Even though Wal-Mart's U.K operations are profitable, sales growth has been down for nearly 4 years, and Asda has missed profit targets for several quarters running and is in danger of slipping from second to third place in the U.K. market.

This result comes on top of Wal-Mart's costly exit from the German market. In 2005, it sold its 85 stores there to rival Metro at a loss of $1 billion. Eight years after buying into the highly competitive German market, Wal-Mart executives, accustomed to using Wal-Mart's massive market muscle to squeeze suppliers, admitted they had been unable to attain the economies of scale it needed in Germany to beat rivals' prices, prompting an early and expensive exist.

Despite these and other setbacks, Wal-Mart has little choice but to persist with its global plans. International outlets account for about 40 percent of the company's total of 6,600 stores, but they bring less than a quarter of total sales. At the same time, only overseas markets offer the world's biggest retailer the kind of room it needs to grow. This is why Wall Street increasingly focuses on the company's international record.[15]

GLOBAL STRATEGY AND RISK

Even with the best planning, global strategies carry substantial risks. Many such strategies represent a considerable stretch of the company's experience base, resources, and capabilities. The firm might target new markets, often in new—for the company—cultural settings. It might seek new technologies, initiate new partnerships, or adopt market share objectives that require earlier or greater commitments than current returns can justify. In the process, new and different forms of competition can be encountered, and it could turn out that the economics model that got the company to its current position is no longer applicable. Often, a more global posture implies exposure to different cyclical patterns, currency, and political risk. In addition, substantial costs are associated with coordinating global operations. As a consequence, before deciding to enter a foreign country or continent, companies should carefully analyze the risks involved. Finally, companies should recognize that the management style that proved successful on a domestic scale might turn out to be ineffective in a global setting.

Types of Risk

The risks a company can encounter in the international business environment can be *political, legal, financial/economic,* or of a *sociocultural nature.*

Political Risk

Political risk relates to politically induced actions and policies initiated by a foreign government. Its assessment involves an evaluation of the stability of a country's current government and of its relationships with other countries. A high level of risk affects ownership of physical assets and intellectual property, security of personnel and, as a consequence, the potential for trouble. Analysts frequently divide political risk into two sub-categories: *global* and *country-specific risk*. Global risk affects all of a company's multinational operations, whereas country-specific risk relates to investments in a specific foreign country. We can distinguish between *macro* and *micro* political risk. Macro risk is concerned with how foreign investment in general in a particular country is affected. By reviewing the government's past use of *soft* policy instruments, such as blacklisting, indirect control of prices, or strikes in particular industries, and *hard* policy tools, such as expropriation, confiscation, nationalization, or compulsory local shareholding, a company can be better prepared for potential future government action. At the micro level, risk analysis is focused on a particular company or group of companies. A weak balance sheet, questionable accounting practices, or a regular breach of contracts should give rise to concerns.

Legal Risk

Legal risk is risk that multinational companies encounter in the legal arena in a particular country. Legal risk often is closely tied to political country risk. An assessment of legal risk requires analyzing the foundations of a country's legal system and determining whether the laws are properly enforced. Therefore, legal risk analysis involves becoming familiar with a country's enforcement agencies and their scope of operation. As many companies have learned, numerous countries have written laws protecting a multinational's rights but rarely enforce them. Entering such countries can expose a company to a host of risks, including the loss of intellectual property, technology, and trademarks.

Financial/Economic Risk

Financial/economic risk in a foreign country is analogous to operating and financial risk at home. The volatility of a country's macroeconomic performance and the country's ability to meet its financial obligations directly affect performance. A nation's currency competitiveness and fluctuation are important indicators of a country's stability—both financial and political—and its willingness to embrace changes and innovations. In addition, financial risk assessment should consider such factors as how well the economy is being managed, the level of the country's economic development, working conditions, infrastructure, technological innovation, and the availability of natural/human resources.

Societal/Cultural Risk

Societal/cultural risk is associated with operating in a different sociocultural environment. For example, it might be advisable to analyze specific ideologies; the relative importance of ethnic, religious, and nationalist movements; and the country's ability to cope with changes that will, sooner or later, be induced by foreign investment. Thus, elements such as the standard of living, patriotism, religious factors, or the presence of charismatic leaders can play a huge role in the evaluation of these risks.

Global Strategy—Exploiting Similarities *and* Differences[16]

As Wal-Mart's international record attests, getting global strategy right is daunting even for the most successful companies. It shows global strategy involves more than taking a superior (by assumption) business model and rolling it out globally to capture economies of scale. Such a narrow perspective on "how much to adapt the business model—how much to standardize from country to country versus how much to localize to respond to local differences" implicitly defines global strategy in terms of exploiting *similarities* across countries, and the potential for the scale economies that such commonalities unlock, as the primary source of added value. Put another way, differences from country to country are viewed as obstacles that need to be overcome.

Although correctly choosing how much to adapt a business model is certainly important for extracting value from international operations, a singular focus on possible tradeoffs between global scale economies and local considerations obscures strategic opportunities based on the exploitation of *differences*. Indeed, global strategies based on the principle of arbitrage, the purposeful exploitation of differences in markets—in terms of cost, market structure, or other key variables—can offer sustainable sources of competitive advantage. In fact, the best global strategies do both; they exploit opportunities to standardize some aspects of the value-creation process while they differentiate the company or brand from rivals on others.

CEMEX—the Mexican global cement producer—provides a good example. It pursued a financial strategy of arbitraging capital cost differences even as it implemented a standardized operational strategy. It set up complete, uniform production-to-distribution chains in most of its major markets, reinforced by cross-border scale economies in such areas as trading, logistics, information technology, and innovation (in the broadest sense of the term). Mixing and matching was possible in this case because, to a large extent, CEMEX can choose how to raise capital independently from the way it chooses to compete in product markets; that is, it could organize its operations into relatively autonomous bundles of activities in which economies of scale and standardization were essential and those where arbitrage economies were being pursued.

As the CEMEX example shows, differences can make arbitrage just as valuable as the similarities that create opportunities for scale economies. This creates real opportunity for companies that have the imagination to see the full range of possibilities.

NOTES

1. P. Krugman, *Geography and Trade*, MIT Press, Cambridge, MA, 1993.
2. M. Porter, *The Competitive Advantage of Nations, The Free Press* (A Division of MacMillan, Inc.), New York, 1990.
3. S. M. Oster, *Modern Competitive Analysis*, Second Edition, Cambridge, Oxford University Press, 1994.

4. Oster, 1994, op. cit.
5. This section is based on George S. Yip, *Total Global Strategy: Managing for Worldwide Competitive Advantage*, Upper Saddle River, NJ, Prentice Hall, 1992, Chapters 1 and 2.
6. Jean-Pierre Jeannet, *Managing with a Global Mindset*, Upper Saddle River, NJ, Financial Times/Prentice Hall, 2000, Chapters 4 and 5.
7. Jeannet. op. cit.
8. C. A. Bartlett and S. Ghoshal, *Managing Across Borders: The Transnational Solution*, Boston, Harvard Business School Press, 1989.
9. Yip, 1992, op. cit., Chapter 4, p. 85.
10. From lectures at Templeton College by Professor Kunal Basu, Spring 2000, with permission.
11. Special Report on Outsourcing, *BusinessWeek,* January 2006.
12. G. Hamel and C. K. Prahalad, "Do You Really Have A Global Strategy?" *Harvard Business Review,* July–Aug. 1985, pp. 139–148.
13. This subsection is based on Turan Khanna, Krishna G. Palepu, and Jayant Sinha, "Strategies That Fit Emerging Markets," *Harvard Business Review,* June 2005, pp. 63–74.
14. This section is based on Vijay Govindarajan and Anil K. Gupta, "Taking Wal-Mart Global: Lessons From Retailing's Giant," *Strategy + Business,* 1999, Fourth Quarter, and company sources.
15. Thomas K. Grose, "Wal-Mart's Rollback—After Retreating from Germany, the Giant Retailer Makes a Last Stand in Britain," *U.S. News & World Report,* October 16, 2006.
16. This section is based on Pankaj Ghemawat, "The Forgotten Strategy," *Harvard Business Review,* Nov. 2003, pp. 76–84.

Chapter 9

Corporate Strategy: Shaping the Portfolio

INTRODUCTION

For single-business companies, the question "What exactly *is* your strategy?" should have a clear, concise answer that can readily be understood by investors, the media, board members, managers, employees, and even suppliers and customers. For multibusiness corporations, the issue is more complex. What is GE's strategy? Should a diversified company have a single, overarching strategy for all of its businesses or can it have unique strategies for each business that share certain characteristics or foci? A number of successful diversified multinationals have concluded that the most effective answer to "What is your strategy?" is to identify three to five strategic themes that are simple to communicate and comprehend. Jeffrey Immelt, CEO of GE, for example, talks about GE's key values, the company's strengths in developing leaders, its ability to integrate businesses on a global scale, and its prowess in making skillful acquisitions rather than about specific businesses or markets.

Distilling corporate strategy into a few simple themes in this way can create a powerful management tool for aligning behaviors and decision making at all levels within the company—the primary purpose of strategy. This, in turn, can provide the basis for communication to the broader stakeholder community. But getting to the *right* strategic themes is easier said than done and requires careful analysis of the company's *portfolio* of businesses and the *rationale* underlying the composition of that portfolio.

Thus, whereas *business unit strategy* deals with the question of *how* to compete in a given industry, *corporate strategy* is concerned with decisions about *which businesses a company operates in*—actions that *shape the corporate portfolio of businesses*—and with decisions about how to create value in the portfolio *by exploiting synergies among multiple business units.*

This chapter focuses on the first dimension—shaping the corporate portfolio. We begin by introducing the concepts of *economics of scale and scope* and ask the question: Is bigger better? We then look at the issue of defining a portfolio's *core* and its potential for growth. Next, we consider the full range of *growth strategies* at the corporate level, including concentrated growth strategies, vertical and horizontal integration, diversification, mergers, acquisitions, and cooperative strategies, such as joint ventures and alliances. Next, we review *divestment options,* defined to include sell-offs, spin-offs, and liquidations. The second dimension of corporate strategy—finding ways to create value in the portfolio by exploiting synergies among the multiple business units—is discussed in Chapter 10.

THE ECONOMICS OF SCALE AND SCOPE

The business historian Alfred D. Chandler argued that, "to compete globally, you have to be big."[1] Looking back over a century of corporate history, he noted that the "logic of managerial enterprise" begins with economics—and the cost advantages that come with scale and scope in technologically advanced capital-intensive industries. Large plants frequently produce products at a much lower cost than can small ones because the cost per unit decreases as volume goes up (*economies of scale*). In addition, larger plants can use many of the same raw and semifinished materials and production processes to make a variety of different products (*economies of scope*). What is more, these principles are not limited to the manufacturing sector. Procter & Gamble, through its multi-brand strategies, benefits from economies of scope because of its considerable influence at the retail level. In the service sector, the scale and scope economies of the major accounting firms have enabled them to dominate the auditing services market for large companies by displacing a number of respectable local and regional accounting firms.

Economies of Scale

More formally, *economies of scale* occur when the unit cost of performing an activity decreases as the scale of the activity increases. Unit cost can fall as scale is increased for reasons such as the use of better technologies in production processes or greater buyer power in large-scale purchasing situations. A different form of scale economics occurs when cost can be reduced as a result of finding better ways to perform a given task. In this scenario, the cumulative number of units processed or tasks performed drives the cost reduction. This is referred to as the *economics of learning*. The graphical representation of this phenomenon is called the *learning or experience curve*.

Economies of Scope

Economies of scope occur when the unit cost of an activity falls because the asset used is shared with some other activity. When Frito-Lay Corporation, for example, uses it trucks to not only deliver its Frito corn chips and Lay's potato chips, but also salsa and other dips to be used with the chips, it creates economies of scope. Decision opportunities for creating economies of scope fall into three broad classes: (1) *horizontal scope*, (2) *geographical scope*, and (3) *vertical scope*.

Horizontal scope decisions mainly concern choices of product scope. GE is a highly diversified company with interests in appliances, medical systems, aircraft engines, financing, and many other areas. Intangible assets such as knowledge—Sony's expertise in miniaturizing products, for example—or brands— think of the Virgin brand—can also be sources of horizontal economies of scope when they are used in the development, production, and marketing of more than one product.

Geographical scope decisions involve choices about geographical coverage. McDonald's has operations in almost 100 countries, Whirlpool has production facilities in a few countries but markets its products in a large number of countries, and Internet-based companies such as eBay and Amazon have achieved geographical scope on a virtual basis.

Vertical scope decisions are concerned with how a company links its value chain activities vertically. In the computer industry, IBM has traditionally been highly vertically integrated. Dell, in contrast, does not manufacture anything. Rather, it relies on an extensive network of third-party suppliers in its value-creation process.

Size alone, of course, is not enough to guarantee competitive success. To capitalize on the advantages that scale and scope can bring, companies must make related investments to create global marketing and distribution organizations. They must also create the right management infrastructure to effectively coordinate the myriad activities that make up the modern multinational corporation.

Timing also is critical. It is no accident that IBM, Intel, Microsoft, Hoechst, and Sony—all dominant in their industries— were *first movers*. First mover advantage explains why American hardware and software companies were successful in building a global presence and why Japanese corporations seized the advantage in many electronics industries. Challengers face a formidable uphill battle. They must build productive capacity while first movers are perfecting their production processes, develop marketing and distribution organizations to compete for market share in already established markets, and attract managerial talent capable of beating entrenched competitors.

WHAT IS "CORE"?

A useful starting point for crafting a corporate strategy is to define *core*. For most companies, the *core* is defined in terms of their most valuable customers, their most valuable products, their most important channels, and their distinctive capabilities. The challenge is to define the company as different from others in a way that builds on real strengths and capabilities—that avoids "strategy by wishful thinking"—in a manner that is relevant to all stakeholders, with room for growth.[2] Here is where the art and science of strategy formulation meet and where CEOs have a unique opportunity to position their companies with customers, suppliers, alliance partners, and financial markets.

Not choosing what is core by default also is a choice. Not making a deliberate choice risks confusion about a company's positioning in its served markets, however, and might make it more difficult to create value on a sustained basis.

Carefully defining a portfolio's core is important because there is a systematic tendency for companies to underexploit the full potential of their strongly performing business units. A common misunderstanding of the relationship between returns and competitive strength is the primary cause of underestimating the future potential of the core business. Rather than being linear—a "somewhat" stronger business should earn "somewhat" higher profitability—the relationship shows *increasing* returns to leadership (Figure 9-1). According to Bain International, a strong leader, defined as a company with a relative market share of greater than 2 times, should earn 18 percent more than its cost of capital, whereas a company with 1 times relative market share will earn 1 percent—a difference of 18 times for a doubling of competitive strength.[3]

The same study suggests that this mistaken view of the relationship between returns and competitive strengths can cause companies to fall into one or more of three strategy "traps": (1) assuming that business units that are performing well have reached their limit, and therefore deciding not to make any further investments in the core business; (2) assuming that there is greater upside potential in underperforming businesses and making

Figure 9-1 The Relationship between Returns and Competitive Strength

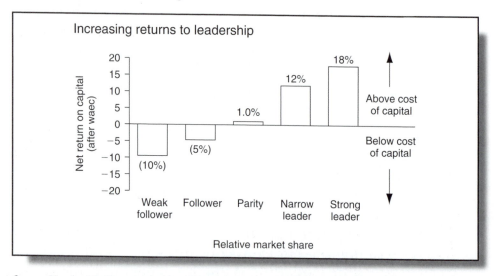

Source: Used with the permission of Bain & Co. © 2005 Bain & Company Inc., 131 Dartmouth Street, Boston, Massachusetts 02116, United States of America. All rights reserved.

unwarranted, more risky investment in underperforming portfolio components; and (3) prematurely abandoning core businesses.

The story of Colgate-Palmolive illustrates what is possible when a company chooses to focus on building its core business and driving it to its full potential. Since 1984, Colgate's share price has outperformed GE and delivered a return three times that of S&P 500. These results are remarkable, because Colgate is a slow-growth company. Its net revenue grew less than 2 percent a year between 1996 and 2000. In the same period, however, its stock price almost tripled. These results were achieved by making major investments in the company's core business and by making it the leader in its industry.[4]

GROWTH STRATEGIES

Achieving consistent revenue and profit growth is hard—especially for large companies. To put this challenge in perspective, for a $30 billion company, about average for a *Fortune* 100 company, to grow 6 percent, it must spawn a new $2 billion company every year. What is more, a growth strategy that works for one company might not be appropriate for another. It might even be disastrous. A high percentage of mergers and acquisitions, for example, fail to meet expectations. Making the right acquisition, successfully integrating an acquired company into the acquirer's operations, and realizing promised synergies is difficult even for experienced players such as GE. Companies that only occasionally make an acquisition have a dismal track record. Relying on internal growth alone to meet revenue targets can be equally risky, especially in years of slow economic growth. Few companies consistently achieve higher-than-GDP growth from internal sources alone.

To formulate a successful growth strategy, a company must carefully analyze its strengths and weaknesses, how it delivers value to customers, and what growth strategies its culture can effectively support. For price-value leaders such as Dell or Wal-Mart, a growth strategy focused on entering adjacent markets is highly suitable. For performance-value players such as Intel or Genentech, on the other hand, continuous innovation might be a more effective platform for revenue growth. Selecting the right growth strategy, therefore, requires a careful analysis of opportunities, strategic resources, and cultural fit.[5]

Whether a company chooses to pursue growth through further investments in its core business or by expanding beyond its current core, it has only three avenues by which to grow its revenue base: (1) organic or internal growth, (2) growth through acquisition, and (3) growth through alliance-based initiatives. This is often referred to as the "Build, Buy, or Bond" paradigm. Wal-Mart and Dell primarily rely on organic growth. GE regularly makes strategic acquisitions in markets it deems attractive in order to achieve its growth objectives. Amazon and eBay have numerous alliances and supplier relationships that fuel their revenue growth.

We can also characterize growth strategies using product-market choice as the primary criterion: (1) concentrated growth (2) vertical and horizontal integration, and (3) diversification.

Concentrated Growth Strategies

Existing product markets often are attractive avenues for growth. A corporation that continues to direct its resources to the profitable growth of a single product category, in a well-defined market, and possibly with a dominant technology, is said to pursue a *concentrated growth* strategy.[6] The most direct way of pursuing concentrated growth is to target increases in market share. This can be done in three ways: (1) increasing the number of users of the product, (2) increasing product usage by stimulating higher quantities of use or by developing new applications, and/or (3) increasing the frequency of the product's use.

Concentrated growth can be a powerful competitive weapon. A tight product-market focus allows a company to finely assess market needs, develop a detailed knowledge of customer behavior and price sensitivity, and improve the effectiveness of marketing and promotion efforts. High success rates of new products also are tied to avoiding situations that require undeveloped skills, such as serving new customers and markets, acquiring new technologies, building new channels, developing new promotional abilities, and facing new competition.

Four specific conditions favor concentrated growth:

1. The industry is resistant to major technological advancements. This is usually the case in the late growth and maturity stages of the product life cycle and in product-markets where product demand is stable and industry barriers, such as capitalization, are high.
2. Targeted markets are not product saturated. Markets with competitive gaps leave the firm with alternatives for growth, other than taking market share away from competitors.
3. The product-market is sufficiently distinctive to dissuade competitors from trying to invade the segment.
4. Necessary inputs are stable in price and quantity and are available in the amounts and at the times needed.

A small sample of corporations that successfully use concentrated growth strategies includes Allstate, Amoco, Avon, Caterpillar, Chemlawn, KFC, John Deere, Hyatt Legal Services,

Goodyear, Giant Foods, Mack Truck, Martin-Marietta, McDonald's, Swatch, and Tenant.

Vertical and Horizontal Integration

If a corporation's current lines of business show strong growth potential, two additional avenues for growth—*vertical* and *horizontal integration*—are available.

Vertical integration describes a strategy of increasing a corporation's vertical participation in an industry's value chain. *Backward integration* entails acquiring resource suppliers or raw materials or manufacturing components that used to be sourced elsewhere. *Forward integration* refers to a strategy of moving closer to the ultimate customer, for example, by acquiring a distribution channel or by offering after-sale services. Vertical integration can be valuable if the corporation possesses a business unit that has a strong competitive position in a highly attractive industry—especially when the industry's technology is predictable and markets are growing rapidly. However, it can reduce a corporation's strategic flexibility by creating an exit barrier that prevents the company from leaving the industry if its fortunes decline.

Decisions about vertical scope are of key strategic importance at both the business unit and corporate levels because they involve the decision to redefine the domains in which the firm will operate. Vertical integration, therefore, also affects industry structure and competitive intensity. In the oil industry, for example, some companies are fully integrated from exploration to refining and marketing, whereas others specialize in one or more "upstream" or "downstream" stages of the value chain.

There are four reasons to vertically integrate:[7]

1. The market is too risky and unreliable and is at risk of "failing." The typical features of a failed vertical market are (1) a small number of buyers and sellers; (2) high asset specificity, durability, and intensity; and (3) frequent transactions.
2. A company in an adjacent stage of the industry chain has more market power. Specifically, if one stage of an industry

chain exerts market power over another and thereby achieves abnormally high returns, it may be attractive for participants in the dominated industry to enter the dominating industry. However, although players in weak stages of an industry chain might have clear incentives to move into the powerful stages, such a move is not without danger. Existing players in an industry often believe they can enter another business within the chain more easily than can outsiders. However, the key skills along an industry chain usually differ so substantially that outsiders with analogous skills from other industries often are superior entrants.

3. Vertical integration also makes strategic sense when used to create or exploit market power by raising barriers to entry or allowing price discrimination across customer segments.

- *Barriers to entry.* When most competitors in an industry are vertically integrated, it can be difficult for nonintegrated players to enter. Potential entrants might have to enter all stages to compete. This increases capital costs and the minimum efficient scale of operations, thus raising barriers to entry. Consider the automobile industry. Auto manufacturers are usually forward-integrated into distribution and franchised dealerships. Those with strong dealer networks tend to have exclusive dealerships. This means that new entrants must establish widespread dealer networks, which is expensive and time-consuming. Without their "inherited" dealer networks, manufacturers such as General Motors would have lost more market share than they already have to the Japanese.

- *Price discrimination.* Forward integration into selected customer segments can allow a company to benefit from price discrimination. Consider a supplier with market power that sells a commodity product to two customer segments with different price sensitivities. The supplier would like to maximize its total profits by charging a high price to the price-insensitive segment and a low price to the price-sensitive segment, but it cannot do so because the low-price customers can resell to the high-price customers and, ultimately, undermine the entire strategy.

By forward-integrating into the low price segment, the supplier prevents reselling. Evidence suggests that the aluminum companies have forward-integrated into fabrication segments with the most price-sensitive demands (such as can stock, cable, and automobile castings) and have resisted integration into segments where the threat of substitution is low.

4. When an industry is young, companies sometimes forward-integrate to develop a market. For example, during the early decades of the aluminum industry, producers were forced to forward-integrate into fabricated products and even end-product manufacture to penetrate markets that traditionally used materials such as steel and copper. This kind of forward integration is successful only when the downstream business possesses proprietary technology or a strong brand image prevents imitation by "free rider" competitors. It is futile to develop new markets if a company cannot capture the economic gains for at least several years.

The most comprehensive study of vertical integration was conducted as part of the PIMS comparative analysis, which was introduced in Chapter 6, of a large number of businesses in a variety of industries. It posed three important questions with respect to vertical and horizontal integration: (1) Are highly integrated businesses in general more or less profitable than less integrated ones? (2) Under what circumstances is a high level of vertical integration likely to be most profitable? (3) Apart from its influence on overall profitability, what are the principal benefits and risks associated with vertical integration strategies?[8]

The answers are intriguing. With respect to the first question—How profitable is vertical integration?—the study found that for both industrial and consumer manufacturing businesses, *backward* integration generally raised ROI but *forward* integration did not, whereas partial integration generally hurt ROI. The findings also show that the impact of vertical integration on profitability varies with the size of the business. Larger businesses tend to benefit to a greater extent than smaller ones. This suggests that vertical integration might be a particularly attractive option for businesses with a substantial market share in which further backward integration has the potential for enhancing competitive advantage and increasing barriers to entry. Finally, with respect to the question of what other factors should be considered, the results suggest that (1) alternatives to ownership, such as long-term contracts and alliances, should actively be considered; (2) vertical integration almost always requires substantial increases in investment; (3) projected cost reductions do not always materialize; and (4) vertical integration sometimes results in increased product innovation.

It is important to note that, although useful as a general guide to crafting strategy, some of these findings might need to be validated before applying them to a specific industry.

Horizontal integration involves increasing the range of products and services offered to current markets or expanding the firm's presence into a wider number of geographic locations. Horizontal integration strategies often are designed to leverage brand potential. In recent years, *strategic alliances* have become an increasingly popular way to implement horizontal growth strategies.

Diversification Strategies

The term *diversification* has a wide range of meanings in connection with many aspects of business activity. We talk about diversifying into new industries, technologies, supplier bases, customer segments, geographical regions, or sources of funds. In a strategic context, however, *diversification* is defined as a strategy of entering product markets different from those in which a company is currently engaged. Berkshire Hathaway is a good example of a company engaged in diversification; it operates insurance, food, furniture, footwear, and a host of other businesses.

Diversification strategies pose a great challenge to corporate executives. In the 1970s, many U.S. companies, facing stronger competition from abroad and diminished growth prospects in a number of traditional industries, moved into industries in which they had no particular competitive advantage. Believing that general management skill could offset knowledge gained from experience in an industry, executives thought that because they were successful in their own industries, they could be just as successful in others. A depressing number of their subsequent experiences showed that these executives overestimated their relevant competence and, under these circumstances, bigger was worse, not better.

Diversification strategies can be motivated by a variety of factors, including the desire to create revenue growth, to increase profitability through shared resources and synergies, to reduce the company's overall exposure to risk by balancing the business portfolio, or an opportunity to exploit underutilized resources. A company might see an opportunity to capitalize on its current competitive position—leveraging a strong brand name, for example—by moving into a related business or market. Entering a new business may also counterbalance cyclical performance or use excess capacity.

Relatedness or the potential for *synergy* is a major consideration in formulating diversification strategies. Related diversification strategies target new business opportunities, which have meaningful commonalities with the rest of the company's portfolio. Unrelated diversification lacks such commonalities. *Relatedness* or *synergy* can be defined in a number of ways. The most common interpretation defines relatedness in terms of *tangible links* between business units. Such links typically arise from opportunities to share activities in the value chain among related business units, made possible by the presence of common buyers, channels, technologies, or other commonalities. A second form of relatedness among business units is based on common *intangible resources*, such as knowledge or capabilities. Sony's expertise in "miniaturizing" products is a good example. A third form of relatedness concerns the ability of business units to jointly *gain* or *exercise market power*. Examples of this form of relatedness include a company's ability to cross-subsidize competitive battles across product markets or geographies; to take advantage of reciprocal buying opportunities; to provide complementary products or "total solutions," rather than individual products; and to confront challenges from societal stakeholder groups or regulatory bodies. *Strategic relatedness* is a fourth type of relatedness. It is defined in terms of the similarity of the strategic challenges faced by different business units. For example, a company might have developed a special expertise in operating businesses in mature, low-tech, slow-growing markets. All these scenarios offer companies an opportunity to exploit the different types of relatedness—which are not available to single-business competitors—for competitive advantage.

A well-known study links a company's performance to the degree of *relatedness* among its various businesses. It identifies three categories of relatedness based on a firm's *specialization ratio*, defined as the proportion of revenues derived from the largest single group of related businesses: *dominant business companies, related business companies,* and *unrelated business companies.*[9] Dominant business companies, such as General Motors and IBM, derive a majority of their revenues from a single line of business. Related business companies, such as General Foods, Eastman Kodak, and DuPont, diversify beyond a single type of business but maintain a common thread of relatedness throughout the portfolio. The components of the portfolios of unrelated business companies, or diversified conglomerates, have little in common. Rockwell International and Textron are examples of conglomerates that lack synergistic possibilities in products, markets, or technologies. The study concluded that companies with closely related portfolios tend to outperform widely diversified corporations.

The following six questions are useful for evaluating the risks associated with a diversification strategy:[10]

1. *What can our company do better than any of its competitors in its current markets?* This question is aimed at identifying a company's unique strategic assets. It forces the organization to think about how it can add value to an acquired company or in a new market.
2. *What strategic assets are needed to succeed in the new market?* Having *some* of the skills needed to successfully stake out a position in a new market is not enough. A company must have, or know where to get, *all* of them.
3. *Can the firm catch or leapfrog competitors?* If a company does not have all of the requisite skills to succeed in a new market, it must know how to buy them, develop them, or make them

unnecessary by changing the rules of competition. When Canon diversified from cameras into photocopiers, it lacked a strong direct sales force capable of challenging Xerox in its customer base of large companies. Rather than investing in a sales force, Canon decided to target small and midsize companies as well as the consumer market through established dealers.

4. *Will diversification break up strategic assets that need to be kept together?* Corporate assets often are synergistic. Cannibalizing one or more carefully developed assets from an integrated set developed for one product-market for use in a new competitive arena can destroy the profit-generating synergies of the parent firm.

5. *Will our firm simply be a player in the new market or will it be a winner?* Diversifying companies risk being outmaneuvered by their new competitors; especially if their strategic assets are more easily imitated, purchased, or replaced than they originally thought.

6. *What can the corporation learn by diversifying, and are we organized to learn it?* Diversification presents a company with an opportunity to learn about new markets and business models and therefore about how to improve existing businesses. Systematically capturing, codifying and embedding such knowledge throughout the company is key to long-term success.

Porter has summarized these considerations in the form of three tests useful for deciding whether a particular diversification move is likely to enhance shareholder value:

1. *The attractiveness test.* Is the industry the company is about to enter fundamentally attractive from a growth, competitive, and profitability perspective, or can the company create such favorable conditions?

2. *The cost of entry test.* Are the costs of entry reasonable? Is the time horizon until the venture becomes profitable acceptable? Are risk levels within accepted tolerances?

3. *The better-off test.* Does the overall portfolio's competitive position and performance improve as a result of the diversification move?[11]

Diversification is a powerful weapon in a corporation's strategic arsenal. It is not a panacea for rescuing corporations with mediocre performance, however. If done carefully, diversification can improve shareholder value, but it needs to be planned carefully in the context of an overall corporate strategy.

Mergers and Acquisitions

Companies can implement diversification strategies through internal development; cooperative ventures, such as alliances; or through *mergers and acquisitions*. Internal development can be slow and expensive. Alliances involve all of the complications and compromises of a renegotiable relationship, including debates over investments and profits. As a result, permanently bonding with another company is sometimes seen as the easiest way to diversify. Two terms describe such relationships: *mergers* and *acquisitions*. A *merger* signifies that two companies have joined to form one company. An *acquisition* occurs when one firm buys another. To outsiders, the difference might seem small and related less to ownership control than to financing. However, the critical difference often is in management control. In acquisitions, the management team of the buyer tends to dominate decision making in the combined company.

The advantages of buying an existing player can be compelling. An acquisition can quickly position a firm in a new business or market. It also eliminates a potential competitor and therefore does not contribute to the development of excess capacity.

Acquisitions, however, are generally expensive. Premiums of 30 percent or more over the current value of the stock are not uncommon. This means that, although sellers often pocket handsome profits, acquiring companies frequently lose shareholder value. The process by which merger and acquisition decisions are made contributes to this problem. In theory, acquisitions are part of a corporate diversification strategy based on the explicit identification of the most suitable players in the most attractive industries as targets to be purchased. Acquisition strategies should also specify a comprehensive framework for the due diligence assessments of targets, plans for integrating acquired companies into the corporate portfolio, and a careful determination of "how much is too much" to pay.

In practice, the acquisition process is far more complex. Once the board has approved plans to expand into new businesses or markets, or once a potential target company has been identified, the time to act is typically short. The ensuing pressures to "do a deal" are intense. These pressures emanate from senior executives, directors, and investment bankers, who stand to gain from *any* deal; shareholder groups; and competitors bidding against the firm. The environment can become frenzied. Valuations tend to rise as corporations become overconfident in their ability to add value to the target company and as expectations regarding synergies reach new heights. Due diligence is conducted more quickly than is desirable and tends to be confined to financial considerations. Integration planning takes a back seat. Differences in corporate cultures are discounted. In this climate, even the best-designed strategies can fail to produce a successful outcome, as many companies and their shareholders have learned.

What can be done to increase the effectiveness of the merger and acquisition process? Although there are no formulas for success, six themes have emerged:

1. Successful acquisitions are usually part of a well-developed corporate strategy.
2. Diversification through acquisition is an ongoing, long-term process that requires patience.
3. Successful acquisitions usually result from disciplined strategic analysis, which looks at industries first before it targets companies, while recognizing that good deals are firm specific.
4. An acquirer can add value in only a few ways, and before proceeding with an acquisition the buying company should be able to specify how synergies will be achieved and value created.
5. Objectivity is essential, even though it is hard to maintain once the acquisition chase ensues.
6. Most acquisitions flounder on implementation—strategies for implementation should be formulated before the acquisition is completed and executed quickly after the acquisition deal is closed.

Cooperative Strategies

Cooperative strategies—*joint ventures, strategic alliances,* and *other partnering* arrangements—have become increasingly popular in recent years. For many corporations, cooperative strategies capture the benefits of internal development and acquisition while avoiding the drawbacks of both.

Globalization is an important factor in the rise of cooperative ventures. In a global competitive environment, going it alone often means taking extraordinary risks. Escalating fixed costs associated with achieving global market coverage, keeping up with the latest technology, and increased exposure to currency and political risk all make risk-sharing a necessity in many industries. For many companies, a global strategic posture without alliances would be untenable.

Cooperative strategies take many forms and are considered for many different reasons. However, the fundamental motivation in every case is the corporation's ability to spread its investments over a range of options, each with a different risk profile. Essentially, the corporation is trading off the likelihood of a major payoff against the ability to optimize its investments by betting on multiple options. The key drivers that attract executives to cooperative strategies include the need for risk sharing, the corporation's funding limitations, and the desire to gain market and technology access.[12]

Risk Sharing   Most companies cannot afford "bet the company" moves to participate in all product markets of strategic interest. Whether a corporation is considering entry into a global market or investments in new technologies, the dominant logic dictates that companies prioritize their strategic interests and balance them according to risk.

Funding Limitations   Historically, many companies focused on building sustainable advantage by establishing dominance in *all* of the business' value creating activities. Through cumulative investment and vertical integration, they attempted to build barriers to entry that were hard to penetrate. However, as the globalization of the business environment accelerated and the technology race intensified, such a strategic posture became increasingly difficult to sustain. Going it alone is no longer practical in many industries.

To compete in the global arena, companies must incur immense fixed costs with a shorter payback period and at a higher level of risk.

Market Access Companies usually recognize their lack of prerequisite knowledge, infrastructure, or critical relationships necessary for the distribution of their products to new customers. Cooperative strategies can help them fill the gaps. For example, Hitachi has an alliance with Deere & Company in North America and with Fiat Allis in Europe to distribute its hydraulic excavators. This arrangement makes sense because Hitachi's product line is too narrow to justify a separate distribution network. What is more, customers benefit because the gaps in its product line are filled with quality products such as bulldozers and wheel loaders from its alliance partners.

Technology Access A large number of products rely on so many different technologies that few companies can afford to remain at the forefront of all of them. Automakers increasingly rely on advances in electronics; application software developers depend on new features delivered by Microsoft in its next-generation operating platform, and advertising agencies need more and more sophisticated tracking data to formulate schedules for clients. At the same time, the pace at which technology is spreading globally is increasing, making time an even more critical variable in developing and sustaining competitive advantage. It is usually beyond the capabilities, resources, and good luck in R&D of any corporation to garner the technological advantage needed to independently create disruption in the marketplace. Therefore, partnering with technologically compatible companies to achieve the prerequisite level of excellence is often essential. The implementation of such strategies, in turn, increases the speed at which technology diffuses around the world.

Other reasons to pursue a cooperative strategy are a lack of particular *management skills;* an *inability to add* value in-house; and a *lack of acquisition opportunities* because of size, geographical, or ownership restrictions.

Cooperative strategies cover a wide spectrum of nonequity, cross-equity, and shared-equity arrangements. Selecting the most appropriate arrangement involves analyzing the nature of the opportunity, the mutual strategic interests in the cooperative venture, and prior experience with joint ventures of both partners. The essential question is: How can we structure this opportunity to maximize the benefit(s) to both parties?

The airline industry provides a good example of some of the drivers and issues involved in forging strategic alliances. Although the U.S. industry has been deregulated for some time, international aviation remains controlled by a host of bilateral agreements that smack of protectionism. Outdated limits on foreign ownership further distort natural market forces toward a more global industry posture. As a consequence, airline companies have been forced to confront the challenges of global competition in other ways. With takeovers and mergers blocked, they have formed all kinds of alliances—from code sharing to aircraft maintenance to frequent flyer plans.

It is widely expected that four major groups will dominate the airline industry before long. The "Oneworld" alliance includes British Airways, American Airlines, Qantas, Canadian Airways, and Cathay Pacific. The "Star" Alliance is led by United Airlines and Lufthansa and includes a number of smaller carriers, including Thai, SAS, Air Canada, Varig, SAA, Singapore, ANA, ANX, and Ansett. A third group, headed by KLM (now part of Air France) and Northwest, has signed up Continental and Alitalia. The final group is composed of Delta, Swissair, Sabena, and Austrian airlines.

The Strategic Logic of Alliances

According to the Booz Allen Hamilton, Inc., a consulting firm, each life cycle phase of a business has its own, unique alliance drivers.[13] Product innovation, credibility, and access to capital are the key drivers of alliance initiatives in the early growth stage (Figure 9-2). An alliance's external value and market and customer reach are the most important factors in both the rapid growth and consolidation phases. In the stability stage, reduced cost, value-chain strengthening, and product extension become the most important factors.

Based on the role the alliance plays in the participants' corporate strategy and the structure of the leadership of the joint venture,

Figure 9-2 Business Life Cycle Phases

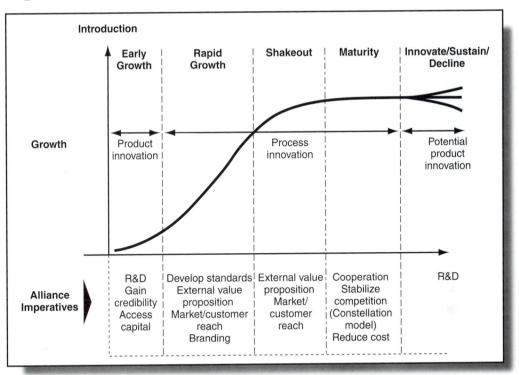

Source: Adapted from Booz-Allen & Hamilton.

they distinguish between four different alliance models: franchise, portfolio, cooperative, and constellation (Figure 9-3):

1. When gaps in an organization's value chain are greater than any one partner can fill, managers can turn to the *franchise* model. In this model, a company develops an alliance structure that can be easily replicated for a class of partnerships. Nintendo uses the franchise model to fill in a key capability need—the development of games for its consoles.
2. The *portfolio* model, also known as *hub-and-spoke,* involves the establishment of multiple alliances managed as a single portfolio. One company acts as the "hub" for the alliances and manages the external partners. AT&T and Time Warner each use this approach.
3. With the *cooperative* model, the alliance is at the center. Customer relationships shift from individual company members to the

Figure 9-3 Alliance Architecture Models

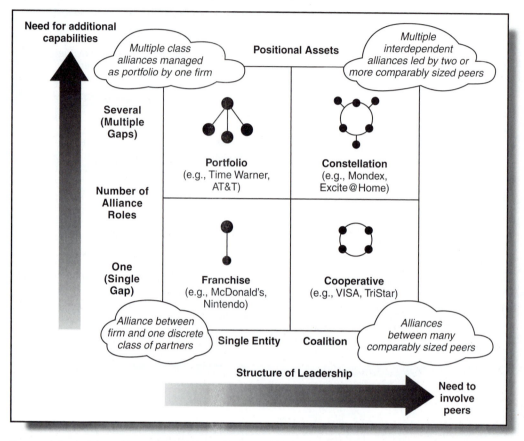

Source: Adapted from Booz-Allen & Hamilton.

alliance center. No one company is in control; instead all partners work together toward the same unifying goal. Tri-Star—an alliance among CBS, Columbia Pictures, and HBO—is an example of the cooperative model.

4. Companies that utilize the *constellation* model develop breakout strategies designed to put competitors on the defensive. A constellation requires its own center, one that is focused on creating value for the extended entity in the areas of strategic leadership, capability brokering, identity, control, and capital. For example, entering the e-procurement industry requires a considerable number of partners that can play multiple alliance roles, which the design of an alliance constellation can facilitate.

Additional insight into the strategic role of alliances is provided by the Boston Consulting Group, which divides alliances into four groups on the basis of whether the participants are competitors and on the relative depth/breadth of the alliance itself (Figure 9-4):

1. *Expertise alliances* typically bring together noncompeting firms to share expertise and specific capabilities. Outsourcing of information technology services provides a good example.
2. *New-business alliances* are partnerships focused on entering a new business or market. Many companies, for example, have partnered when venturing into new parts of the world (e.g., China).
3. *Cooperative alliances* are joint efforts by competing firms to attain critical mass or economies of scale. Competitors combining to seek cheaper health insurance for employees, for example, or combined purchasing arrangements illustrate this kind of alliance.
4. *M&A-like alliances*, as the name implies, focus on near-complete integration but are prevented from doing so, either because of legal regulatory constraints (airline industry) or because of unfavorable stock market conditions.

Figure 9-4 Alliance Types

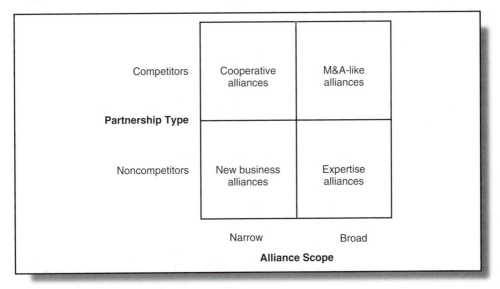

Source: Copyright © 2005 Boston Consulting Group. All rights reserved.

BCG found that whereas *new-business* alliances comprise a clear majority (over 50 percent), *expertise-based* alliances are most favored by the stock market, and *M&A-like* alliances are the least favored. That M&A-like alliances perform poorly is not surprising considering that such alliances are created in response to unfavorable regulatory or market conditions.[14]

Growth and Strategic Risk[15]

Different growth strategies entail different kinds and levels of strategic risk. A study by Bain International suggests that strategic risk can be measured in terms of how far a growth initiative takes a company away from the established strengths of its core business. Distance from the core is measured on five key dimensions (see Figure 9-5). Each growth initiative is characterized in terms of the number of steps away from these core dimensions that is implied by a particular strategic move. This is calculated

Figure 9-5 Distance from the Core

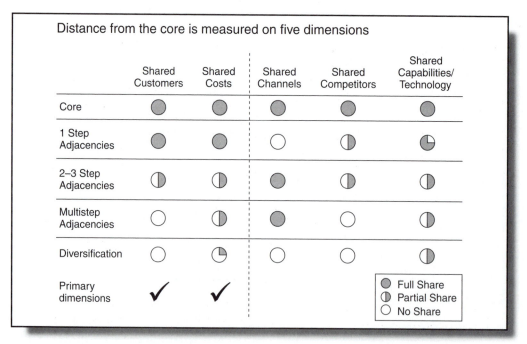

Source: Used with the permission of Bain & Co. © 2005 Bain & Company Inc., 131 Dartmouth Street, Boston, Massachusetts 02116, United States of America. All rights reserved.

Figure 9-6 Adjacency and Strategic Risk

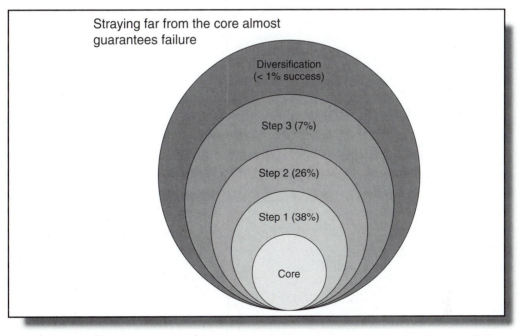

Straying far from the core almost guarantees failure

- Diversification (< 1% success)
- Step 3 (7%)
- Step 2 (26%)
- Step 1 (38%)
- Core

Source: Used with the permission of Bain & Co. © 2005 Bain & Company Inc., 131 Dartmouth Street, Boston, Massachusetts 02116, United States of America. All rights reserved.

by assessing the degree of sharing between the core business and the growth opportunity.

As a company moves away from its core, typically its success rate drops and strategic risk increases (Figure 9-6). What is more, the chances of success vary by the *type* of adjacency that defines a particular growth initiative. A geographic expansion or the introduction of a new product within an existing geography, for example, is generally less risky than targeting new customers and/or channels. Forward or backward integration across the value chain or entering a completely new business are more risky yet (Figure 9-7).

Together, these two dimensions of strategic risk—distance from the core and the type of strategic adjacency represented by a particular growth initiative—define a strategic risk "heat map," which is useful for managing the risk profile of an overall corporate growth strategy (Figure 9-8). It suggests, for example, that a growth strategy made up of "Step 3" adjacency moves alone is dangerous and should be reexamined with an eye toward reducing strategic risk.

Figure 9-7 Types of Adjacency and Strategic Risk

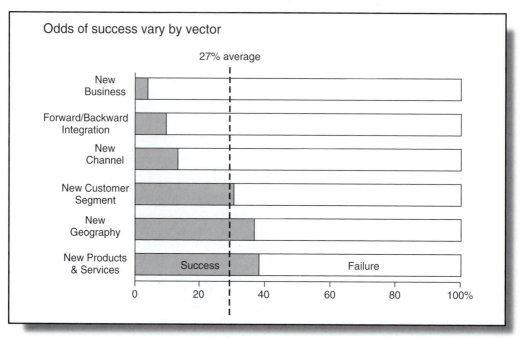

Source: Used with the permission of Bain & Co. © 2005 Bain & Company Inc., 131 Dartmouth Street, Boston, Massachusetts 02116, United States of America. All rights reserved.

Figure 9-8 Strategic Growth Success Profile

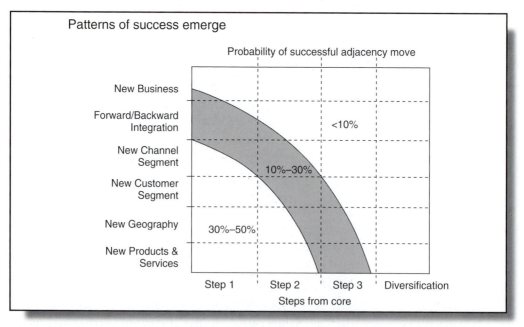

Source: Used with the permission of Bain & Co. © 2005 Bain & Company Inc., 131 Dartmouth Street, Boston, Massachusetts 02116, United States of America. All rights reserved.

DISINVESTMENTS: SELL-OFFS, SPIN-OFFS, AND LIQUIDATIONS

At times, companies are faced with the prospect of having to retrench in one or more of their lines of business. A sell-off of an SBU to a competitor or its spin off into a separate company makes sense when analysis confirms the corporation is the wrong corporate parent for the business. In such circumstances, value can be realized by giving the markets the opportunity to decide the fate of the business. If there are no potential buyers, liquidation might have to be considered.

A good example is provided by the recent sale of Chrysler to Cerberus, the private equity firm, for $7.4 billion, 3 months after DaimlerChrysler announced that "all options" were on the table for its struggling U.S. Chrysler unit. Cerberus beat out two other bidders: a partnership between rival private-equity players Blackstone Group and Centerbridge Capital Partners, and Canadian auto-parts maker Magna International.

The new company's name is Chrysler Holding, with the former German parent changing its name to Daimler, pending approval at a future special shareholders meeting. Daimler-Benz spent $36 billion for Chrysler in 1998 in what was then called a "merger of equals." The spin-off unwinds what turned into a very unhappy marriage. Under the terms of the deal, Cerberus will invest $5 billion in the new company, with $1.45 billion going to DaimlerChrysler, which, in turn, said it would invest $600 million in the new Chrysler company. Cerberus will also invest $1.05 billion in Chrysler's financial arm—an attractive synergy for the private-equity firm, which already has 51 percent stake in GMAC, General Motors' financing business.

Pitfalls

A key motivation for splitting a major company into two or more freestanding units is to unlock value for shareholders. Value, however, can be elusive. For every successful spin, there are two that fail to live up to their potential. It is vital, therefore, that boards of directors, executives, and especially senior managers of the spin-offs themselves understand the special pressures under which spin-offs labor, so that they can develop and execute growth strategies that will fulfill the promise.

What distinguishes a successful spin-off? Analysis of spins that yielded excellent returns for shareholders, such as the 1993 split of Marriott into the Host Marriott Corporation and Marriott International Inc. or the American Express Corporation's spin-off of Lehman Brothers Holdings Inc., which took place in 1994, suggests three major success factors:

1. *Ensure that both the parent corporation and the unit spun off have viable business and financial structures.* A company's decision to spin off a division is often triggered by the parent's poor performance. A lagging financial performance can tempt parent companies to improve their balance sheets by burdening the offspring. In that case, spun companies are more likely to fall into bankruptcy than the parent, because the parent saddles them with excessive debt, onerous contracts, or impaired assets.

2. *Meet or exceed earnings expectations.* This is important for all companies, but even more so for a spin-off, especially during the first 2 years when Wall Street is forming its view of the quality and reliability of the newly independent company's management team. An earnings shortfall during this critical period has a greater effect on the stock price of a spin than on the average publicly traded company's stock.

3. *Continue growth.* The third step in a successful spin is continued growth. Reliable earnings growth on par with GNP growth usually implies below-average returns to shareholders, and therefore it is not good enough to attract new investors.[16]

NOTES

1. A. D. Chandler, "The Enduring Logic of Industrial Success," *Harvard Business Review,* March–April 1990, pp. 130–140.
2. Paul Calthrop, "Define the Core: Strategy as Choice," *Management Ideas in Action,* Bain International, November 2001.
3. Paul Calthrop, "Driving a Business to Its Full Potential," *Management Ideas in Action,* Bain International, December 2001/January 2002.

4. Ibid., op. cit.
5. George S. Day, "Which Way Should You Grow?" *Harvard Business Review,* July–August 2004, pp. 24–26.
6. J. A. Pearce II and J. W. Harvey, "Concentrated Growth Strategies," *Academy of Management Executive,* February 1990, pp. 61–68.
7. John Stuckey and David White, "When and When Not to Vertically Integrate," *Sloan Management Review,* Spring 1993, pp. 71–83.
8. R. D. Buzzell and B. T. Gale, *The PIMS Principles: Linking Strategy to Performance*, New York, The Free Press, 1987.
9. R. P. Rumelt, *Strategy, Structure, and Economic Performance*, Cambridge, MA, Harvard University Press, 1974.
10. C. C. Markides, "To Diversify or Not to Diversify?" *Harvard Business Review,* November–December 1997, pp. 93–99.
11. Michael E. Porter, "From Competitive Advantage to Corporate Strategy," *Harvard Business Review,* May–June 1987, p. 46.
12. "A Practical Guide to Alliances: Leapfrogging the Learning Curve," Los Angeles, CA, Booz Allen & Hamilton, 1993.
13. This section is based on J. R. Harbison, A. Viscio, P. Pekar, Jr., and D. Moloney, "The Allianced Enterprise: Breakout Strategy for the New Millennium," Los Angeles, CA, Booz-Allen & Hamilton, 2000.
14. Kees Cools and Alexander Roos, *The Role of Alliances in Corporate Strategy*, The Boston Consulting Group, 2005.
15. This section is based on Paul Calthrop, "A Common Language of Strategic Risk," *Management Ideas in Action,* Bain International, October 2003.
16. Chuck Lucier, Jan Dyer, and Gerald Adolph, "Breaking Up Is Hard to Do—and to Manage," *Strategy + Business,* 2002, Third Quarter.

Chapter 10

Corporate Strategy: Managing the Portfolio

INTRODUCTION

The focus of Chapter 9 was on choosing *which businesses and markets to enter or exit*; that is, making decisions about *shaping the portfolio of businesses* a firm is engaged in. In this chapter, we deal with the second component of corporate strategy—finding ways to create value by *making choices about how to manage the portfolio*. Three perspectives are identified—the portfolio, value-based, and resource-based points of view—and their relative merits are assessed. Next, we look at the importance of a corporation's parenting style in managing and maintaining a portfolio of businesses. This is followed by a description of strategic planning practices at the corporate level and a discussion of horizontal strategies aimed at realizing potential synergies and at creating a boundaryless culture in a portfolio of businesses. We conclude the chapter with a discussion of how to evaluate strategy options at the corporate level.

MANAGING A PORTFOLIO OF BUSINESSES

Research by the Ashridge Strategic Management Center suggests that most multibusiness corporations destroy rather than create shareholder value in at least part of their portfolios.[1] Four causes of value destruction are cited: (1) negative effects of central executive influence on the companies, (2) the pursuit of elusive synergies in constructing a portfolio of businesses, (3) the constraining behavior of corporate staffs, and (4) inopportune acquisitions. Large mergers in general, and high-tech combinations in particular, have a tendency to derail. Fusing the different corporate cultures and product lines may take years—an eternity in the hypercompetitive high-tech world. This does not mean that opportunities to realize economies of scale and scope should be ignored. Rather, these findings suggest that bigger is not always better and that a trade-off exists between size and the organizational complexity in running a multibusiness corporation.[2]

Early Perspectives: Management as "Structure Follows Strategy"

Early research on the challenges associated with managing a diverse portfolio of businesses focused on the relationship between the strategy and the organizational structure of large, diversified corporations. This research documented the evolution of the *multidivisional* (the so-called M-form) organizational structure in the 1960s and urged managers to create a *fit* between structure and strategy so that "structure followed strategy."[3] In part, this theory was developed to justify the existence of the "pure" conglomerate form in which business units have little or nothing in common and therefore do not have the potential for realizing economies of scope. It justified unrelated diversification on the grounds that conglomerates still can generate efficiencies based on governance characteristics such as a multidivisional organization.[4] The thesis was that conglomerate M-form firms could allocate capital resources and coordinate divisional activities more effectively than the external capital market and that corporate management had information and control advantages over private investors, which allowed it to create superior returns.

The BCG Approach to Portfolio Management

In the 1990s, the Boston Consulting Group (BCG) introduced the well-known *growth/share matrix*, which remains one of the most enduring portfolio analysis techniques.[5] It also was developed to assist corporate executives who struggled with creating a rationale and formulating a coherent strategy for their diverse array of semi-autonomous divisions, about which they often knew little.

The BCG approach to portfolio analysis is based on the premise that multidivision, multiproduct companies have a distinct advantage over nondiversified companies: The ability to channel resources into the most productive units. A diversified company can use the strength of one division to fuel the expansion of another. This ability to integrate investment patterns between different businesses makes it possible to optimize the performance of the portfolio as a whole rather than focus on the performance of individual units. To achieve this optimal allocation of resources, the BCG approach recognizes a role for each of a corporation's strategic business units and integrates these roles into one overall portfolio approach. Product roles are assigned on the basis of a unit's cash flow potential and cost position relative to its principal competitors. Differences in growth and in cash flow potential determine how funds are allocated across the portfolio.

The analysis begins with the construction of a *growth/share matrix* for the company and its major competitors. Each business unit is plotted on a two-dimensional graph according to the relative market share it commands and the growth rate that characterizes its market, as shown in Figure 10-1.

Although placement of business units on the matrix is usually done subjectively, it is possible to enhance the sophistication of the model by depicting a business unit by a circle, the size of which is proportional to the annual dollar sales of the total

Figure 10-1 The Boston Consulting Group's Approach to Portfolio Analysis

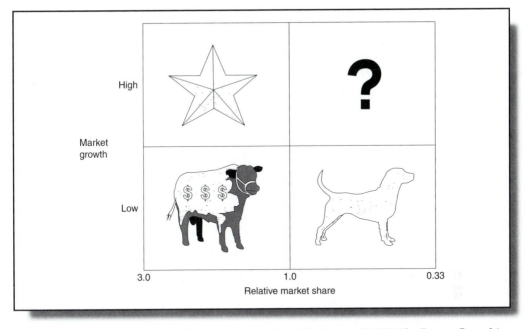

Source: The BCG Portfolio Matrix from the Product Portfolio Matrix, © 1970, The Boston Consulting Group.

market. A segment of the circle can then be shaded to indicate the firm's relative market share.

It is also possible to be more specific about the proper placement of a firm within a quadrant. High-growth markets typically show growth rates of greater than 10 percent per year, and high-share products occupy leadership positions in their markets (i.e., they have a relative market share of at least 1.0). Therefore, the midpoints on the vertical and horizontal axes can be shown as 0.10 and 1.00, respectively.

The BCG matrix is divided into four quadrants, each representing a different growth/share position. *Question marks* are low-share/high-growth businesses. They typically offer new products with potentially large future sales volumes. Substantial cash investments are needed to improve each business' share position from one of a me-too entry to one of market leadership. *Stars* are high-share/high-growth businesses that might or might not be self sufficient in terms of their cash needs. If handled successfully, they are the company's future cash cows. *Cash cows* are high-share/low-growth businesses that generate large amounts of cash—far more than they can profitably reinvest, and therefore a source of funds. *Dogs* are low-share/low-growth businesses; they neither generate nor require much cash. Because some level of reinvestment is needed, and because returns are usually modest at best, they often are "cash traps."

As conceptualized by BCG, the way businesses move across the chart over time reflects the strategic moves by the company and the evolutionary forces acting on the industry. For example, if only share-maintenance-level investments are made, market forces will cause all businesses to move downward and to eventually end up as dogs. The major strategic task, therefore, is redirecting excess cash generated by cash cows to fund market share increases for the most promising businesses in the portfolio—selected question marks whose positions are strong enough for them to become stars. Under this philosophy, question marks with a relatively weak competitive position should be divested or continued under a "no cash in" doctrine. Dogs can remain in the portfolio as long as they contribute to cash flow and do not tie up disproportionate amounts of working capital that can be put to better use.

These perspectives on strategy are based on the finding that high market share and profitability are strongly correlated in many stable market situations. Market dominance, therefore, becomes an appropriate strategic goal in high-growth markets, and maximizing cash generation is desirable in low-growth markets where market share gains are more costly to obtain. How many and which businesses to select for growth depends on their relative competitive strengths, the cost of gaining market leadership, and the cash flow generated by other businesses in the portfolio.

Experience curve effects are an important factor in explaining the correlation between market share and profitability. For many manufacturing businesses, for example, a large percentage of the variances in profitability can be explained by competitive cost differentials that reflect differences in competitors' experience. The company with the largest cumulative volume of production often has the lowest unit cost, which translates into higher cash flow.

The assumption of a strong correlation between market share and profitability is not always justified, however, and therefore must be applied with care. Poor investment decisions can erode a market leader's capacity to generate cash. Experience in related products or a technology—the so-called shared experience—is sometimes as important as direct experience. Additionally, for service companies, experience effects might be less pronounced.

General Electric Business Screen

Shortly after BCG pioneered its portfolio approach, General Electric and McKinsey & Company developed a slightly more complex matrix. Shown in Figure 10-2, the *General Electric Business Screen* uses nine cells to describe a company's portfolio. Instead of classifying a market based only on growth rate, it uses long-term *industry attractiveness*, defined to include such factors as the industry's growth rate, investment intensity, technological intensity, governmental influences, and other regulatory factors. Also, instead of characterizing a business' position in terms of market share alone, it defines *business strength* in terms of market share, technical strength, management cohesiveness and depth, and access to financial resources. Based on the intersection of a firm's ratings on industry attractiveness and business strength, the *Business Screen* prescribes growth/investment, selective investment/earnings, or harvesting/divestment strategies.[6]

MACS: McKinsey's Market-Activated Corporate Strategy Framework[7]

BCG's growth/share matrix and McKinsey's nine-box strategy matrix were created to map product markets in which companies sell goods and services to customers. Because a comprehensive strategy must also help a parent company win in the market for corporate control—where business units themselves are bought, sold, spun off, and taken private—McKinsey developed an additional

Figure 10-2 General Electric's Business Screen

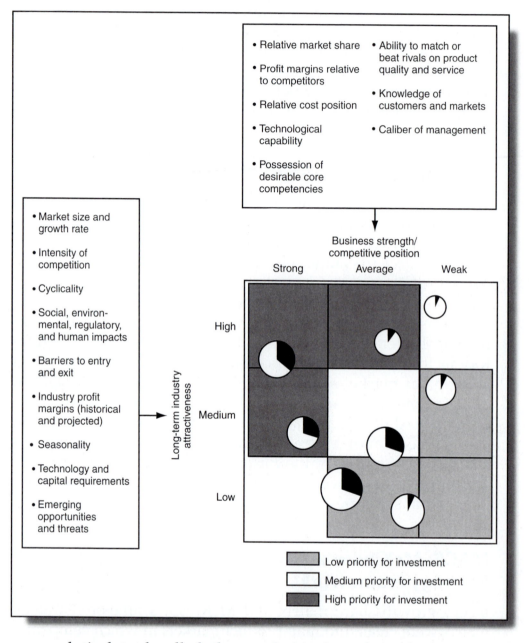

- Relative market share
- Profit margins relative to competitors
- Relative cost position
- Technological capability
- Possession of desirable core competencies

- Ability to match or beat rivals on product quality and service
- Knowledge of customers and markets
- Caliber of management

- Market size and growth rate
- Intensity of competition
- Cyclicality
- Social, environmental, regulatory, and human impacts
- Barriers to entry and exit
- Industry profit margins (historical and projected)
- Seasonality
- Technology and capital requirements
- Emerging opportunities and threats

Business strength/ competitive position

Strong   Average   Weak

Long-term industry attractiveness

High

Medium

Low

Low priority for investment

Medium priority for investment

High priority for investment

analytical tool called the market-activated corporate strategy (MACS) framework.

Like the old nine-box matrix, MACS includes a measure of each business unit's stand-alone value within the corporation, but it adds a measure of a business unit's fitness for sale to other companies. This new measure is what makes MACS especially useful.

The key contribution of the MACS framework is that it recognizes that a corporation's ability to extract value from a business unit should be benchmarked externally relative to that of other potential owners and should be taken into account in deciding whether to sell or hold onto the unit in question. The basic premise is that such a decision should not solely be made on the basis of a valuation of the business unit in isolation. Rather, under the MACS point of view decisions about whether to sell off a business unit might have less to do with how unattractive it really is (the main concern of the nine-box matrix) and more with whether a company is, for whatever reason, well suited to run it.

In the MACS matrix, the axes from the familiar nine-box framework measuring the industry's attractiveness and the business unit's ability to compete have been collapsed into a single horizontal axis, representing a business unit's *potential for creating value as a stand-alone enterprise*. The vertical axis in MACS represents a parent company's *ability, relative to other potential owners, to extract value* from a business unit. It is this second measure that differentiates the MACS framework from other valuation methods.

As in the nine-cell model, each business unit in MACS is represented as a bubble whose radius is proportional to the sales, the funds employed, or the value added by that unit. The resulting chart can be used to plan acquisitions or divestitures and to identify the kinds of institutional skill-building efforts that the parent corporation should be engaged in.

The horizontal dimension of a MACS matrix shows a *business unit's potential value as an optimally managed stand-alone enterprise* (not the actual value). Often, this estimate will involve qualitative considerations. To gain a measure of comparability between business units, one can calculate the maximum potential net present value (NPV) of the business unit and then scale that NPV by some factor—such as sales, value added, or funds employed—to make it comparable to the values of the other business units. If the business unit might be better run under different managers, its value is appraised as if they already do manage it, because the goal is to estimate optimal, not actual, value.

That optimal value depends on three factors:

1. *Industry attractiveness* is a function of the structure of an industry and the conduct of its players, which reflects the external forces impinging on an industry, such as new technologies, government policies, and lifestyle changes, as well as the industry's structure, including the economics of supply, demand, and the industry chain and the conduct and financial performance of the industry's players.
2. The *position of the business* unit within its industry depends on its ability to sustain higher prices or lower costs than the competition. This can be assessed by considering the business unit as a value delivery system, where "value" means benefits to buyers minus price.
3. *Chances to improve* the attractiveness of the industry or the business unit's competitive position within it come in two forms: opportunities to do a better job of managing internally and possible ways of shaping the structure of the industry or the conduct of its participants.

The vertical axis of the MACS matrix measures a corporation's *relative ability to extract value* from each business unit in its portfolio. The parent is classified as "in the pack" if it is judged no better than other companies to extract value from a particular business unit or as a "natural owner" if it is uniquely suited for the job.

Being a "natural owner" of a certain business unit can have multiple dimensions. The parent corporation might be able to better envision the future shape of the industry and leverage that vision though asset restructuring. It might be better at exercising internal control: cutting costs, leveraging suppliers, and so on. It might have other businesses that can share resources with the new unit or transfer intermediate products or services to and from it. GE, for example, has profitably used its finance arm to create competitive advantage within other business units. Finally, financial or technical factors might determine, to one extent or other, the natural owner of a business unit. These can include taxation, owners' incentives, imperfect information, and differing valuation techniques.

Once a company's business units have been located on the MACS matrix, decisions about whether a unit should remain part of a company's portfolio can be entertained.

The strategic prescriptions suggested by the MACS framework include the following:

- Consider divesting structurally attractive businesses if they are worth more to another company.
- Consider retaining structurally mediocre (or even poor) businesses if the company can extract more value out of them than other owners could.
- Give top priority to business units that are positioned toward the far left of the matrix—either by developing them internally or by selling them.
- Consider improving a business unit and selling it to a "natural owner" if the value of the business unit can be enhanced through internal improvements but if the company is not the "natural owner" once it is in top shape.

A cautionary note is in order at this point. Like other portfolio models, the MACS matrix only provides a snapshot. Sometimes, a parent company can change the way it extracts value, and in so doing it can become the natural owner of a business even if it was not previously. But such a change will come at a cost to the parent and to other units in its portfolio. The manager's objective is to find the combination of corporate capabilities and business units that provides the best overall scope for creating value.

Life Cycle Matrix

Another variant of the portfolio methodology that has gained some currency was developed at Arthur D. Little, Inc. This *life cycle matrix approach* plots businesses based on the stage of an industry's evolution and the strength of the company's competitive position, as shown in Figure 10-3.[8]

Figure 10-3 Arthur D. Little's Life Cycle Approach to Portfolio Analysis

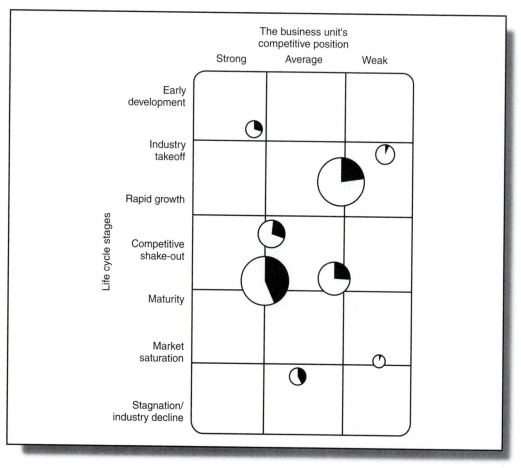

Limitations of Portfolio Analysis Techniques

Although portfolio analysis is useful in describing the current portfolio of a corporation, it has limitations as a technique for strategy development or for assisting in the management of a corporate portfolio. Labeling businesses, especially as cash cows or dogs, is dangerous, because it can lead to self-fulfilling prophecies; milking a cash cow business will almost certainly limit its growth, and classifying a business as a dog can discourage creativity in charting its future. Portfolio analysis also has prescriptive limitations. It does not answer such questions as how do we grow overall revenues? What new businesses should be added to the portfolio? Moreover, as ownership of large corporations dispersed and shares became traded more freely, the assumption that companies should be self-sufficient in capital, a central premise of the BCG matrix, lost its validity. New options had to be considered, such as paying out "excess" free cash flow to shareholders in the form of dividends and raising additional investment funds in the capital markets. At the same time, the rapid growth in the corporate headquarters staffs at many corporations prompted investors to ask what value these corporate resources contributed to the semiautonomous operations of the divisions.

The Value-Based Approach to Portfolio Management

Changes in the competitive environment set the stage for the emergence of the *value-based approach* to corporate strategy, with its focus on maximizing shareholder value. This approach treats strategic business units as separate entities that are valued according to their cash flows. It raises questions about how much economic value each division creates and what the optimal structure of the corporation is. Implicitly, the value-based approach imputes a *share price* for each business unit. If the market value of the corporation as a whole is less than the sum of the valuations of the different business units, action is required, often in the form of a sell-off of those business units that are implicitly undervalued.

Figure 10-4 shows the "pentagon" framework that depicts the value-based approach.[9] It shows several levels of analysis, starting with internally available data and restructuring options within the current portfolio. In the first step, the current market valuation of the company is compared with an objective assessment of the value of the company generated with its current corporate strategy. If the "as is" discounted cash flow analysis of the current portfolio produces a higher value than shareholders are willing to pay, management needs to improve its communications with shareholders. Moreover, to show its confidence in its corporate strategy it must consider moves such as a share repurchase program. If the internally developed cash-flow analysis

Figure 10-4 The Pentagon of Value-Based Management

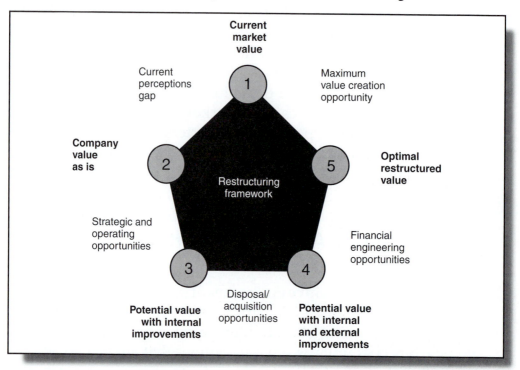

Source: Valuation: Measuring and Managing the Value of Companies, by Tom Copeland, Tim Keller, and Jack Murrin. Copyright © John Wiley & Sons, Inc. This material is used by permission of John Wiley & Sons, Inc.

shows that the company is overvalued by the market, it might mean shareholders are anticipating a possible takeover or break up. This outcome is a clear warning signal that management needs to revisit its corporate strategy and improve shareholder value.

Depending on the outcome of the overall valuation of the company, it is logical to consider strategic and operating improvements within the current portfolio as the second step. Such improvements can be targeted at the business unit level, for example, by focusing on increasing sales growth and operating margins or by decreasing working-capital requirements. At the corporate level, improvements can include reducing overhead or reexamining the strategies for managing the portfolio. If the problems uncovered at this stage are manageable, simple turnaround strategies involving one or more business units are appropriate.

If the problems are pervasive, or if they can be dealt with better by a different corporate parent, more drastic action might be needed.

If straightforward business unit improvements or a turnaround strategy are not likely to improve shareholder value sufficiently, portfolio adjustments must be considered as the third step. As part of this process, management must revisit the rationale for the corporation's diversified posture. Portfolio adjustments to consider include shrinking the scope of the company's activities through sell-offs, spin-offs, and liquidations or expanding it through diversification.

The fourth and final step in the value-based approach involves *financial engineering* of the reconfigured corporate portfolio. Among the options that have provided troubled corporations with increased value for their shareholders are recapitalization, tax favorable reorganization of global ownership structures, and changes in the corporation's debt-to-equity ratio.

The Resource-Based Approach to Portfolio Management

In their influential article, "The Core Competence of the Corporation," C. K. Prahalad and Gary Hamel argue that companies should build core capabilities that transcend the boundaries of traditional business units.[10] They urge corporations to center their portfolios on *core businesses* and adopt goals and processes aimed at enhancing *core competencies*. This core-competency perspective was later extended to what is known today as the *resource-based view* of the firm. This point of view focuses on the fit between corporate resources and product markets, on the corporation as a collection of tangible and intangible assets, and on organizational capabilities that collectively define the corporation's distinctive competence.

Three elements—*resources; businesses;* and *structure, systems, and processes*—define the pillars of the resource-based approach to corporate strategy. It holds that when these three elements are aligned in pursuit of a carefully articulated *vision*, and motivated by the right *goals* and *objectives*, a *corporate advantage* can be created that justifies the corporation's existence as a multibusiness entity.[11]

Using a Portfolio Approach for Managing Alliances

Today, at any given time, the corporate strategy of large companies might include as many as 100 or more alliances. Increasingly, therefore, companies need a process to actively monitor the effectiveness of such arrangements to identify which alliances create or destroy value. By taking a portfolio approach to managing alliances, a company can protect itself from the consequences of the failure of any single initiative and position itself to take advantage of options that may carry a higher degree of risk but that also can deliver above-average returns.[12]

To manage its alliance portfolio, Royal Philips Electronics, for example, uses a simple matrix to divide its alliances into four groups on the basis of the amount of synergy between the partners and the potential long-term value of the alliance to Philips:

- *Business alliances* are largely operational and tactical and often focused on logistics or purchasing.
- *Strategic alliances* usually are created to develop a new product, service, or business.
- *Relationship alliances* are long-lasting partnerships that span multiple divisions.
- *Corporate alliances* are 10 board-designated partnerships of particular strategic interest to the future of the company.

Business and *strategic* alliances are managed by the sponsoring business units, whereas *relationship* and *corporate* alliances are directed by a specially created corporate *alliance office*. The portfolio management approach to managing alliances has the advantage of focusing senior management's time and attention on the most important cooperative arrangements. At the same time, the creation of the corporate alliance office has helped Philips create a new core competence critical to the execution of its corporate strategy.[13]

THE ROLE OF THE CORPORATE OFFICE

The management style of the corporate office determines the organizational structure, systems, and processes a company uses to implement a strategy. It defines the roles of corporate executives in shaping and executing divisional strategies, the methods by which they control the activities of the various semiautonomous business units, and how they provide coherence to the various corporate activities as a whole.

In a study of large, British multibusiness companies, Goold and Campbell identified five management styles based on an analysis of the *role of the corporate office* and whether the company exercised *strategic* or *financial* control.[14] Companies in which headquarters exercised a high level of influence in shaping and coordinating business unit and division strategies could be characterized as having either a *strategic planning* or *centralized* style of management, depending on whether they used a strategic or financial form of control. Companies with largely autonomous business units were characterized as having either a *holding company* or a *financial control* style of management. A fifth—labeled *strategic control*—was found to be the most common management style. This style is defined by an intermediate position on both dimensions. Only a few pure cases of a centralized or holding company management style were found.

A different way to characterize a corporation's management style is based on the distinction between *behavior* and *outcome* control. Some companies, such as Textron or ABB Brown Bovary, operate with a small headquarters staff, give substantial autonomy to their operating units, and exercise control primarily by setting financial standards of performance. In other words, they exercise *outcome* control. Others, such as Cooper Industries, take a much more active role in running divisional operations and exercise control by getting involved in "how to" decisions. This management style is based on *behavior* control.

Figure 10-5 Outcome and Behavior Control Key Dimensions

Outcome Control	Behavior Control
• Structure: Independent, self-contained units	• Rewards, Incentives: Focus on long-term career progression; performance measurement based on multiple quantitative and qualitative goals
• Rewards, Incentives: Substantial part of overall compensation, tied to a single, quantifiable objective	• People: Internal career paths; active career development focused on industry and company-specific experience
• Resource Allocation: Tight expenditure controls	
• People: Focus on industry experience, aligning incentives with performance	• Culture: Focus on common corporate culture designed to allow managers to move freely among divisions
• Corporate Office: Small, focused on analyzing results	• Corporate Office: Experienced corporate managers function as advisors and monitors

Figure 10-5 summarizes the key differences between these two approaches as evidenced by how a company's structure, systems, and procedures are aligned with its chosen strategic direction. In reality, companies practicing outcome control will also ask behavioral control questions, and vice-versa. The differences between the two philosophies are real, however. They affect how corporate systems and processes are used, and they shape a company's culture.

Most companies employ a mixture of behavior and outcome control. For example, in many corporations, executives base their divisional performance evaluations primarily on financial measures (outcome control), but are more involved in initiatives such as upgrading manufacturing processes or implementing total quality programs (behavior control).

Outcome control is typically more appropriate when a single measure of current financial performance, such as cash flow, is appropriate to assess a unit's strategic position; when factors outside the business unit have only a minor effect on performance; and when there is little need for coordination between the various business units. For these reasons, outcome control is typically more relevant to companies with a portfolio of unrelated businesses, whereas parenting styles involving substantial behavior control are more likely to be found in companies made up of related businesses.

CORPORATE STRATEGIC PLANNING

Thirty years ago, elaborate planning processes, supported by dedicated staff groups, could be found in almost every *Fortune* 500 company. Then a backlash developed, and strategic planning fell out of favor. Disappointing corporate results, erosion in competitiveness, a lack of innovation, and a failure to take risks all were blamed on strategic planning. An overreliance on simplistic planning models, which generated dubious numbers, was also cited as a major cause of failure. In response, formal, bureaucratic processes were replaced by simpler, more effective ones; elaborate planning systems gave way to leaner, more decentralized forms of strategy development; and staff groups that had been the backbone of many corporate planning processes were eliminated. Strategy formulation became a line management function once again, and processes that were exclusively top-down in nature were replaced by approaches that involved managers at all levels, reflecting the new culture of empowerment. In the process, thick strategic planning documents were exchanged for more easily grasped and communicated five-page strategic plans.

Although the sentiments behind these changes—making strategy development a line responsibility once again, restoring the balance between top-down and bottom-up influences, and simplifying planning processes—were laudable, their implementation often left a lot to be desired. As a result, for many companies these changes exacted a heavy price. In the frenzy of catching up with their competitors, executives became preoccupied with tactics and operational issues such as reengineering, benchmarking, downsizing, total quality initiatives, teamwork, and empowerment. Execution and implementation became the focal point of managerial effort. Strategy was easy, thought some who believed that implementation was the real challenge.

Long-term, sustained superior performance requires strategic thinking *and* strategic planning. *Strategic thinking* is focused on creating a vision for the future of the organization and on crafting a clear, concise blueprint for realizing that vision. *Strategic planning* is a process used to develop supporting analyses and to communicate and implement the chosen strategy. Only a CEO or senior management can drive the strategic-thinking process. Strategic thinking starts at the top of the organization and is an iterative process that through a series of exchanges works its way down to involve every level of the organization.

From Strategic Planning to Strategic Management

To create a true strategic planning core competency, companies typically progress through four discrete phases of development. The first phase focuses on *financial planning*; it is the most basic task and can be found at all companies. Financial planning is simply the process of setting annual budgets and using them to monitor progress against objectives. As financial planners extend their time horizons beyond the current year, they often cross into *forecast-based planning*, which is the second phase. The third phase represents a profound leap forward and can be characterized as *externally oriented planning*, because it derives many of its advantages from more thorough and creative analyses of market trends, customers, and the competition. In the fourth phase— characterized by a systematic, company-wide embodiment of externally oriented planning—strategic planning morphs into *strategic management*.

At its highest level of development, strategic planning melds with everyday management into a single, seamless process. At that level, planning techniques are not necessarily more sophisticated, but they are fully integrated into the process of management itself.

No longer is planning a yearly, or even quarterly, activity. Instead, it is woven into the fabric of operational decision making.

Only a few of the world's companies—one of which is multinational GE—have reached this level of competence. Perhaps the need to plan for hundreds of fast-evolving businesses serving thousands of product markets in dozens of nations has accelerated evolution at these companies. Five attributes distinguish the planning process in such strategically managed companies from their counterparts:

1. *A well-understood conceptual framework that sorts out the many interrelated types of strategic issues.* This framework is defined by tomorrow's strategic issues rather than by today's organizational structure. Top management supervises the process and decides which issues it must address and which should be assigned to operating managers.

2. *Strategic-thinking capabilities that are widespread throughout the company, not limited to the top echelons.* This provides evidence that strategic thinking in the company has evolved from a planning ritual into a core competence, and that bottom-up strategic thinking complements top-down strategic direction setting.

3. *A process for negotiating trade-offs among competing objectives that involves a series of feedback loops rather than a sequence of planning submissions.* A well-conceived strategy plans for the resources required and, where resources are constrained, seeks alternatives.

4. *A performance review system that focuses the attention of top managers on key problem and opportunity areas, without forcing those managers to struggle through an in-depth review of each business unit's strategy every year.* Top management should be focused on emerging trends, new competitive developments, leadership development, and innovation.

5. *A motivational system and management values that reward and promote the exercise of strategic thinking.* Contrary opinions, out-of-the-box thinking, and purposeful experimentation with new ideas and business models should be welcomed and encouraged; occasional failure should be anticipated and treated as a learning experience.

Developing a strong strategic-planning capability pays off. True strategic management has been shown to improve a company's long-term business success. And top executives in strategically managed companies know the value of effective business strategies supported by coherent functional plans. In every case, they can identify individual successes that have repaid many times over the company's increased investment in planning.

Corporate Strategic Planning as a Process

An effective strategic-planning process requires explicit consideration of strategy development at the corporate, or "group," level and at the strategic business unit (SBU) level. It also requires explicit analysis of possible synergies and trade-offs between and among the various components of the portfolio.

The *corporate strategy* encompasses the following:

1. It defines the boundaries of the corporate portfolio (i.e., which industries the company is currently in or might enter) and provides the rationale for this definition. It also outlines how resources are to be acquired and then allocated among the different businesses.
2. It establishes a group structure, delineates roles, and stipulates the interrelationships among the various business units.
3. It sets the fundamental shared values and culture of the group.
4. It identifies "shared" resources, functions, and responsibilities.
5. It sets performance metrics and target achievement levels for individual business units.

SBU strategies are focused on determining how an individual SBU can compete most effectively within its own business area. Specifically, SBU strategies encompass the following:

1. They define the boundaries of the business and assess their competitive position.
2. They outline how they plan to move to more attractive industry segments, improve their competitive position in the industry, and grow the business.
3. They specify what their competitive advantage will be and how it can be sustained.

The process usually is iterative in nature and follows the three steps introduced in Chapter 1. The first, a "Where Are We Now?" analysis, is focused on a hard-edged evaluation of the constraints and opportunities contained in the company's environment at the SBU and corporate levels. In this step, the task for individual business units is to develop a sound understanding of their marketplace and its competitive dynamics, to conduct an objective and rigorous analysis of their strengths and weaknesses, and to identify opportunities for growth and profit improvement. To permit a comparative analysis at the group level, each SBU also should summarize its strategic situation using a common set of factors that reflect corporate values. Next is the "Where Do We Want To Go?" phase, in which the portfolio is reviewed in detail. Portfolio analysis is used to evaluate broad strategic thrusts, growth opportunities, investment options, and limits on the future scope for business units. The group then establishes a preliminary strategic direction for each SBU and the group. The third step, focused on "How Do We Get There?" is directed at establishing the ways and means required to coordinate and integrate the actions of management throughout the company. In this phase, business units are asked to develop a sound, detailed set of strategies. Once each SBU has formulated plans, group management positions them on a portfolio grid and evaluates their relative contributions to the overall corporate goals, their resource and management requirements, and opportunities for synergy. Finally, an outline for implementing the overall strategy is developed, and the ways and means required to coordinate and integrate the actions of management throughout the company are identified. The final product, the strategic plan, should be a straightforward document—concise enough to provide direction but flexible enough to allow for the timely adaptation to changed market circumstances.

Experience suggests a few guidelines that help the process stay focused and effective: (1) keep the process participative and interactive; (2) separate primary responsibilities—the corporate office should carry out the overall group assessment, individual SBUs should perform their own strategic analysis; (3) ask for concise, factual documentation; (4) do not try for perfection the first time around, instead use the iterative nature of the process to advantage.

Limitations of Strategic Planning

A lean, effective strategic-planning process can provide much-needed focus to the strategy-development process. Nevertheless, an overreliance on strategic planning has major pitfalls:

1. Formal planning techniques cannot always deal effectively with emerging or unanticipated issues. Scenario analysis, which was discussed in Chapter 3, helps, but is no substitute for managerial insight and flexibility.
2. Planning techniques too often focus on extrapolating current (known) trends rather than on a creative exploration of alternative futures.
3. The quality of the data on which many strategic plans are based often is poor. Most planning models require detailed estimates ranging from market share data to growth estimates to productivity judgments. Getting accurate numbers for all these variables is difficult and costly. As a result, shortcuts often are made and "guestimates" find their way into the analysis. This skews results and creates unwarranted illusions of certainty. More dangerous, if goals and incentives are based on such analyses and conclusions, counterproductive behavior can result.
4. The relationship between formal planning and long-term performance is weak. Good planning processes are undoubtedly helpful, but ultimate performance is more closely associated with effective strategic thinking than with strategic planning.

HORIZONTAL STRATEGIES FOR MANAGING A PORTFOLIO

Eliminating artificial barriers imposed by organizational structure, functional domains, or formal processes and procedures has become increasingly critical to successful strategy implementation and to value creation in a portfolio of businesses. Encouraging *resource sharing, cross-functional and cross-divisional learning, and transferring critical skills* across the organization are the key foci of a *horizontal strategy.*

Resource Sharing

The central provision of key functions or services by corporate headquarters is an example of resource sharing at the corporate level. Many corporations have central human resource departments; provide financial, accounting, research, purchasing, and planning services for their businesses; and offer specialized services, such as shareholder relations, on behalf of the entire corporation. Which services should be centralized is a simply a trade-off between costs and benefits. Large-scale centralized services might be less expensive, but they also might be less responsive to the demands of the individual businesses. Market-based incentives for shared service units, such as letting them compete with independent suppliers, are useful for maintaining responsiveness and keeping costs down.

Learning and Transferring Critical Skills

Learning and transferring critical skills from one part of the corporation to another are critical to creating a culture of continuous improvement and improving the competitiveness of different businesses in a corporate portfolio. *Benchmarking*, the identification of *best practices*, and *total quality management* (TQM) are well-known examples of techniques developed to foster and implement a continuous improvement philosophy.

Benchmarking is a multistep technique that is focused on a comparative evaluation of a process, product, service, or strategy. Initially an internal exercise that companies undertook to improve their efficiency, it was later extended to the identification of *best practices* within or even outside a company's industry. By finding out what competitors or best-in-class companies do better and how they do it, these techniques allow companies to (1) enhance competitiveness through continuous improvement of products and processes; (2) foster positive attitudes toward teamwork, cooperation, self-examination, and accepting new and different ideas; and (3) identify ways to redirect a company's strategy for greater effectiveness. *Total quality management* (TQM) is a set of management processes and systems developed in the 1950s by quality advocates such as W. Edwards Deming, Joseph Juran, Philip Crosby, and Armand Feigenbaum. It is focused on product and process quality as key drivers behind creating a competitive advantage. TQM relies on five fundamental premises: (1) total commitment, (2) focus on customers, (3) focus on processes, (4) making decisions based on facts, and (5) continuous improvement.[15] It extends to suppliers and other partners in the value-creation process and relies heavily on the use of statistical quality-control methods.

Creating a Learning Organization

In a *learning organization*, everyone—from the lowest-ranking employee on the shop floor to the most senior executive—is involved in identifying and solving problems, enabling the organization to continuously experiment, change, and improve, thereby increasing its capacity to grow, learn, and achieve its purpose.[16] The concept does not imply a specific structure. Rather, it is a vision of and an attitude about what an organization can become.

Senge identifies five areas that managers should concentrate on in developing a learning organization:

1. Encouraging more *systems thinking*—letting employees know how the company really works and how and where they fit in.
2. Fostering a *shared vision*—developing a common purpose and commitment.
3. *Challenging existing mental models*—questioning old ways of doing things and encouraging "outside-the-box" thinking.
4. Enhancing *team learning*—emphasizing collective over individual contributions and learning.
5. Motivating employees to improve their *personal mastery* of their job.[17]

There can be little question that the pursuit of these objectives will help companies adapt more effectively to a changing competitive environment and improve the chances of successfully implementing strategic change.

The Boundaryless Organization

General Electric has been at the forefront of developing new organizational learning concepts and implementing horizontal strategies aimed at value creation. In the 1980s, its CEO, Jack Welch, saw that rigid, hierarchical organizations were poorly structured to compete in the fast-moving, information-centric, customer-focused competitive environment that had just begun to emerge. He also realized that people were GE's most important strategic resource, and that the diversity of knowledge, talents, and ideas they brought would become the principal driver of competitive advantage in the new competitive environment. *Work-Out*, GE's program aimed at eliminating unnecessary bureaucracy, launched *boundarylessness* as a principal management philosophy. Welch described boundarylessness this way:

> GE's diversity creates a huge laboratory of innovation and ideas that reside in each of the businesses, and mining them is both our challenge and awesome opportunity. Boundaryless behavior is what integrates us and turns this opportunity into reality, creating the real value of a multibusiness company—the big competitive advantage we call Integrated Diversity.[18]

GE's Work-Out initiative provided a forum in which employees and executives could work out new ways of responding to competitive challenges. With outside consultants playing a facilitating role, groups of 40 to 100 employees in each of GE's businesses met for several days to share views about what improvements could be made and how. The rules of the process required managers to make on-the-spot decisions on proposed changes or charter a team to evaluate a proposal by an agreed-on date. Almost half of GE's workforce participated, and considerable productivity increases were realized. The most important benefits probably were not of an operational nature, however. The meetings encouraged front-line employees to challenge the status quo and take the initiative in proposing new ways of doing things. In the process, the Work-Out initiative helped redefine GE's corporate culture in terms of values such as speed, simplicity, and self-confidence. Quick decision-making modeled speed, the focus on eliminating bureaucracy reinforced simplicity, and the protected decision-making environment and process created self-confidence.[19]

The Work-Out sessions also revealed the importance of having the right reward systems. To create congruence between its system of incentives and desired behavior, GE allowed managers to base compensation at all levels on results, not position. Jack Welch documented this important aspect of creating a boundaryless culture in GE's 1994 Annual Report:

> Boundaryless behavior has become the "right" behavior at GE, and aligned with this behavior is a rewards system that recognizes the adapter or implementer of an idea as much as its originator. Creating this open, sharing climate magnifies the enormous and unique advantage of a multibusiness GE, as our wide diversity of service and industrial businesses exchange an endless stream of new ideas and best practices.[20]

Knowledge Management

The success of horizontal strategies is directly related to the effectiveness of the corporation's system of knowledge management. For many years, the primary focus of efforts to improve productivity or enhance value was on getting the most out of physical and financial assets. Today, a firm's most important strategic resource is *knowledge*.[21]

Horizontal strategy implementation is complex because knowledge comes in many forms and resides in many places—within as well as outside of the organization. Conventional information systems cannot always access or effectively integrate the knowledge needed for a specific task. The knowledge required to develop the next-generation microprocessor, for example, or the process to manufacture it, is extremely diverse, complex, and specific. A key challenge, therefore, is to integrate multiple forms of knowledge in the most effective manner while maintaining the efficiencies associated with specialized knowledge creation.

Knowledge comes in two basic forms: *explicit* and *tacit*. Explicit knowledge is codified and therefore can be transferred across the organization at relatively low cost. Tacit knowledge, in contrast, is recognizable only when it is used. An example is the collective 20-year experience of a worker on the assembly line. Such knowledge is extremely valuable to an organization, but it is difficult to codify and transfer.

Many horizontal strategy initiatives depend on a company's ability to *convert* tacit into explicit knowledge, and vice versa. Converting tacit into explicit knowledge is the process of *systematizing* knowledge. This can be achieved by encouraging the sharing of tacit knowledge between individuals (e.g., sharing "experiences") or by documenting existing (tacit, implicit) knowledge (e.g., conducting an information audit). The reverse—encouraging the conversion of explicit knowledge into tacit knowledge—can also be useful. For example, when a particular organizational culture is critical to a company's strategy, the focus should be on stimulating the *internalization* of explicit knowledge into a shared set of norms; that is, a desired set of tacit, implicit behaviors.

EVALUATING STRATEGY OPTIONS AT THE CORPORATE LEVEL

The sheer number and enormous diversity of viable strategy options at the corporate level complicates the determination of the best option. Is internal growth better than external growth? Is concentrated growth preferable to diversification? Are cooperative strategies the answer? Do we have the capacity to successfully manage an acquisition? These questions raise important issues about the evaluation of strategic alternatives at the corporate level.

The complexity of putting a numerical value on a corporate strategy is daunting. The simple fact is that, many popular press accounts not withstanding, there is no single, fully developed financial theory that can produce unambiguous estimates of value in dynamic strategic environments. Techniques such as *discounted cash flow* analysis are helpful in valuing well-defined, relatively predictable alternatives for which reasonably accurate cash-flow forecasts can be generated. However, valuing strategic alternatives in situations characterized by higher levels of uncertainty is another matter entirely.

Timothy Luehrman distinguishes among three classes of valuation problems. Valuing *operations* is the most common valuation issue. It involves putting a value on an ongoing business or deciding on a specific strategic investment. Here, discounted cash flow methods can be used.[22] Valuing *opportunities*—the second type of valuation problem—is akin to valuing options rather than an underlying stock. It places a value on possible future operations. Deciding on how much to spend on R&D and on what kind is an example; such a decision foreshadows future alternatives. Here, *option pricing* methods are more appropriate than discounted cash flow schemes, although their application is far from straightforward. Finally, valuing *ownership claims*, which is important in assessing such strategic options as joint ventures and alliances, involves assessing the value of the venture as well as the equity cash flows associated with it. *Equity cash flow* analysis is the preferred technique under this scenario.

Deciding on an overall, theoretically consistent, quantitative methodology for evaluating a complex corporate strategy proposal involving multiple options is not a simple undertaking. Even though progress has been made with user-friendly computer models, specialized skills will always be needed to successfully implement these techniques. Another reason is that valuation necessarily has a subjective element. Quantitative analysis provides the underpinning for executive forecasting. It narrows the executives' field of vision so that their conceptual powers can be focused on the most-promising options. To the extent that the future behaviors of customers, competitors, and other stakeholders are best predicted by their past behaviors, executives with relevant experience are best prepared to help the corporation see "around the corner," as all strategy formulation requires. Therefore, formulating effective corporate strategies always will require more than in-depth quantitative analysis; it will also demand keen managerial insight, intuition, and creativity.

NOTES

1. A. Campbell and D. Sadtler, "Corporate Breakups," *Strategy + Business*, 1998, (12): 64–73.
2. P. C. Davis and A. Kamra, "The Value of Big in Banking," *Strategy + Business*, 1998, (12): 7–9.
3. A. Chandler, *Strategy and Structure*, Cambridge, MIT Press, 1960.
4. O. E. Williamson, *The Economic Institutions of Capitalism*, New York, The Free Press, 1985.
5. "Note on the Boston Consulting Group Concept of Competitive Analysis and Corporate Strategy," Boston, Harvard Business School, 1975.
6. *Strategic Management in GE*, Corporate Planning and Development, General Electric Corporation.
7. Frederick W. Gluck, Stephen P. Kaufman, A. Steven Walleck, Ken McLeod, and John Stuckey, "Thinking Strategically," *McKinsey Quarterly*, 2000.
8. C. D. Hofer and D. Schendel, *Strategy Formulation: Analytical Concepts*, St. Paul, MN, West Publishing, 1978.
9. T. Copeland, T. Koller, and J. Marrin. *Valuation: Measuring and Managing the Value of Companies*, New York, John Wiley & Sons, 1995.
10. C. K. Prahalad and G. Hamel, "The Core Competence of the Corporation," *Harvard Business Review*, May–June 1990, pp. 79–91.
11. D. J. Collis and C. A. Montgomery, *Corporate Strategy; Resources and Scope of the Firm*, Homewood, IL, Irwin, 1997.
12. Kees Cools and Alexander Roos, *The Role of Alliances in Corporate Strategy*, The Boston Consulting Group, 2005.
13. Ibid.
14. M. Goold and A. Campbell, *Strategies and Styles*, Boston, Blackwell Publishing, 1987.

15. B. Bergman and B. Klefsjö, *Quality: From Customer Needs to Customer Satisfaction*, London, McGraw-Hill, 1994.
16. Richard L. Daft, *Management*, New York, The Dryden Press, 1997, p.751.
17. Ibid., p. 750.
18. GE Annual Report, 1992.
19. "GE's Two-Decade Transformation: Jack Welch's Leadership," Harvard Business School Case Study 9–399–150, Rev. Jan. 2000.
20. GE Annual Report, 1994.
21. I. Nonaka and H. Takeuchi, *The Knowledge Creating Company*, Cambridge, Oxford University Press, 1995.
22. T. A. Luehrman, "What's It Worth? A General Manager's Guide to Valuation," *Harvard Business Review,* May–June 1997, pp. 132–142. Luehrman recommends replacing traditional *discounted cash flow analysis using the weighted-average cost of capital* with the *adjusted present value* approach to facilitate adjustments for items such as tax shields and changes in capital structure.

INDEX

C

E

F

Johns, J., 115
Johnson & Johnson, 16
Jonash, R. S., 170
Jones, John, 51
Joyce, William, 27, 31, 51
Jump$tart Coalition, performance metrics, 18
Juran, Joseph, 256

K

Kamra, A., 261
Kaplan, Robert, 25, 44, 52
Kaufman, Stephen P., 261
Khanna, Parrag, 76
Khanna, Turan, 191, 202
Kiley, D., 115
Klefsjö, B., 262
Kletter, David, 44, 51
Knowledge dissemination, and globalization, 64–65
Knowledge management, 258–259
Knowledge, as a strategic asset, 106–107
Kocourek, Paul F., 51, 52
Koller, Tim, 25, 244, 261
Kotter, John P., 25, 51
Koudal, P., 167, 170, 171
Krugman, Paul, 76, 201

L

Lagon, Mark P., 76
Leadership, 38
    4 + 2 formula for sustained business success, 35
    product leadership, 132–133, 135
    role of board of directors, 48–51
    role of in *Good to Great* transition, 28–29

Learning organizations, 256
Learning/experience curve, 205
Legal risk, 199
Lehn, K., 115
Level 5 leaders, 28–29
Levels of strategy, 13
Leverage ratios, 99
Levien, Roy, 24
Lifecycle matrix, 241–242
Liquidations, 229–230
Liquidity ratios, 99
Loene, Pierre M., 177
Lucier, Chuck, 231
Luehrman, Timothy A., 24, 260, 262

M

M&A-like alliances, 225–226
MACS (market-activated corporate strategy) framework, 237–241
Maintaining strategic focus, 12
Makhija, A. K., 115
Management
    portfolios. *See* Portfolio (of businesses) management
    role of board of directors, 48–51
    role of leadership in *Good to Great* transition, 28–29
    strategic planning to strategic management, 250–252
    structure follows strategy, 233–234
Market analysis, 93–94
Market drivers, industry globalization, 178–179
Market share, importance of, 118–119
Market value added (MVA), 102–104

Strategy–structure–systems
  paradigm, 38
Strebel, P., 115
Stretch, 16, 17
Stringer, R., 170
Structure
  4 + 2 formula for sustained
    business success, 33–34
  and organizational change, 39–41
Structure follows strategy, 233–234
Stuckey, John, 231, 261
Substitute products and services, in
  Porter's five forces model, 81
Suppliers, in Porter's five forces
  model, 80
SVA (shareholder value approach),
  23–24
Switchboard Profit model, 137
Synergy, 215
Systems, and organizational
  change, 41

T

Tacit knowledge, 107
Tactics versus strategy, 5
Takeuchi, H., 262
Talent, 4 + 2 formula for sustained
  business success, 34
Technological globalization, 55
Technological tectonics, 59
Technology
  and globalization, 65–66
  upgrading, 160–161
Terrorism, and globalization, 66
Time Profit model, 137
Total quality management (TQM),
  255–256
Trade-offs, 5–7
Transnational global strategy, 181

Treacy, M., 132, 135, 139
Tully, S., 115

U

Uncertainty, 69–73
  Global Scenario Group, 71–73
  scenario analysis, 70–71
Unique competitive positioning, 7
UPS, 43
Urbanization, 61

V

Vahlenkamp, T., 151, 169
Value chain analysis, 122–125
Value creation
  focus on, 7–10
  through innovation, 161–169
Value disciplines, 132–135
  customer intimacy, 134–135
  operational excellence,
    133–135
  product leadership, 132–133, 135
Value-based approach to portfolio
  management, 243–245
Value-based management (VBM), 23
Values
  shared, 42
  shareholder value approach
    (SVA), 23–24
van de Heijden, C. A. J. M., 76
Van Lee, Reggie, 25
VBM (value-based
  management), 23
Vertical integration, 211–214
Vertical scope decisions, 206
Vesey, T., 170
Viguerie, S. P., 154–155, 169
Vinelli, A., 139

Viscio, A., 231
Vision statements, 14–16

W

Walleck, A. Steven, 261
Wal-Mart, supply-chain
  ecosystem, 12
Wal-Mart, global strategy
  formulation, 192
  gains and setbacks,
    197–198
  global opportunity, 192–193
  global transfer of skills, 195
  local adaptation, 195–196
  local competition, 196–197
  mode of entry, 194–195
  target markets, 193–194
Waterman, R. H., Jr., 115
Webb, J., 139
Webb, J. W., 171
Welch, Jack, 15, 257–258

*What Really Works: The 4 + 2 Formula
  for Sustained Business Success,*
  27, 31. *See also* 4 + 2 formula
White, David, 231
White, J. B., 115
Wiersema, F., 132, 135–139
Williamson, David, 25
Williamson, O. E., 261
Wolcott, R. C., 170

X

Xerox, 107

Y

Yip, George S., 177, 202
Yoshino, Michael E., 177

Z

Zerillo, P. C., 170